£6.r

# THE MORAY BOOK

# THE
# MORAY BOOK

*Editor*

*Donald Omand*

Paul Harris Publishing

Edinburgh

First published 1976 by
Paul Harris Publishing
Edinburgh

ISBN 0 904505 05 7

Printed in Scotland by The Shetland Times Ltd., Lerwick,
Shetland

# CONTENTS

# LIST OF ILLUSTRATIONS

29. Kynoch's Wool Mill, Keith. *(D. Stronach)*
30. Ramsay Macdonald, first Labour Prime Minister. *(Mrs I. Peterkin)*
31. Two Lead Hearts: said to have been used in the parish of Forres and neighbourhood for curing heart ailments of children. *(National Museum of Antiquities of Scotland)*
32. 6d. of George II, from Banffshire, placed in a pail before milking to preserve the milk from witchcraft. *(National Museum of Antiquities of Scotland)*
    Pendant (found on the Culbin Sands) formed of a small quartz pebble in a mount of copper strips. *(National Museum of Antiquities of Scotland)*
33. Old Gravestone, Michael Kirk, Gordonstoun. *(D. Stronach)*

# FIGURES

# ACKNOWLEDGEMENTS

I wish to thank the following people for kindnesses in many ways, in particular for supplying relevant material and giving advice on chapter content.

Officers of the Archaeology Division of the Ordnance Survey for help while using their records; the many owners of farm buildings and Doo-Cots; Mr. A. J. Soutar for assistance with the chapter on Plant Life; Mr. S. Maxwell, National Museum of Antiquities of Scotland; Messrs. G. Tuley, J. Frater, J. Maxtone, G. Reid and J. Vallance, Elgin; Mr. D. J. Guthrie, Elgin Library; Mr. J. K. Butler, Thurso.

Due debt is paid to the late Professor M. L. Anderson and his work *A History of Scottish Forestry*.

Much of the information contained in the chapter on Climate was obtained from relevant references listed in the Bibliography (Part 1.).

I am grateful to the following for permission to use their plates: The National Museum of Antiquities of Scotland, Plates 13(1), 31 and 32; The British Museum, Plate 13(2); Aerofilms Ltd., 1, 4 and 19; The Elgin Society, Plate 11; M. Proctor, Plates 5 and 6; C.O. R.A.F., Kinloss, Plate 3.

All figures for the text were drawn by Mr. R. Bremner, Department of Geography, University of St. Andrews, except for Figure 8 (Miss A. Henshall) and Figure 9 (Mr. A. Small).

The dustjacket was designed and painted by Mrs. B. Myatt, Halkirk.

Mrs. E. Gore, Elgin and Mrs. J. Mowat, Halkirk, provided valuable secretarial assistance.

Finally, I wish to thank the former Education Committees of Banff, Moray and Nairn for taking an interest in this project and for their joint financing of the many initial costs incurred.

DONALD OMAND

February 1976.

# INTRODUCTION

The place name Moray or Moravia originally applied to an area much more extensive than the recently formed Moray District. It is a name well known and honoured in Scotland's history.

This new administrative unit (Fig. 1.), part of the Grampian Region, comprises a natural and man made landscape of remarkable diversity. Here is scenery to suit all tastes: from the high dissected plateau of the Cairngorms through rolling hills to the Laich of Moray, a fertile tract of lowland of some 48 km (30 miles) in length and varying from 8-19 km (5-12 miles) in width. Great contrasts of coastal form and evolution occur: from the cliffs of the eastern part of the District to rock stacks at Cullen and Portknockie's Bow Fiddle, westwards along the great parallel shingle ridges from Portgordon to Lossiemouth and ending in the massive sand dunes of Culbin. This is a land with extensive forests, of powerful rivers and clear mountain streams. This is distillery country: "Rome was built on seven hills, and Dufftown built on seven stills!"

Climatically this is one of the most favoured Dictricts in the Kingdom. The Foreword to the 3rd Statistical Account of Moray points out that the climate is so mild, dry and fog free that the lighthouses have no foghorns! The large airfields at Kinloss and Lossiemouth, built on what was once flat forming land, take advantage of weather conditions which, from the aviation point of view, rank among the finest in the country.

The Moray District has attracted settlement from early times, as instanced by the archaeological finds near Fochabers (see Chapter 6) and the kitchen "middens" in Culbin Forest which yielded interesting artifacts now on display in Elgin and Forres Museums. Moray appears to have been a buffer area at least since Pictish times and intruding Vikings in search of timber may have been attracted by the widespread forests which must have had an abundance of game, as they were the hunting grounds of the kings of Scotland. From medieval times is a rich architectural heritage in Cathedral, Church and Castle (e.g. at Elgin, Cullen and Birnie, and at Balvenie, Dufftown). The small harbours which at one time sheltered behind the river bars of the Spey, Lossie and Findhorn were gradually

Fig. 1 Moray in the Grampian Region (Inset: the Regions of Scotland)

abandoned as the rivers silted up. The original fishing communities set up their small villages on the old raised beach platforms and from these the more substantial fishing villages evolved, but the emphasis of the industry is now in the bustling ports of Buckie and Lossiemouth. Over the centuries the major inland settlements of Forres, Elgin and Keith developed as agricultural and trading centres. The distribution of population in Moray parallels the trend of the other Districts of northern Scotland, viz. a growth of town size and a decline in rural population density.

With the reorganisation of Local Government the identity of the old counties has gone but let us hope that the diverse elements of the new Moray may evolve into a unity that will add further lustre to this historic name.

DONALD OMAND
Editor

# THE NATURAL ENVIRONMENT

# 1

# THE PHYSICAL BACKGROUND

## SINCLAIR ROSS

### THE ORIGIN OF THE ROCKS OF MORAY

Geological processes act over very considerable periods of time, and before they can be fully appreciated any evidence must be considered in relation to a realistic time scale — one where a unit of a million years is not too large. For example, a rate of erosion of 1 millimetre in 20 years does not at first sight appear to be of much significance, but in geological terms this means that a mountain range 3000m (10000ft) in height can be eroded away in a period of 60 my (million years). Using a time scale of this order, the magnitude of the processes involved in the development of the present day landscape becomes immediately obvious.

From before 800 mybp (million years before the present) a large ocean basin covering the present position of the Scottish Highlands had been filling with sediments which slowly consolidated into rocks such as sandstones, mudstones and limestones. In a mountain building period termed the Caledonian Orogeny, which was at its peak between 510 and 480 mybp, these rocks were crumpled into a fold mountain system which lay from Scandinavia across Scotland to Ireland and beyond and which was at least as high as the Alps. Throughout the orogeny the sedimentary rocks were subjected to varying degrees of heat, pressure and movement and were converted into crystalline metamorphic rocks. Two main groups were recognised: what were originally shallow water sediments being known as the Moinan assemblage and a younger deep-water series as the Dalradian assemblage. The former group consists mainly of quartzose granulites and the latter a much more diverse group of quartzites, schists and marbles. In places temperatures had been sufficiently high to lead to the formation of granitic magma from the complete melting of the sedimentary rocks, while at

B

the peak of the orogen basic magma from a greater depth was intruded into some parts. These magmas remained at depth, usually in or below the cores of the folds of the mountains, but some penetrated to the surface during volcanic eruptions.

With the formation of this new mountain chain, the cycle of erosion commenced again, continuing throughout the long Devonian Period (410 to 345 mybp). The sediments collecting on the northern side of the range were being deposited in what has been termed 'Lake Orcadie'. Here, under an arid climate the lake at times had the proportions of a huge inland sea but shrunk periodically to a collection of shallow lakes, mudflats and dried up watercourses. With the continuing deposition the basin slowly subsided and the sediments reached immense thickness, consolidating into the rocks which are now known as the Old Red Sandstone Series. The prolonged erosion wore the mountains down to the roots, revealing the coarse-grained granites and gabbros which had originally solidified at great depth.

Sediments of progressively younger groups continued to be deposited on top of the older series under widely varying subaerial and marine conditions. There was no major folding from Old Red Sandstone times onward, but there was some crustal warping and movement on fault systems. During several periods of uplift and erosion which followed, a large proportion of the sedimentary strata was stripped off the old land surface, so that today in Moray the outcrops of the Old Red Sandstone are confined to the north of the District, with a few exposures in inland areas. Almost a complete series of the younger strata is to be found on the floor of the Moray Firth, but on land the only remnants of these of any size are the desert sandstones of Permo-Triassic age (280 to 195 mybp) which are found between Elgin and the coast.

Additional notes on the geology of Moray appear in the Appendix to this chapter. Readers wishing a more detailed treatment of the subject are referred to the publications listed in the Bibliography.

## THE DEVELOPMENT OF THE MODERN LANDSCAPE

By the end of the Cretaceous period, some 64 mybp, the land surface of the Highlands had been worn away to a featureless peneplain. The surface sloped gently eastwards and was composed of metamorphic and igneous rocks of the old mountain chain and probably very considerable areas of younger sedimentary strata. The Atlantic Ocean had not yet opened so a continental climate prevailed. During the following Tertiary period the surface underwent a pulsed uplift in three or four stages accompanied by deep subaerial erosion (Fitzpatrick 1972). The interval between each stage was sufficient for a distinct erosional surface to develop, resulting in a stepped profile descending northeastwards as a series of pediments. Simultaneously a river system was developing, draining eastwards from the Hebridean volcanic plateau which built as the Atlantic opened. Holgate (1969) has shown that the original continuity of this river system was destroyed by a lateral movement of 29 km (18 miles) on the Great Glen fault system, which occurred around 52 mybp. His reconstruction of the drainage prior to this dislocation brings all the major valleys on both sides of the Great Glen into excellent alignment, and shows that the River Moriston was at one time continuous with the Findhorn and that the Garry and other rivers to the south fed into the Spey. These Tertiary rivers with their very large catchment areas and draining the high rainfall areas to the west, were very much more powerful than the present rivers of the Highlands. Their valleys are still the major valley systems of today, in spite of the drainage modifications subsequent to the dislocation.

RELIEF

The oldest and highest of the pediments formed in the Tertiary Period and therefore the one which has been most deeply dissected, is now represented by the Grampian Mountains, where the peaks and ridges tend to rise up to the same general level. Part of this group, the Cairngorms, dominates the south of Moray. Here erosion has carved a landscape of wild grandeur from the old granite plateau, with tor-capped ridges, savage corries and deep valleys, flanked by precipitous cliffs and scree slopes. A considerable area of the Cairngorms lies above 1100 m (3600 ft) and several peaks rise above 1200 m (3950 ft). The highest is Ben Macdui with two peaks of 1309 m (4296ft) and 1293m (4244ft) respectively, while Cairngorm reaches 1245m (4084ft). From this height the panoramic view of the more distant mountains confirms the general level of the

mountain tops throughout the area. To the east the peaks of
Beinn a' Bhuird 1196m (3924ft) and Ben Avon 1171m (3843ft)
mark the District boundary. In this part of Moray there are
24 mountain tops of sufficient height to be classed as "Munro's".
The rounded summits with their tors survive from the deeply
weathered pre-glacial landscape, while the deep valley holding
Loch Avon (Plate 1), the corries and the steep cliffs date from
the glacial period. Over much of the summit plateau the granite
has disintegrated into a coarse sand and large solifluction lobes,
formed by the downhill slumping of sand and loose granite
blocks, are common.

To the northeast of the Cairngorms the country rocks are
Moinian and Dalradian (Fig. 2) and the landscape is quickly
taken over by northeastward orientated ridges and valleys. Here
erosion has led to the formation of longitudinal streams running
in valleys carved out of the weaker members of the metamorphic
rocks and controlled by their strike direction, while the ridges
are formed of the more resistant bands, usually of quartzite
(Johnstone 1973). There is a noticeable drop in elevation and
the scenery becomes hilly rather than mountainous with most
of the higher hills reaching to around 730m (2400ft). In the
west these include the ridge of the Cromdale Hills which separates
the Spey from the Avon, and in the east the long line of the
Ladder Hills passing north into the hills of the Glen Fiddich
and Blackwater Forests with the Buck of Cabrach standing in
more open ground. The prominent granite peak of Ben Rinnes,
840 m (2755 ft) in height, with its sgurrans or tors, stands almost
in the centre of the district, flanked by the deep valleys of the
Spey and Glen Rinnes, while northwards the other hills quickly
fall below 500m (1640 ft).

Nearer the coast the country rock is largely of slate and
quartzite of more uniform composition, and similarly over almost
all the area to the northwest of the Spey the rock type is a
uniformly weathering granulite. The strike changes to east-
northeast and Strath Isla and lesser valleys which were continuing northeastwards turn away to the east and broaden out
to give a much more open landscape with widely spaced rounded
hills. The quartzite cone of Knock Hill rising to 429m (1409 ft)
marks where the northeast-trending bands of the varied metamorphic rocks pass out of the eastern boundary of the District.
The land continues to fall away towards the north, so that near

the coast few hill tops exceed 300m (980 ft). The result is a more gently undulating topography as seen on the Dava and Dallas moors and on the Aultmore. This smoother landscape is cut by the deep fault-controlled valleys on the southern flanks of the Hill of the Wangie and Heldon Hill and where the Spey has carved its wide strath on a more northerly course to the sea.

Between the hilly ground and the Moray Firth there is a low lying coastal plain (Plate 4), much of which is covered by deep superficial deposits of glacial origin. Here rocks of Old

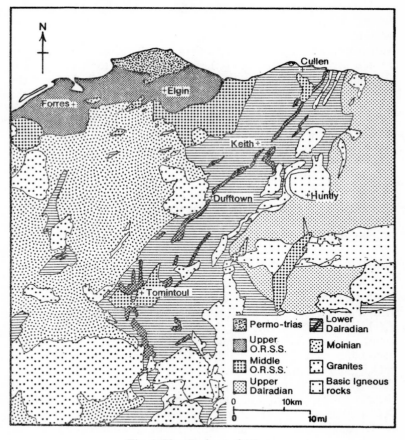

Fig. 2 The Geology of Moray

Red Sandstone age lie unconformably on a platform of metamorphic rocks, while sandstones of Permian and Triassic age form low ridges to the north and northwest of Elgin and on the coast between Burghead and Lossiemouth. This coastal platform narrows eastwards from the Spey and much of the cover of sedimentary rock has been eroded away exposing the metamorphic rock. The orientation of the coastline is controlled by east-west faulting and by the strike of the strata.

## GLACIATION

The suggestion that Scotland had at one time been covered by an ice sheet was first put forward in 1840 by Louis Agassiz who also considered that this event was followed by a period of valley glaciation. As valley glaciers could be seen in the Alps, people accepted this part of the theory, but it took many years for the ice sheet concept to be generally recognised. Over the years theories have been advanced depicting the retreat of the ice as being interrupted by as many as three readvances. Even today when a much better understanding of glaciation and deglaciation processes is emerging, there is little agreement as to the exact sequence of events in the Highlands during the ice age. Some glaciologists now challenge the readvance theories and consider that there was but one single, rapid downwasting of the ice sheet. It is therefore better to keep an open mind on the subject until such time as the true pattern emerges. (A list of publications summarising the glaciation of Northeast Scotland is contained in the bibliography.)

*Glaciation Processes*

At very low temperatures the sole of a glacier freezes to the land surface and ice movement takes place by deformation within the ice above this level with little erosion taking place. At higher temperatures the land/ice interface is lubricated by water and the ice slides over the land surface abrading it and producing rock flour and other debris. As well as picking up rocks, under some conditions of permafrost ice can pluck large slabs of normally unconsolidated materials from the surface and these can be moved up shear planes into the ice with little deformation. Huge quantities of waste material are produced by freeze-thaw action and fall on to or are picked up by the ice. All these materials are transported away from their source areas by the ice, to be dumped at a later date as the ice melts. The large areas of till and the deposits of water-sorted sands and gravels found in the Highlands today originated in this way. The mapping of erratic trains and glacial striae are methods of deducing the direction of ice movement, but geologists urge caution in the slavish use of information deduced from erratics because of the large areas where geological mapping is conjectural due to extensive drift cover and the lack of uniformity in individual rock masses.

The most powerful of all erosion processes associated with glaciation is the effect of meltwater. During the downwasting of the ice sheet, the equivalent of many years accumulated snowfall melted each summer leading to torrential streams being channeled between the slope of the land surface and the ice edges as well as flowing in tunnels through and under the ice. These torrents were heavily charged with rock debris of all sizes which increased their erosive power tremendously. They actively deepened the valleys below the ice, cut V-shaped channels through the solid rock on the shoulders of the hills and transported waste material far and wide. Wherever the flow of meltwater slackened, sand and gravel were dumped on the beds of these streams, and in places where temporary lakes were formed against the ice margins, layers of the finer silts and clays were deposited. Today the former marginal channels can be traced by series of terrace features on the valley sides and the sub-glacial deposits are seen forming hummocks and ridges on the lower ground. The points where meltwater channels ended are often marked by large outwash spreads of sand and gravel.

*Glaciation in Moray*

As far as Moray is concerned, it is generally agreed that there was a strong push of ice from the high precipitation areas farther west as well as from the higher ground to the south. For at least the latter part of its history the ice sheet did not cover the Buchan area and parts of eastern Moray (Fig. 3). In this area the evidence of glaciation is far from fresh. The surface drift has been more deeply weathered than in the surrounding areas and the topography is smooth and generally rounded due to downhill creep of material under periglacial conditions. Where bedrock is exposed it is usually seen to be frost shattered. Outwith this 'moraineless' area the evidence of glaciation is

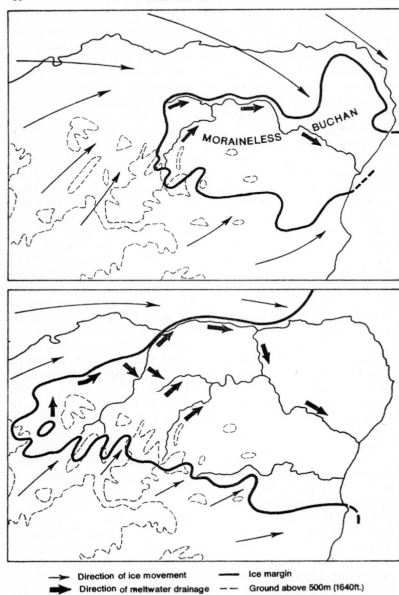

Fig. 3 Stages in Ice Sheet Decay of N.E. Scotland (After Synge 1956)

much more striking, in particular to the west of the Spey, where some workers suggest the freshness of the glacial evidence is due to a readvance.* Very fine examples of hummocky moraine and kettle hole topography are to be seen in the Lhanbryde area.

The deglaciation of Moray is pictured as being a steady retreat westwards of the Moray Firth Ice with the ice edge maintaining an orientation roughly parallel to the coast. A buried soil horizon discovered at Tiendland just southeast of Elgin has been dated at 28,000 bp, indicating that that area has been free of ice since that date. There is no fresh evidence of glaciation in the lower Spey valley and the Spey glacier may have retreated as far as Grantown at this stage. In the south of the District the larger hilltops were freed of ice and valley glaciers retreated steadily until the corrie glaciers in the Cairngorms were all that remained.

The mapping of the meltwater features of Moray helps to unravel the retreat stages of the ice sheet. At the time when ice stood at the stage depicted in Fig. 3a the main meltwater streams were being channeled via Strath Isla and the Deveron into the Ythan. By the stage shown in Fig. 3b they were also escaping along the coast where deposits of sand, silt and clay south of Buckie and Cullen mark the sites of temporary ice marginal lakes. Although the main river valleys carried the bulk of the glacial meltwaters there were numerous other drainage channels. Some are recognisable as wide, gently sloping valleys draining towards the main rivers or the coast, but now containing only small streams or even no water at all, while others are in the form of narrow, steep-sided gullies. Many bear the old names "den", "glack" or "slog". Scarcely any part of the District is without them but good examples are the den carrying the A96 road on the southeast outskirts of Keith, Glack Harnes between Ben Rinnes and Meikle Conval, the Glen of Rothes and the deep valleys now dammed to form the reservoirs at Loch Park and Romach Loch.

Marginal terrace features can be seen in most of the river

*More recently Clapperton and Sugden (1975) suggest that apart from minor fluctuations in the higher corries of the Cairngorms, the main deglaciation of the District was complete by or soon after 12,000bp. They also consider that the term 'moraineless' Buchan should be dropped because it suggests the area was unglaciated.

valleys and particularly fine examples occur in the lower reaches of the Avon, in the Spey from Ballindalloch to the sea and again in the Findhorn from where it enters Moray to the sea. Bremner (1934) considers that the Spey was dammed by ice downstream from Knockando and a lake was formed reaching a level of 202m (620 ft), which rapidly filled with sediment. As the ice retreated and the water level fell, the river cut a series of alluvial terraces in this material. Other lake stages occurred at lower levels at Rothes and at Fochabers, while at Dounduff on the Findhorn a similar series of terraces indicate a lake level there also of 202m (620 ft). From the Knockando and Rothes lakes the overflow could escape into the Isla, while that from the Fochabers lake flowed towards Buckie. The meltwaters from the Findhorn flowed eastwards along the ice via Romach Hill and Dallas into Lossie, whence for a time via Rothes Glen into the Spey, but later eastwards through the Blackhills channel. Subsequently the waters were channeled into the Black Burn and then via Rafford, Burgie and Forres. Other stages can be followed near Darnaway and the Muckle Burn.

A great depth of fluvio-glacial material covers lower Moray from the Spey to the western boundaries of the District and beyond. Some indication of the thickness of these deposits which were dumped against the ice edge can be gauged from the heights of Cluny Hill at Forres and the Binn Hill near Garmouth which are composed of some 70m (230 ft) of these materials. These deposits have been extensively reworked by marine action at the higher sea levels of the late-glacial and post-glacial eras as well as that of the present day, producing complex terrace features which merge with those of the lower reaches of the Spey and the Findhorn. The extensive storm beach shingle ridges near the coasts also date from this period. Several large erratic masses of Jurassic sediments which were deposited on lowland Moray by the ice were formerly worked as a source of lime, but are not now visible.

DRAINAGE

The drainage pattern of Moray is better studied from a simplified map such as Fig. 4 which shows only the main streams. As described previously, the solid geology of the district controls the drainage and most of the river valleys are extremely wide in relation to the streams they contain, pointing to their great age. From west to east the main systems are: -

Findhorn - Divie - Dorback Burn - Muckle Burn.
Lossie - Black Burn.
Spey - Avon - Livet - Dullan Water - Fiddich.
Deveron - Blackwater - Isla.

The largest river in Moray is the Spey, rising far to the southwest. For its valley to have attained the proportions it now boasts, the river must have cut back to intercept the old Tertiary drainage system at a very early stage in its history. However, perhaps the most quoted case of river-capture in the District

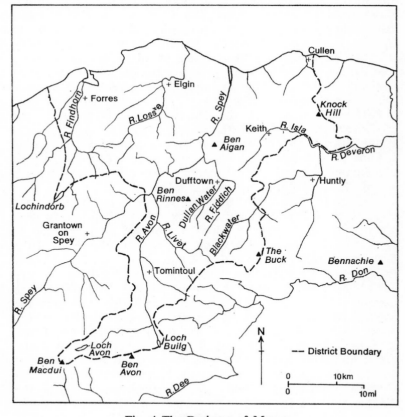

Fig. 4 The Drainage of Moray

is the beheading of the Don by the Avon, which cut back along the strike to capture the headwaters of the older, eastward-draining river at Inchrory. Fault systems too have altered the drainage and the Spey is diverted northwards at Craigellachie by a fault which runs from Dufftown to the Glen of Rothes. The weakened rocks of this fault zone also offered an easier path for the waters of the Fiddich and Dullan Water, which at one time flowed along the strike into the Isla, but are now diverted into the Spey.

In their middle reaches the Findhorn and the Spey meander in wide bottomed valleys with little gradient. In contrast, by the time these rivers pass into Moray both are actively cutting down into the country rock. The Findhorn runs in a scenic gorge which is in places not much wider than itself, while the Spey is cutting a fresh one in the wide floor of its old valley. This rejuvenation is probably due to slight crustal warping. Once these rivers reach the low ground, like the Lossie, they begin to meander as they flow over the unconsolidated material which forms the coastal plain.

The headwaters of the Deveron and its tributary the Blackwater rise in the southeast of Moray and soon pass out of the District, re-entering it near Rothiemay where the Deveron is joined by the Isla which has been meandering through a wide alluvium-filled strath. The combined rivers continue eastwards out of Moray in a deep picturesque valley.

Many of the minor streams have cut surprisingly deep channels in drift or soft country rock, while others run in deep glacial meltwater channels which are out of all proportion to the size of the streams. The catchment areas of the rivers of the District are considerable, and prolonged heavy rainfall can lead to severe flooding in their valleys and the low-lying country nearer the river mouths. The unconsolidated 'haughlands' are particularly vulnerable to erosion by floodwaters and here the banks have been strengthened in areas of known risk. In the lower reaches of the Findhorn and the Lossie the river banks have been heightened to contain the rivers in time of spate. Local historians have written vivid descriptions of the great floods of the last century, which underline the destructive powers of these rivers when in full spate. At Randolph's Leap on the Findhorn, where the river is channeled through a narrow gorge, a stone marks the spot reached by the floodwaters in 1829,

15m (50 ft) above the normal level of the river.

One great difference between the landscape of Moray and that of the Highlands farther to the west is the almost total absence of deep valley lochs. Loch Avon (Plate 1) and Loch Builg in the Cairngorms, though small, are in this class, but elsewhere the lochs are mostly of the kettle-hole type. Typical examples of these are the many lochans on the Dava and Dallas Moors. In general these lochs are very small, being at the most only a few hundred metres across; however, Lochindorb which occupies a shallow depression on the Dava Moor, is some 3½ km (2 miles) in length. Some of the lochs have been dammed for use as reservoirs and some for sporting purposes, but all are shallow.

### Coastal Features

About half of the coastline of Moray is made up of fine sandy beaches while the remainder is of rock or shingle. One of the more attractive stretches is that between Burghead and Covesea where interesting rock formations and cliff features alternate with small picturesque sandy coves. Here the Permo-Triassic sandstones show a large variety of erosional features such as the exploitation of the jointing in the rocks by wave action, the formation of potholes of all sizes and the differential weathering of the hard and soft portions of the sandstones. All stages in the development, enlargement and collapse of caves can be examined including a sea stack called Gow's Castle. Some of the caves have been excavated at sea levels slightly above that of the present day.

From Buckie to the eastern boundary of the District the coast is mostly formed of Cullen Quartzite and the orientation of the coastline is controlled by the strike of these rocks. There are one or two small caves along the coast and a very fine arch, the Bow Fiddle Rock (Plate 2) at Portknockie and another in the headland nearby. Evidence of an old sea level at a height of just oves 5 m (17 ft) can be found in most parts of the Moray coast, usually in the form of a raised beach backed by a cliff feature. The original fishing villages between Portgordon and Cullen were built on this platform, later to expand to the higher ground above the old cliff line, giving rise to the term "seatown" for the lower parts of the villages. Old sea stacks dating from this higher sea level can be seen on the Cullen golf course.

As the post-glacial sea level fell, the glacial sands and gravels were extensively reworked by wave action and there are splendid examples of storm beach shingle ridges between Portgordon and Lossiemouth which are in places over 800 m ($\frac{1}{2}$ mile) in width, and others at Findhorn and on the Culbin foreland. The longshore drift moves beach material westwards building bars across the mouths of the rivers Spey, Lossie and Findhorn. The one at Speymouth is particularly troublesome as it diverts the river closer to Kingston, which is constantly threatened by erosion, and periodically cuts have to be made through the spit to channel the river away from the village. The last cut was made in 1962 and at the time of writing (1974) it is being cut again. Though tradition has it that at one stage prior to 1798 this bar had reached a length of 5 km (3 miles), it does not appear on old maps, but it certainly was long enough to provide a sheltered anchorage. The earlier shingle ridges moving west from the Binn Hill area had enclosed the Spynie basin and diverted the drainage of the Lossie into Burghead bay. The river later breached these ridges near Caysbriggs and thereafter Spynie Loch, Fig. 5, was

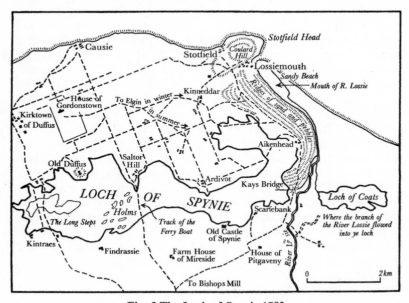

Fig. 5 The Loch of Spynie 1783

an arm of the sea until the 15th century with a harbour at Spynie Palace. The entrance slowly silted up and after a series of attempts the loch was finally successfully drained in 1880 (Mackintosh 1928).

Like the Spynie basin, the Roseisle — Kinloss area is largely made up of estuarine sands, silts and clays, and was at one time protected on the seaward side by a series of storm beach shingle ridges. In Burghead Bay most of the storm beach has been eroded away and waves attacking the unprotected sands have enlarged the bay into a semi circular form with some 10 km (6 miles) of sandy beach. Considerable spreads of peat are revealed from time to time and point to the former presence of shallow lakes in the area. The bay is backed by an area of sand-dunes now planted with trees. Over the centuries the material eroded from Burghead Bay has been moved westwards to build the various bar features across the mouth of the River Findhorn. The present hooked spit (Plate 3) forces the exit channel to cut deeper into the opposite shore at the Culbin Forest. Findhorn Bay empties almost completely at low water and is very slowly silting up; it provides a fine sheltered stretch of water for yachting. The tidal race in the narrow entrance to the bay is very swift and the sand bar across the mouth has to be negotiated with care as it frequently shifts its position during storms.

Until it was stabilised by afforestation, the Culbin foreland was a wide expanse of dune-covered, sandy wasteland with old storm beach shingle ridges showing here and there through the sand. The area is famous because of the engulfing of the Culbin estates by drifting sands in the year 1695, an event much dramatized in literature, but now considered to have been a more gradual process on which the great storms of 1694-95 put the final seal. Many artefacts dating from prehistoric to recent times have been discovered amongst the dunes.

Ogilvie (1923) and Steers (1937) have discussed the evolution of the foreland. More recent information from aerial photographs and the distribution of the soil and peat deposits confirms that the Findhorn originally drained westwards on the south side of the main shingle deposits which formed a westward growing bar system, and reached the sea just west of Cloddiemoss. As the bar continued to grow, the river broke through it somewhere near the present opening to Findhorn Bay, leaving the old exit

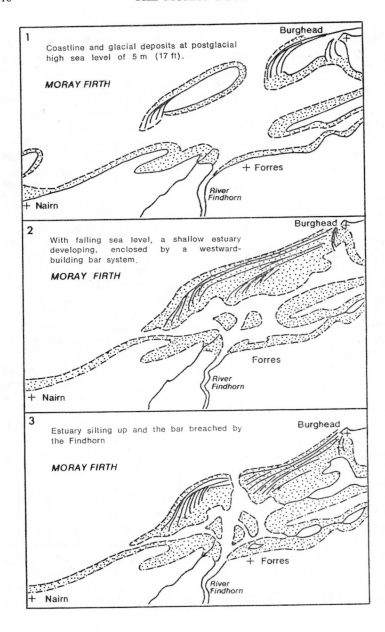

**1** Coastline and glacial deposits at postglacial high sea level of 5 m (17 ft).

MORAY FIRTH

Burghead

+ Forres

River Findhorn

+ Nairn

**2** With falling sea level, a shallow estuary developing, enclosed by a westward-building bar system.

MORAY FIRTH

Burghead

Forres

River Findhorn

+ Nairn

**3** Estuary silting up and the bar breached by the Findhorn

MORAY FIRTH

Burghead

+ Forres

River Findhorn

+ Nairn

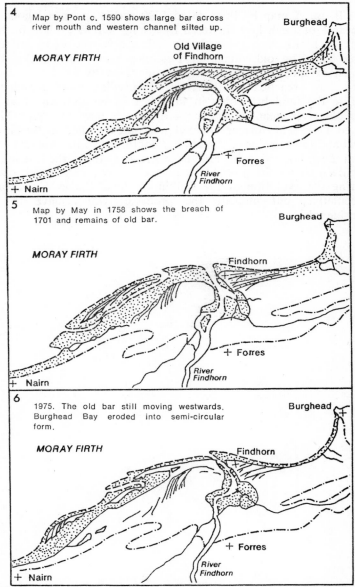

**4** Map by Pont c. 1590 shows large bar across river mouth and western channel silted up.

Burghead

MORAY FIRTH

Old Village of Findhorn

+ Forres

River Findhorn

+ Nairn

**5** Map by May in 1758 shows the breach of 1701 and remains of old bar.

Burghead

MORAY FIRTH

Findhorn

+ Forres

River Findhorn

+ Nairn

**6** 1975. The old bar still moving westwards. Burghead Bay eroded into semi-circular form.

Burghead

MORAY FIRTH

Findhorn

+ Forres

River Findhorn

+ Nairn

Fig. 6 Stages in the Development of Culbin Foreland and Burghead Bay

C

to silt up. A map by Pont dated 1590 shows an open lagoon in the area of Loch Loy sheltered by a long sandbar, while farther east the Findhorn is shown being deflected westwards by another long bar. The old village of Findhorn was built on this bar which extended 8 km (5 miles) or more westwards before it in turn was breached by the river. The village was abandoned before the final breaching in 1701 but its position and that of the old river channel are marked on the map by Peter May dated 1758. The former channel was quickly filled in by blown sand and the remains of the old bar continued to move westwards with new hooked spits and bars growing from the breaches. Figure 6 shows the probable sequence of events that took place during the evolution of the Culbin foreland. Stages 1 to 3 are speculative, but indicate the processes which have to be considered.

APPENDIX

*Additional notes on the Geology of Moray*

Geologists of international repute were being attracted to Moray as long ago as 1840. Their interest was initially in the fossil fish beds of the Old Red Sandstone, but these finds were partially eclipsed by the discovery of reptilian remains in the Permo-Triassic rocks of the Elgin and Lossiemouth areas, which are the only known localities for such remains in the country. This activity led to the development of a considerable interest in geology among the local inhabitants, some of whom made significant contributions to the science. Fine collections of fossils were made, the most famous being the Altyre Collection, now housed in Edinburgh. After the turn of the century more attractive problems in other parts of Scotland shifted the focus of attention away from the fossils of Moray and work on them gradually declined. The massive nature of the sandstones of the District does not lend itself to easy quarrying by the amateur, and today, with all but one of the quarries closed, little fresh material comes to light.

The Dalradian rocks have played a leading part in the understanding of metamorphic processes ever since Barrow's pioneer work at the end of the last century. He was first to map the occurrence of certain minerals and use them as indicators of different zones of metamorphism. Geologists have been paying increasing attention to the Dalradian series in Moray over recent years as well as to the basic and granitic intrusions, and their findings are helping to unravel the complex tectonic processes involved in the Caledonian Orogeny. The more uniform Moinian granulites and quartzites on the other hand have not proved attractive to the investigators and very little work has been done on them.

## SUMMARY OF SOLID GEOLOGY OF MORAY

### SEDIMENTARY ROCKS

#### JURASSIC

LOWER LIASSIC:               Sandstones, siltstones, mudstones, shales.

#### PERMIAN AND TRIASSIC

UPPER TRIASSIC:              Cherty rock, standstones.
TRIASSIC:                    Pebbly sandstones.
LOWER TRIASSIC OR
UPPER PERMIAN:              Sandstones.

#### OLD RED SANDSTONE

UPPER:                       Sandstones, pebbly sandstones, cornstone.
MIDDLE:                      Sandstones, conglomerate, nodule beds.
MIDDLE OR LOWER:             Sandstones, breccia, limestones.

## METAMORPHIC ROCKS

DALRADIAN ASSEMBLAGE

| | |
|---|---|
| PORTSOY GROUP: | Dark schists, mica-schists, calcareous flagstones, limestones. |
| DURN HILL QUARTZITE: | Quartzites (flaggy and massive), quartz-schist, mica-schist, calcareous schists. |
| SANDEND GROUP: | Black Schist (carbonaceous garnetiferous mica-schists and slates locally passing into clay slates), limestones. |
| GARRON POINT GROUP: | Actinolite-schist. |
| CRATHIE POINT GROUP: | Calc-biotite-schist. |
| FINDLATER FLAGS: | Semi-pelitic flagstones with quartzite. |
| WEST SANDS GROUP: | Garnet-mica-schist. |
| CULLEN QUARTZITE: | Quartzite. |
| MOINIAN ASSEMBLAGE: | Psammitic granulites, pelitic schists, striped schists, quartzite. |

## IGNEOUS ROCKS

| | |
|---|---|
| SMALL INTRUSIONS, DYKES, SILLS AND VEINS: | Andesites, lamprophyres, microdiorite, microgranite, pegmatite, quartz-porphyry, felsite, aplite. |
| LARGER INTRUSIONS: ACID | Granites plus associated small masses of diorite of varied composition. |
| BASIC AND ULTRABASIC | Peridotite, gabbro, norite. (May be represented by serpentine, amphibolite, epidiorite, hornblende-schist.). |
| LAVAS: | Basic pillow lavas. |

## NOTES ON ECONOMIC RESOURCES

From about 1728 to 1737 iron ore was mined in the Conglass area to the east of Tomintoul. The ore was mostly hematite which was found in a narrow vein running in a 5km (3 miles) long fault zone in the black schists. The ore was carried by packhorse to Strath Nethy where it was smelted using charcoal from the local forests. The mine was then abandoned but reopened in 1840 to extract the manganese ores psilomelane and wad. Around 1870 veins of similar composition were investigated at Arndilly north of Craigellachie, but were not considered worth exploiting.

Mineralization involving galena, hematite, fluorspar, barytes, calcite and quartz occurs in the fault zones and rocks of the area between Rothes, Burghead and Buckie. Attempts were made to work the galena deposits in the cherty rock at Stotfield during the last century but the extraction proved too difficult. The possibility of extracting the fluorspar which is the cementing material in some of the sandstones of Hopeman has also been examined. More recently low grade ore deposits in the east of the district have also been evaluated.

In lower Moray the fossiliferous nodule beds of the Old Red Sandstone and the Cornstones of Cothall on the Findhorn and of the Elgin area were used at one time as a source of lime. In addition the large erratic blocks of Jurassic sediments were exploited. Farther to the east and south the much purer metamorphic limestones of the Dalradian (depicted in black in Fig. 2) were used and quarries were opened along the entire length of the series. With the advent of railways and modern transport, the quarries in the impure limestones slowly went out of business and today the main ones in the District are at Keith, Dufftown and Tomintoul.

The sandstones of the Permo-Triassic and Upper Old Red Sandstone deposits of the Hopeman and Elgin areas for long supplied most of the building stone for lower Moray, and the area is dotted with quarries. With the increase in the use of concrete for building these gradually closed, so that today the only working quarry is at Hopeman. The softer rock of the Middle Old Red deposits was also used, particularly in the Tomintoul area. Flagstones of the Aultmore and other areas and some of the mica schists provided building material elsewhere, with the finer beds being used for paving and roofing. The slaty bands in the black schists of Glenlivet and Mortlach were also exploited at one time.

Roadstone and aggregate quarries have been opened in several places in the Moine granulites, while fluvio-glacial gravel deposits and inland storm beach shingle ridges have also been extensively worked in lower Moray.

Clays from the glacial lake deposits were worked for tile and brick making in the Spynie basin, at Cullen and at Craigellachie where there was also a pottery.

There are still considerable areas of hill and basin peat in the District, but its use as a fuel is now very limited. The distillers are the main users, Scottish Malt Distillers for example using some 20,000 cu m (26,000 cu yd) annually. To this end only a few peat mosses are now worked and additional supplies are brought from outside Moray, if required.

## APPENDIX

*SOME LOCALITIES FOR EXAMINING THE ROCKS OF MORAY*

| Rock Type | Location | National Grid Reference* |
|---|---|---|
| Actinolitic flags | Burn of Cairnfield | 420614 |
| Andesite | Gollachy Burn | 405644 |
| | Burn of Rannas | 464645 |
| | Corinacy | 396294 |
| Aplite | Glen Builg | 179052 |
| | Dà Dhruim Loin | 142048 |
| Blackschist | Avon Valley | 185080 |
| | | 160137 |
| | Slateford | 224216 |
| | Tomnavoulin | 213264 |
| | Dufftown | 328405 |
| | Braehead | 425491 |
| Breccia | Cone Rock | 267473 |
| | Burn of Mulben | 325517 |
| Calc-silicate | Tullochallum | 340395 |
| Chiastolite slate | Ardwell | 376303 |
| Conglomerate | Delnabo Bridge | 161171 |
| | Fochabers | 367567 |
| | Cullen Golf Course | 497678 |
| Diorite | Netherly | 243482 |
| | Leids Hill | 418266 |
| | Reekimlane | 360253 |
| Epidiorite | Blackwater | 376307 |
| | Glenmarkie | 398387 |
| Felsite | Muckle Fergie Burn | 171138 |
| | Inchrory | 179084 |
| Gabbro | Blackwater | 346291 |
| Granite | Cairngorm | 006041 |
| | Braes of Glenlivet | 250226 |
| | Ben Rinnes | 255355 |
| Granulite | Randolph's Leap | (NH)999496 |
| | Wester New Forres Quarry | 062578 |
| Hornblende Schist | Blackwater | 376307 |
| Hornfels | Blackwater | 370304 |
| | Blue Hill | 294428 |
| | Knock Hill | 537543 |
| Lamprophyre | Aikenway | 302499 |
| | Ardmachie Burn | 412591 |

*All prefixed NJ unless otherwise stated.

Some Localities for Examining the Rocks of Moray — Continued

| Rock Type | Location | National Grid Reference* |
|---|---|---|
| Limestone | Tomintoul | 155194 |
| | Dufftown | 332407 |
| | Keith | 439482 |
| | Limehillock | 515519 |
| Mica Schist | Bridge of Brown | 125206 |
| | Dullan Water | 313380 |
| Micro Diorite | Portessie | 436665 |
| Norite | Ternemny | 558528 |
| | Meikle Cairn | 419254 |
| Pillow Lava | Blackwater | 370304 |
| Phyllite | Burn of Mulben | 343517 |
| | Den of Pitlurg | 433452 |
| Quartzite | Ess of Glenlatterach | 193533 |
| | Portnockie to | 496685- |
| | Portessie | 440666 |
| | Cullen Bay | 518677 |
| Sandstone (Middle O.R.) | River Spey | 338594 |
| | Burn of Tynet | 383621 |
| (Upper O.R.) | Sluie | 003532 |
| | Carden Hill | 143623 |
| | Knock of Alves | 162629 |
| | Quarry Wood | 175635 |
| (Permo-Trias) | Covesea to | 187710- |
| | Cummingstown | 123692 |
| | Burghead Pier | 108691 |
| (Jurassic) | Stotfield between tidemarks | 229712 |
| Serpentine | Blackwater Lodge | 336287 |
| | Drumnagorach | 520520 |
| Slate | Slateford | 224216 |
| | The Scalp | 358370 |
| | Tarrymount Quarry | 411585 |
| Troctolite | Upper Fowlwood | 527528 |

*All prefixed NJ unless otherwise stated.

## SOME FEATURES OF GEOGRAPHICAL/GEOLOGICAL
## INTEREST IN MORAY

| Feature | Location | National Grid Reference* |
|---|---|---|
| Arch | Portknockie | 494689 |
| | | 497686 |
| Caves | Cummingstown | 130691 |
| | Hopeman | 160702 |
| | Covesea | 181708 |
| | Findochty | 474683 |
| Clay Galls | Leggat Quarry | 175635 |
| | Burghead | 108692 |
| Dune bedding | Hopeman | 160702 |
| Earth Pillars | Alt Dearg | 334565 |
| Fault | Burghead | 122692 |
| | Gipsies Cave | 160702 |
| | Rosebrae Quarry | 173633 |
| Folding | | |
| (in Black Schist) | Ailnack Gorge | 155160 |
| | Dullan Water | 325384 |
| | Dufftown | 332407 |
| | Braehead | 425491 |
| (in Quartzite) | Pitchroy Mill | 173378 |
| (in Sandstone) | Hopeman | 152701 |
| Fossils† | | |
| (Fish remains) | Altyre Burn | |
| | Carden Hill | |
| | Knock of Alves | |
| | Quarry Wood | |
| | Scaat Craig | |
| | Dipple | |
| | Burn of Tynet | |
| (Reptile remains) | Carden Hill | |
| | Quarry Wood | |
| | Lossiemouth | |
| (Reptile Footprints) | Clashaig Quarry | 162702 |
| Fossil Glacial Till | Muckle Fergie Burn | 317814 |
| Glacial Striae | Carden Hill | 143622 |
| | Quarry Wood Hill | 184636 |

*All prefixed NJ unless otherwise stated.

†A detailed list is contained in "The Geology of the Elgin District." The supply of fossil material is almost completely exhausted due to the closing of the quarries.

Some Features of Geographical/Geological Interest in Moray—Continued

| Feature | Location | National Grid Reference* |
|---|---|---|
| Kettleholes | Dava Moor | (NH)990394 |
|  | Lhanbryde | 280600 |
| Mudcracks | Leggat Quarry | 175635 |
| Potholes | Giant's Chair | 322383 |
|  | Randolph's Leap | (NH)999496 |
| Raised Beach | Portgordon | 405648 |
|  | Cullen | 500676 |
| Ripple Marks | Leggat Quarry | 175635 |
| Rodding in |  |  |
| Quartzite | Ess of Glenlatterach | 193533 |
|  | Wester New Forres |  |
|  | Quarry | 063578 |
| Sea Stack | Gow's Castle | 181708 |
|  | Cullen Golf Course | 497678 |
| Shearplanes | Cliffs of Hopeman | 166704 |
| Slickensiding | Dufftown | 332407 |
|  | Gipsies Cave | 160702 |
| Solifluction Lobes | Cairngorm | 006033 |
| Storm beach shingle |  |  |
| ridges | West of Kingston | 315662 |
|  | Findhorn | 060643 |
|  | Culbin | (NH)992627 |
| Terraces | River Findhorn | (NH)997495 |
|  |  | 013545 |
|  | River Avon | 159279 |
|  |  | 189339 |
|  | River Spey | 186380 |
|  |  | 277503 |
|  | River Lossie | 118495 |
| Tors | Ben Rinnes | 255355 |
|  | Meall Gaineimh | 166051 |
| Unconformity | Portknockie | 497686 |
|  | Ailnack Gorge | 154157 |
|  | Ardmachie Burn | 402594 |
|  | Burn of Buckie | 420651 |
| Varved Clays | Spey North of |  |
|  | Ordiequish | 340575 |
| Wind-faceted pebbles | Burghead | 108691 |
|  | Sluie | 012528 |

*All prefixed NJ unless otherwise stated.

# 2
# CLIMATE

SINCLAIR ROSS

The District of Moray is well sheltered by the mountains of the Scottish Highlands from the prevailing southwest to west winds blowing from the Atlantic. These winds deposit most of their moisture in the form of rain on the windward slopes of the mountains, and on the lee side the descending air is dried and warmed by the föhn effect — a name originally given to dry winds descending on the lee side of the Alps. This leads to much of Moray having a drier, warmer and sunnier climate than the comparatively high latitude of the District might suggest. When comparing the climate of the favoured Laich area with that of other places of similar latitude in the Northern Hemisphere, perhaps only the south coast of Sweden enjoys better conditions.

The climate does, however, vary considerably throughout Moray due to differences in exposure and altitude. Eastwards along the coast there is increasing exposure to winds from between northwest and east; southwards conditions become less genial as the effects of altitude on temperature, cloud cover and precipitation come into play. This continues to the sparsely populated southern borders of the District, where the higher hill tops have a much more rigorous climate than the valleys below, and in winter, in the windswept Cairngorm area, arctic conditions of great severity may be encountered.

Long-term climatological records for Moray are scarce, particularly for upland parts, and, in discussing the separate aspects of the climate, use has been made of estimates based on what short-term records are available, and some data for stations just outside the District have been included.

### RAINFALL

The District as a whole, and the coastal area in particular, has a much lower average rainfall than parts of Scotland farther to the west. Not only is there shelter from rain-bearing winds coming from the prevailing direction of west to southwest, but also from those blowing from the south and southeast. However, as the wind backs from southeast to east, this shelter is gradually lost, and in the sector from east to northwest, Moray is completely exposed to any rain-bearing winds. A considerable proportion of the annual rainfall, particularly in the winter months, comes from showers associated with winds from directions between

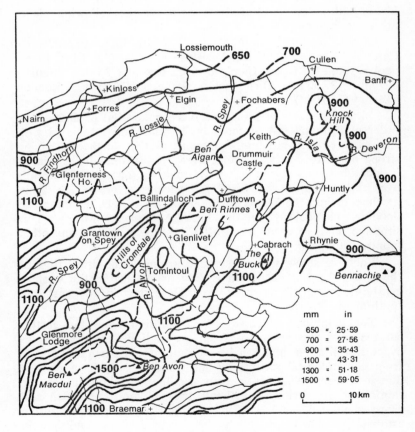

Fig. 7 The Rainfall of Moray. Annual average 1916-1950

northeast and northwest, but western parts of the District get some shelter from the high ground of northwest Scotland.

The lowland area of Moray has an annual rainfall of less than 800 mm (31 in) on average, and in parts of the Laich less than 650 mm (25 in), making the area one of the driest in Scotland (Fig. 7). Inland, rainfall increases in elevation to reach a maximum somewhat in excess of 1500 mm (60 in) per annum in the Cairngorm area. Comparison with places in the west of Scotland with similar latitude shows annual averages of 1300 mm (50 in) at sea level and of more than 3900 mm (155 in) over the higher hills. Annual rainfall averages for the following places are given for comparison:

Kinlochewe 1798 mm (70.79 in), Glasgow 1018 mm (40.08 in), Cardiff 1069 mm (42.09 in), Aberdeen 836 mm (32.91 in), Liverpool 891 mm (35.08 in), Cambridge 552 mm (21.73 in), Edinburgh 699 mm (27.52 in), Birmingham 780 mm (30.71 in), London 639 mm (25.16 in).

Nearly all cases of prolonged heavy rainfall at Kinloss of the order of 25 mm (1 in) or more in 24 hours are associated with stationary or slow-moving depressions in the North Sea, giving strong north to northeast winds over Moray. Inland the rainfall is identified by orographic uplift, making for substantial falls over the catchment areas of the various rivers which drain northwards into the Moray Firth, and often results in widespread flooding, particularly in the lowland area of Moray. This situation tends to occur more often in August that in any other month of the year.

Table 1a shows that on average, spring is the driest time of the year. The wettest period is July or August in the western coastal area but October or even December in the east and south of the District.

The combined processes of evaporation from the earth's surface and transpiration from vegetation are known as evapotranspiration, and can be estimated for a particular period from climatological records, or measured directly by a method due to Green (1963). It is then possible, by allowing for the rainfall of the period, to estimate the soil moisture deficit and assess the need for irrigation at any site. Evapotranspiration estimates, (Table 1b), highlight the risk of drought conditions in lowland Moray in spring and early summer.

## Table 1a
## MONTHLY AND ANNUAL AVERAGES OF RAINFALL (MILLIMETRES) FOR STATIONS IN AND BORDERING MORAY — 1916-1950

| | Height (metres) | (feet) | Jan | Feb | Mar | April | May | Jun | Jul | Aug | Sept | Oct | Nov | Dec | Year | Year (ins.) |
|---|---|---|---|---|---|---|---|---|---|---|---|---|---|---|---|---|
| Nairn | 6 | 20 | 51 | 38 | 35 | 41 | 50 | 48 | 70 | 70 | 59 | 69 | 56 | 48 | 635 | 25.00 |
| Forres | 37 | 122 | 52 | 40 | 38 | 44 | 53 | 56 | 80 | 76 | 67 | 76 | 60 | 49 | 691 | 27.20 |
| Kinloss | 5 | 15 | 46 | 34 | 32 | 40 | 48 | 50 | 71 | 69 | 59 | 68 | 54 | 43 | 614 | 24.17 |
| Glenferness House | 214 | 700 | 82 | 60 | 58 | 72 | 74 | 77 | 104 | 99 | 89 | 102 | 81 | 69 | 932 | 36.69 |
| Ballindalloch | 192 | 630 | 76 | 56 | 53 | 67 | 65 | 66 | 93 | 87 | 84 | 92 | 79 | 66 | 883 | 34.76 |
| Gordon Castle | 32 | 105 | 60 | 47 | 43 | 47 | 53 | 57 | 78 | 79 | 77 | 80 | 73 | 57 | 751 | 29.57 |
| Drummuir Castle | 189 | 620 | 73 | 56 | 57 | 71 | 73 | 75 | 96 | 95 | 97 | 102 | 89 | 71 | 957 | 37.68 |
| Banff | 24 | 79 | 62 | 49 | 41 | 45 | 52 | 53 | 73 | 76 | 76 | 75 | 79 | 63 | 744 | 29.29 |
| Braemar | 338 | 1110 | 104 | 68 | 57 | 57 | 66 | 48 | 76 | 78 | 75 | 105 | 97 | 96 | 927 | 36.49 |
| Lossiemouth* | 6 | 20 | 47 | 36 | 35 | 40 | 47 | 51 | 70 | 68 | 63 | 68 | 58 | 49 | 633 | 24.92 |
| Elgin, Kirkhill* | 11 | 36 | 51 | 39 | 38 | 45 | 51 | 57 | 76 | 75 | 70 | 74 | 63 | 50 | 689 | 27.13 |
| Keith* | 110 | 360 | 75 | 59 | 55 | 65 | 68 | 71 | 94 | 96 | 96 | 99 | 91 | 73 | 943 | 37.13 |
| Cullen House* | 46 | 151 | 63 | 47 | 43 | 48 | 54 | 58 | 79 | 79 | 79 | 81 | 77 | 83 | 768 | 30.24 |
| Glenlivet* | 330 | 1085 | 91 | 65 | 56 | 67 | 68 | 65 | 87 | 82 | 84 | 100 | 86 | 75 | 925 | 36.42 |
| Cabrach* | 317 | 1040 | 96 | 72 | 63 | 75 | 76 | 71 | 99 | 90 | 95 | 111 | 98 | 85 | 1031 | 40.59 |
| Glenmore Lodge* | 341 | 1120 | 111 | 76 | 62 | 70 | 69 | 65 | 97 | 85 | 88 | 112 | 96 | 85 | 1016 | 40.00 |

NOTE: Averages marked * have been estimated from short-term records.

## Table 1b
## ESTIMATED AVERAGE EVAPOTRANSPIRATION (P.T.) IN MILLIMETRES FOR COASTAL DISTRICTS OF MORAY

| Jan | Feb | Mar | Apr | May | Jun | Jul | Aug | Sep | Oct | Nov | Dec | Summer Apr/Sep | Winter Oct/Mar |
|---|---|---|---|---|---|---|---|---|---|---|---|---|---|
| 6 | 12 | 32 | 60 | 83 | 93 | 87 | 62 | 43 | 25 | 8 | 6 | 427 | 91 |

TEMPERATURE

During winter the temperature of the waters of the Moray Firth can fall to around 4°C, but this is still high enough to have a considerable warming effect on cold air reaching the area from the north. As a result, average winter temperatures in the coastal areas of Moray compare favourably with those of places much farther south. Inland the warming influence of the sea is more than offset by the decrease of temperature with increasing altitude, so winter temperatures are lower.

When spring sets in in England, winter is still lingering on in the north. The sea warms but slowly and cold east to southeast winds are rather persistent, making spring in Moray later and cooler than in the south. Due to the effect of latitude, southern parts of the British Isles have a higher heat intake from the sun, and by summer, temperatures there quickly outstrip those of Moray. The sea remains comparatively cool in these northern parts, reaching a maximum of around 13°C in August, so throughout summer sea breezes have a cooling effect on the coastal districts. During the autumn, predominantly westerly winds bring mild air in from the Atlantic and delay the onset of winter with its cold northerly outbreaks.

For any site, the temperature pattern is very dependent on exposure. Some sheltered inland places, especially those on south-facing slopes, can enjoy surprisingly high temperatures in summer. In winter on the other hand, in valleys in particular, but also on open undulating ground, cold air drainage and frost hollow effect are widespread, and lead to very low temperatures being recorded when the ground is snow-covered.

Some temperature averages are given in Table 2a. These show little variation throughout lower Moray, but that the temperatures in upland districts are considerably lower than those near the coast, because of the decrease in temperature with increase in altitude.

The length of the growing season for the common crops and vegetation of northwest Europe can be measured by the accumulation of day-degrees Celsius above a daily mean temperature of 5.6°C, (Birse and Dry, 1970). In the lower parts of Moray, the growing season begins, on average, in the last week in March and lasts until mid November, while on ground

**Table 2a**

AVERAGES OF DAILY MEAN TEMPERATURES IN DEGREES CELSIUS
AT STATIONS IN OR BORDERING MORAY

| | Jan | Feb | Mar | Apr | May | Jun | Jul | Aug | Sep | Oct | Nov | Dec | Year |
|---|---|---|---|---|---|---|---|---|---|---|---|---|---|
| Nairn | 2.8 | 3.3 | 5.2 | 7.2 | 9.5 | 12.5 | 14.1 | 13.7 | 12.1 | 9.5 | 5.6 | 3.9 | 8.3 |
| Forres | 2.7 | 2.9 | 5.1 | 7.2 | 9.7 | 12.7 | 14.0 | 13.7 | 12.3 | 9.3 | 5.3 | 3.7 | 8.3 |
| Kinloss | 2.9 | 3.1 | 5.3 | 7.3 | 9.7 | 12.7 | 14.1 | 13.8 | 12.3 | 9.5 | 5.7 | 3.9 | 8.3 |
| Gordon Castle | 2.9 | 3.2 | 5.2 | 7.4 | 9.7 | 12.7 | 14.1 | 13.9 | 12.3 | 9.5 | 5.7 | 4.0 | 8.4 |
| Braemar | 0.4 | 0.5 | 2.7 | 5.2 | 8.2 | 11.5 | 12.7 | 12.3 | 10.3 | 7.5 | 3.4 | 1.7 | 6.4 |
| Lossiemouth* | 2.8 | 3.2 | 5.2 | 7.1 | 9.6 | 12.5 | 14.3 | 13.9 | 12.1 | 9.1 | 5.8 | 4.1 | 8.3 |
| Elgin* | 3.4 | 3.8 | 5.4 | 7.5 | 10.2 | 12.9 | 15.1 | 14.5 | 12.6 | 9.4 | 6.3 | 4.4 | 8.8 |
| Banff* | 3.1 | 3.6 | 5.2 | 7.3 | 9.7 | 12.5 | 14.9 | 14.1 | 12.3 | 9.3 | 6.2 | 4.4 | 8.4 |
| Glenmore Lodge* | 0.7 | 1.1 | 3.2 | 5.4 | 7.9 | 11.2 | 12.6 | 12.3 | 10.3 | 7.5 | 3.8 | 2.2 | 6.5 |
| Glenlivet* | 0.3 | 0.5 | 2.7 | 5.1 | 8.1 | 10.9 | 12.6 | 12.2 | 10.1 | 6.9 | 3.5 | 1.7 | 6.2 |

NOTE: The averages for Nairn, Forres, Kinloss, Gordon Castle and Braemar are for the
period 1941-1970, while those for the other stations are for 1931-1960.
*Estimates from short-term records.

**Table 2b**

AVERAGE MONTHLY MAXIMUM AND MINIMUM TEMPERATURES
IN DEGREES CELSIUS

(30 Years Period 1941-1970)

| | Jan | Feb | Mar | Apr | May | Jun | Jul | Aug | Sep | Oct | Nov | Dec | Year* |
|---|---|---|---|---|---|---|---|---|---|---|---|---|---|
| **Nairn** | | | | | | | | | | | | | |
| Maximum | 11.5 | 11.6 | 14.4 | 17.3 | 20.4 | 23.8 | 23.5 | 23.3 | 21.1 | 18.3 | 13.6 | 12.0 | 25.7 |
| Minimum | -8.0 | -7.0 | -4.7 | -2.9 | -0.1 | 2.9 | 5.4 | 4.5 | 2.5 | -0.5 | -4.3 | -5.6 | -9.7 |
| **Forres** | | | | | | | | | | | | | |
| Maximum | 11.5 | 11.5 | 15.1 | 17.9 | 21.2 | 23.9 | 23.8 | 23.5 | 21.7 | 18.5 | 13.5 | 12.0 | 25.6 |
| Minimum | -7.0 | -6.4 | -4.4 | -2.5 | -0.4 | 2.8 | 5.2 | 4.7 | 2.7 | -0.4 | -3.8 | -5.5 | -9.0 |
| **Kinloss†** | | | | | | | | | | | | | |
| Maximum | 11.8 | 11.8 | 14.9 | 17.6 | 21.2 | 23.7 | 24.0 | 23.4 | 21.6 | 18.8 | 13.9 | 12.3 | 25.8 |
| Minimum | -8.0 | -7.5 | -4.9 | -3.2 | -0.5 | 2.5 | 4.9 | 4.1 | 3.3 | -0.8 | -4.5 | -6.1 | -10.5 |
| **Gordon Castle** | | | | | | | | | | | | | |
| Maximum | 11.7 | 11.7 | 15.3 | 18.1 | 20.9 | 24.3 | 24.3 | 23.7 | 22.1 | 18.9 | 13.8 | 12.1 | 26.2 |
| Minimum | -6.5 | -5.9 | -3.6 | -2.0 | 0.3 | 3.4 | 5.6 | 5.1 | 3.4 | 0.4 | -2.7 | -4.6 | -8.7 |
| **Braemar** | | | | | | | | | | | | | |
| Maximum | 8.9 | 8.7 | 13.0 | 16.2 | 21.1 | 23.7 | 23.3 | 22.7 | 20.1 | 16.5 | 11.6 | 9.9 | 25.4 |
| Minimum | -13.3 | -13.3 | -9.6 | -6.0 | -2.9 | 0.5 | 2.5 | 0.9 | -0.8 | -4.0 | -9.0 | -10.8 | -17.1 |

*Average of highest/lowest in each year

†Some breaks in observations

## Table 2c

### ABSOLUTE MONTHLY MAXIMUM AND MINIMUM TEMPERATURES IN DEGREES CELSIUS

(30 Years Period 1941-1970)

| | Jan | Feb | Mar | Apr | May | Jun | Jul | Aug | Sep | Oct | Nov | Dec | Year |
|---|---|---|---|---|---|---|---|---|---|---|---|---|---|
| **Nairn** | | | | | | | | | | | | | |
| Maximum | 15.0 | 16.7 | 21.1 | 22.2 | 25.0 | 29.4 | 27.2 | 30.6 | 25.0 | 24.4 | 20.0 | 16.1 | 30.6 |
| Minimum | -13.3 | -16.7 | -11.1 | -6.7 | -3.3 | -2.2 | 2.2 | 1.0 | -1.7 | -5.6 | -12.2 | -12.2 | -16.7 |
| **Forres** | | | | | | | | | | | | | |
| Maximum | 14.4 | 16.1 | 20.6 | 22.8 | 25.0 | 27.8 | 28.3 | 30.6 | 25.6 | 24.4 | 16.1 | 13.9 | 30.6 |
| Minimum | -13.3 | -14.4 | -10.6 | -6.1 | -2.2 | -0.6 | 1.7 | 1.1 | -1.1 | -5.6 | -11.7 | -16.7 | -16.7 |
| **Kinloss†** | | | | | | | | | | | | | |
| Maximum | 13.9 | 15.6 | 22.2 | 22.2 | 23.9 | 30.0 | 30.6 | 30.0 | 25.6 | 24.4 | 20.0 | 17.2 | 30.6 |
| Minimum | -15.6 | -16.1 | -11.1 | -7.3 | -2.8 | -1.1 | 1.5 | 1.1 | -1.1 | -6.7 | -8.9 | -16.0 | -16.1 |
| **Gordon Castle** | | | | | | | | | | | | | |
| Maximum | 15.0 | 16.1 | 22.2 | 22.2 | 26.7 | 29.4 | 30.0 | 30.0 | 26.1 | 23.9 | 19.4 | 15.6 | 30.0* |
| Minimum | -15.0 | -16.1 | -12.2 | -6.1 | -2.2 | -0.6 | 2.8 | 3.3 | -1.1 | -3.3 | -9.4 | -16.1 | -16.1 |
| **Braemar** | | | | | | | | | | | | | |
| Maximum | 11.7 | 13.3 | 20.6 | 21.1 | 27.2 | 27.8 | 29.4 | 27.8 | 23.9 | 21.1 | 15.6 | 12.8 | 29.4 |
| Minimum | -22.2 | -25.0 | -21.7 | -10.0 | -6.7 | -2.2 | -0.6 | -2.2 | -6.1 | -8.3 | -16.1 | -19.4 | -25.0 |

NOTES: †Some breaks in observations.

*The absolute maximum temperature of 32.2 degrees Celsius was recorded at Gordon Castle on 1st September, 1906.

D

with elevations approaching 300 m (1000 ft) it is late April before growth begins, and the season ends in late October. In the higher hills this growth factor may be reduced to zero, and here, with the increased rainfall and full exposure to stronger winds, only hardy wild plants and mosses survive. The cooling effect of the combination of strong winds and low temperatures is of great importance to human survival in the mountain area in winter. MacInnes (1972, p. 190) gives a table for calculating this effect.

The averages and extremes of maximum and minimum temperatures in Tables 2b and 2c again show only small differences between places in the coastal area. At upland sites, such as Braemar, temperatures are generally lower than those near the coast, but in early summer the maximum can exceed those at the lower level stations where the sea breezes have a cooling effect. The extremes of temperature given in Table 2d have been recorded at upland sites during periods of broken or short-term records.

### Table 2d
### EXTREMES OF TEMPERATURE RECORDED AT UPLAND SITES DURING PERIODS OF BROKEN OR SHORT-TERM RECORDS

|  | Period | Altitude | | Max. | Min. |
|---|---|---|---|---|---|
|  |  | (m) | (ft) | (°C) | (°C) |
| Cairngorm | 1963-72 | 1090 | 3580 | 21.4 | −15.6 |
| Coire Cas | 1964-73 | 763 | 2500 | 24.5 | −15.0 |
| Glenmore Lodge | 1964-73 | 341 | 1120 | 27.4 | −14.9 |
| Grantown on Spey | 1965-73 | 229 | 750 | 28.5 | −20.6 |
| Glenlivet | 1964-73 | 215 | 700 | 28.3 | −17.9 |

Air frost occurs on average on some 65 days per year in lower parts of Moray and on over 100 days per year in some of the upland parts (Table 2E). Near the coast, western districts are more sheltered from northwest winds than those farther east, and the way in which the winds more readily fall light overnight in the west is reflected in the increase in frequency of air frost from east to west. The minimum temperature on the ground is nearly always lower than that of the air, and over grass surfaces on inland sites ground frosts can be recorded during any month of the year, and are twice as frequent as air frosts.

**Table 2e**

## AVERAGE NUMBER OF DAYS WITH AIR FROST†
### DURING THE 16 YEARS 1956-1972

| | Jan | Feb | Mar | Apr | May | Jun | Jul | Aug | Sep | Oct | Nov | Dec | Year |
|---|---|---|---|---|---|---|---|---|---|---|---|---|---|
| Nairn | 14 | 15 | 10 | 6 | 1 | <1 | 0 | 0 | <1 | 1 | 9 | 13 | 70 |
| Forres | 15 | 16 | 9 | 6 | 1 | <1 | 0 | 0 | <1 | 1 | 9 | 12 | 69 |
| Kinloss | 15 | 15 | 10 | 6 | 1 | 0 | 0 | 0 | <1 | 1 | 9 | 13 | 70 |
| Elgin | 12 | 14 | 8 | 5 | <1 | 0 | 0 | 0 | <1 | <1 | 8 | 10 | 57 |
| Gordon Castle | 13 | 14 | 7 | 5 | <1 | <1 | 0 | 0 | 0 | <1 | 7 | 10 | 57 |
| Banff | 9 | 11 | 4 | 2 | <1 | 0 | 0 | 0 | 1 | 0 | 4 | 7 | 41 |
| Glenlivet* | 15 | 16 | 15 | 10 | 3 | <1 | <1 | <1 | 1 | 4 | 11 | 13 | 90 |
| Glenmore Lodge* | 19 | 19 | 20 | 13 | 5 | <1 | <1 | 1 | 2 | 6 | 15 | 17 | 115 |
| Grantown on Spey* | 19 | 20 | 17 | 13 | 5 | <1 | <1 | <1 | 1 | 5 | 15 | 17 | 113 |

NOTES: †'Air frost' occurs when the temperature at therometer screen level, 1.25 m (4 ft),
      is below the freezing point of water.

      *Averaged from shorter term/broken records.

## SUNSHINE

Cloud is generally well broken in the coastal areas of Moray due to the föhn effect, and these parts of the District are sunnier than the rest although the seasonal increase in coastal cloud due to haar in the months of May to August has an adverse effect on the totals.

Only general statements can be made on the variation of sunshine throughout the District as records are scarce, and so much depends on the exposure of any one site under consideration. For example, in mid winter, places on the north side of a hill with an elevation of more than 8 degrees would have practically all the sunshine cut off, an effect which is of considerable importance to valley sites. Cloudier conditions in the hilly areas result in lower sunshine averages as illustrated in Table 3.

The annual average of 1347 hours recorded at Forres is not as high as that at some of the more favoured places on the east Scottish coast, such as St. Andrews (1461) and Dunbar (1480), but is similar to that of Aberdeen (1342) and Edinburgh (1330). The smoke pollution which can reduce the sunshine in industrial areas does not affect Moray to any great extent, and it is of interest to note that the annual average for Greenock is only 1220 hours.

Seasonally the Moray coast has more sunshine in the winter months of November to March, than does London, but is reversed in the summer period in spite of there being some two hours more daylight in the north at midsummer.

## WIND

The prevailing wind in Moray is southwesterly, but winds from other quarters can be quite persistent, such as spells with northwest winds in winter, cold easterlies in spring and light northeast sea-breezes on the coasts in summer months. The very varied topography of the District makes for many local variations in the wind régime, but there are few detailed long period wind records available for study.

The wind pattern at Kinloss (Table 4A) can be taken as typical of the coastal area, although the eastern parts are more exposed to winds from the northwest. The table shows that the

**Table 3**

AVERAGES OF SUNSHINE DURATION IN HOURS — MONTHLY TOTALS

(30 Years 1931 - 1960)

| Station | Jan | Feb | Mar | Apr | May | Jun | Jul | Aug | Sep | Oct | Nov | Dec | Year |
|---|---|---|---|---|---|---|---|---|---|---|---|---|---|
| Nairn | 49 | 72 | 113 | 142 | 173 | 171 | 139 | 133 | 123 | 93 | 53 | 37 | 1298 |
| Forres | 54 | 74 | 114 | 139 | 179 | 179 | 149 | 144 | 120 | 93 | 58 | 44 | 1347 |
| Kinloss* | 48 | 74 | 112 | 142 | 178 | 174 | 147 | 141 | 121 | 85 | 52 | 41 | 1315 |
| Elgin* | 45 | 76 | 116 | 147 | 185 | 166 | 155 | 151 | 125 | 92 | 47 | 36 | 1341 |
| Gordon Castle | 45 | 71 | 109 | 137 | 176 | 169 | 144 | 142 | 119 | 89 | 51 | 35 | 1287 |
| Banff | 45 | 70 | 108 | 144 | 176 | 173 | 147 | 142 | 122 | 86 | 50 | 33 | 1296 |
| Braemar | 25 | 56 | 95 | 127 | 165 | 166 | 140 | 126 | 103 | 66 | 31 | 18 | 1118 |
| Glenmore Lodge* | 26 | 76 | 107 | 125 | 162 | 157 | 121 | 117 | 111 | 80 | 34 | 14 | 1130 |

*The averages for these stations have been estimated from short term records

## Table 4a

## ANNUAL PERCENTAGE FREQUENCY ANALYSIS OF WIND DIRECTION AND VELOCITY AT KINLOSS

### (8 Years 1964 to 1971)

| Mean Wind Speed | | Wind Directions in Degrees (True) | | | | | | | | | | | | Total |
|---|---|---|---|---|---|---|---|---|---|---|---|---|---|---|
| Force | Knots | 350–010 | 020–040 | 050–070 | 080–100 | 110–130 | 140–160 | 170–190 | 200–220 | 230–250 | 260–280 | 290–310 | 320–340 | % |
| 0 | 0 | – | – | – | – | – | – | – | – | – | – | – | – | 2.8 |
| 1 | 1–3 | – | – | – | – | – | – | – | – | – | – | – | – | 8.2 |
| 2 | 4–6 | 1.0 | 0.6 | 0.9 | 1.7 | 1.0 | 0.9 | 1.6 | 3.7 | 2.6 | 0.7 | 0.4 | 0.5 | 15.7 |
| 3 | 7–10 | 1.4 | 1.2 | 1.9 | 2.9 | 1.2 | 1.2 | 2.4 | 5.8 | 4.6 | 1.3 | 1.2 | 0.9 | 26.0 |
| 4 | 13–18 | 1.2 | 1.3 | 2.0 | 2.3 | 1.4 | 1.2 | 1.4 | 4.3 | 7.6 | 2.3 | 2.9 | 1.1 | 18.9 |
| 5 | 17–21 | 0.6 | 0.2 | 0.3 | 0.5 | 0.5 | 0.3 | 0.2 | 1.1 | 4.1 | 1.3 | 1.4 | 0.7 | 11.2 |
| 6 | 22–27 | 0.4 | 0.1 | 0.1 | 0.1 | 0.2 | 0.1 | 0+ | 0.5 | 2.3 | 0.9 | 0.5 | 0.4 | 5.5 |
| 7 | 28–33 | 0.1 | 0+ | 0+ | 0+ | 0+ | 0+ | 0+ | 0.1 | 0.5 | 0.3 | 0.1 | 0.1 | 1.3 |
| 8 | 34–40 | 0+ | | | | 0+ | 0+ | 0+ | 0.1 | 0.1 | 0.1 | 0.1 | 0+ | 0.3 |
| 9 | 47–54 | 0+ | | | | | | 0+ | 0+ | 0+ | 0+ | 0+ | 0+ | 0+ |
| 10 | 55–63 | | | | | | | | 0+ | 0+ | 0+ | | | 0+ |
| Total | | 4.7 | 3.4 | 5.2 | 7.5 | 4.3 | 3.7 | 5.6 | 15.5 | 21.8 | 6.9 | 6.6 | 3.7 | 99.9 |

NOTES:
1. Adding the columns of the above table vertically gives the percentage amount of time in the average year with winds from the stated directions.
2. Adding the columns of the above table horizontally gives the percentage amount of time in the average year with winds in the stated speed ranges.
3. The above table has been calculated from values of wind direction and associated speed averaged over each hour during the eight year period.

**Table 4b**

**NUMBER OF DAYS WITH GALES AT KINLOSS**

(24 Years 1951-1973)

| | Jan | Feb | Mar | Apr | May | Jun | Jul | Aug | Sep | Oct | Nov | Dec | Year |
|---|---|---|---|---|---|---|---|---|---|---|---|---|---|
| | 38 | 39 | 25 | 25 | 11 | 6 | 7 | 8 | 18 | 34 | 37 | 56 | 304 |
| 24 Year Mean | 1.6 | 1.6 | 1.0 | 1.0 | 0.5 | 0.3 | 0.3 | 0.3 | 0.7 | 1.4 | 1.5 | 2.3 | 12.7 |

wind blows from between south and west for about 45% of the time in the average year. A very large proportion of the stronger winds blow from the southwest or west, but over the 23 year period 1951-1973 there were on average only 12.7 days per year with gales, so lower Moray cannot be classed as a windy area by Scottish standards.

Anemographs (instruments which make continuous recordings of wind direction and speed on graduated charts) have been in use at Lossiemouth since 1960 and Kinloss since 1963. Prior to this date the only records available are those made at Kinloss from an anemometer registering direction and speed on dials from which the mean wind direction and speed were noted every hour on the hour. Since the installation of the anemographs the highest hourly mean speed recorded in this area, a southwest wind of 60 kt, was recorded at Lossiemouth, as was the highest gust, 89 kt, also from the southwest. However, during the exeptionally severe northwest to north gale of 31st January, 1953, a north-northwest wind with a mean speed of 70 kt and a highest gust of 98 kt was measured at Kinloss on a non-recording instrument.

It is of interest to note that many of the strong southwest winds in lower Moray are associated with föhn conditions, and in spring, when the light sandy soils in parts of the Laich are very dry, quite severe soil blowing can occur. Spectacular dust clouds darken the sky as soil is stripped from the newly sown land, and fields can be overrun and roads blocked by drifting sand — a phenomenon recorded throughout the history of Moray.

Inland, with the increase in altitude, windiness increases quickly in the hilly areas, but there is often a considerable degree of shelter in some valleys, where, as in the lower parts of Moray, there are extensive areas of woodland. The only records available for the upland parts of the District are from the Cairngorm, where an anemograph was installed in 1964. Although these records have been interrupted on many occasions by adverse winter conditions, they go a long way to confirm what climbers in that area have reported over the years, namely that severe and extremely gusty wind conditions are frequently met with, both on the summits and on the lee slopes of these mountains. In spite of the gaps in the records, some years have shown more than 100 days with gale force 8 or more on

Cairngorm, mostly in the winter six months of the year. The highest hourly wind recorded is 74 kt from the southwest, and the highest gust 124 kt from west-southwest. It is quite probable that higher speeds have been missed, and that the figure of 100 days per year with gales is very conservative. These prolonged gales, lasting for days at a time, lead to blizzard conditions of great severity in winter, and the importance of the chilling effect of the combination of such winds and low temperatures must never be underestimated.

## SNOW

In winter, northerly winds can bring air from the polar regions directly into the District, sometimes with heavy snowfall. However, the western parts of Moray do get some shelter from airstreams bringing snowstorms from the northwest.

Because of the falling off of temperature with height there can be considerable variation between snowfall on the low lying coastal area and the higher inland parts, and appreciable amounts of snow can be falling on high ground while lowland Moray has rain or sleet. The number of days with snow falling increases rapidly inland, an approximate rule being that there is one day more per year with snow falling for every 15 m (50 ft) of elevation above 60 m (200 ft). Table No. 5A, which refers to

### Table 5a
### AVERAGE NUMBER OF DAYS WITH SNOW FALLING
### AT ANY TIME OF DAY AT KINLOSS
#### (22 Years 1952-1973)

| Jan | Feb | Mar | Apr | May | Jun | Jul | Aug | Sep | Oct | Nov | Dec | Year |
|-----|-----|-----|-----|-----|-----|-----|-----|-----|-----|-----|-----|------|
| 9.4 | 10.0 | 6.8 | 3.7 | 0.9 | 0 | 0 | 0 | 0 | 0.9 | 5.1 | 7.4 | 44.3 |

Kinloss, can be used as a general guide to snowfall in other parts of the District if this rule is applied. Comparison with other parts of the country shows the Moray coast to be one of the "snowiest" lowland areas on the mainland of the British Isles, but the snow does not lie for long.

Tables 5B and 5C highlight the differences between snowfall in lowland and upland areas. In general, the higher the ground the more persistent is the lying snow. Distance from the modifying influence of the sea is also an important factor, while

Table 5b

AVERAGE NUMBER OF DAYS PER WINTER WITH SNOW LYING

AT 0900 HOURS G.M.T.

AT DEPTHS BETWEEN SPECIFIED LIMITS

| Station | Height (m) | No. of Winters | Depth (cm) | | | | | | | | All depths | Max depth |
|---|---|---|---|---|---|---|---|---|---|---|---|---|
| | | | 0-2 | 3-5 | 6-10 | 11-15 | 16-20 | 21-30 | 31-40 | Over 40 | | |
| Nairn | 6 | 1958-71 (13) | 12.5 | 1.9 | 3.0 | 0.1 | 0.5 | | | | 18.1 | 20 |
| Forres | 50 | 1956-71 (15) | 13.2 | 3.7 | 4.7 | 1.3 | 0.5 | 0.6 | 0.2 | | 24.1 | 41 |
| Kinloss | 5 | 1953-74 (21) | 9.8 | 2.8 | 3.0 | 0.9 | 0.6 | 0.2 | | | 17.3 | 30 |
| Lossiemouth | 6 | 1958-71 (13) | 7.2 | 1.9 | 1.6 | 1.1 | 0.2 | | | | 12.0 | 18 |
| Elgin | 15 | 1956-71 (15) | 10.9 | 2.5 | 2.3 | 1.0 | 0.9 | 1.1 | 0.1 | | 18.6 | 33 |
| Banff | 24 | 1961-69 ( 8) | 8.5 | 1.9 | 2.6 | 1.1 | 0.1 | 0.1 | | | 14.4 | 23 |
| Glenlivet (Old Site) | 331 | 1951-61 (10) | 13.1 | 4.6 | 7.9 | 5.8 | 5.8 | 4.7 | 2.8 | 2.7 | 47.4 | 68 |
| Glenlivet (New Site) | 215 | 1963-71 ( 8) | 22.8 | 10.2 | 8.6 | 3.0 | 2.6 | 2.2 | 0.1 | | 49.5 | 33 |
| Braemar | 333 | 1947-58 (11) | 15.7 | 9.6 | 15.1 | 7.3 | 3.5 | 3.6 | 1.1 | 0.8 | 56.7 | 61 |
| Glenmore Lodge | 341 | 1956-71 (15) | 24.0 | 6.5 | 9.1 | 4.9 | 2.9 | 7.9 | 2.9 | 1.7 | 59.9 | 63 |

**Table 5c**

**AVERAGE NUMBER OF DAYS IN EACH MONTH, NOVEMBER TO APRIL,**

**WITH SNOW LYING AT 0900 HOURS G.M.T. — DEPTH NOT SPECIFIED**

| | No. of winters | Nov | Dec | Jan | Feb | Mar | Apr | Total |
|---|---|---|---|---|---|---|---|---|
| Nairn | 13 | 1.0 | 3.5 | 5.6 | 6.1 | 1.6 | 0.3 | 18.1 |
| Forres | 15 | 1.7 | 3.5 | 7.7 | 7.4 | 3.3 | 0.6 | 24.1 |
| Kinloss | 21 | 1.0 | 2.5 | 5.7 | 6.1 | 1.7 | 0.3 | 17.3 |
| Lossiemouth | 13 | 0.5 | 1.8 | 3.8 | 4.5 | 1.4 | 0.1 | 12.0 |
| Elgin | 15 | 1.1 | 2.7 | 6.1 | 5.5 | 2.7 | 0.5 | 18.6 |
| Glenlivet (Old Site) | 10 | 1.6 | 6.8 | 14.7 | 15.2 | 7.5 | 1.6 | 47.4 |
| Glenlivet (New Site) | 8 | 5.7 | 11.4 | 10.5 | 12.4 | 6.7 | 2.7 | 49.5 |
| Banff | 8 | 1.4 | 2.9 | 4.7 | 3.4 | 1.7 | 0.4 | 14.4 |
| Braemar | 11 | 2.3 | 10.8 | 15.8 | 16.1 | 10.1 | 1.7 | 56.8 |
| Glenmore Lodge | 15 | 5.5 | 10.7 | 14.6 | 15.3 | 10.0 | 3.8 | 59.9 |

a north or northeast aspect means less heating from the sun to aid thawing.

The following observations on snow cover in the Cairngorm area over 13 winter seasons up to the end of May (1955-1967) are given by Manley (1971a).

Average number of days with snow cover observed at various levels.

| Altitude | (m) | 300 | 460 | 610 | 760 | 910 | 1070 | 1220 |
|----------|-----|------|------|------|------|------|------|------|
|          | (ft)| 1000 | 1500 | 2000 | 2500 | 3000 | 3500 | 4000 |
| Days     |     | 60 | 79 | 116 | 153* | 178* | 191* | 200* |

* A few days should be added for June.

He suggests that whereas in lowland areas a snowfall of 30 cm (12 in) of snow in a 24 hour period is decidedly infrequent and that one of 60 cm (24 in) lies close to the limit that can be expected, orographic snowfalls in the mountain areas could exceed this by a factor of two at least.

Over the bare hilly areas and in particular on the windswept Cairngorm Plateau the snow is blown on to the lee slopes and into the gullies where it can accumulate to considerable depths. The length of the skiing season is extended by the persistence of this snow, and in the higher parts some of these snow beds last throughout most summers. The persistence of the snow depends not only on the amount that falls and on drift accumulation, but on the chances of removal by heavy warm rainfall. Manley (1971b) gives examples where the snow line on Cairngorm rose rapidly from 300 m (1000 ft) to 1070 m (3500 ft) during two days of warm rainy weather. Historical accounts of flooding in Moray show several major floods to have occurred in winter through rapid thawing of snow by rain.

Although the snowfall in the Cairngorm area is slight when compared, say, with that of the Alps, the ever present wind can cause snow accumulations of the types suitable for the formation of avalanches. The hazards caused by these and the problems of forecasting their occurrence have been discussed by Langmuir (1970) and MacInnes (1972). Because of the extreme wind conditions mentioned earlier, the severity and duration of blizzard conditions in this area must not be misjudged from the comfort of the valley below, and memorial cairns form a grim reminder of this aspect of mountain weather.

## FOG

In Moray, the air at low levels is usually too dry for overnight cooling to produce radiation fog. However, if moister air has been brought into the coastal areas by onshore winds, radiation fog may form, but it is usually of a patchy nature. Inland, this type of fog is more frequent in valleys and river basins, but is still not a common occurrence.

Most fogs affecting the lowland areas are sea fogs, known as "haar" on the east coast of Scotland. They form in the spring and summer months, when warm air from the Continent moves over the comparatively cold waters of the North Sea. The lowest layers of the air are cooled by the sea and extensive banks of fog or very low cloud are formed, which move on to the coasts. Because the haar is generally shallow, temperatures overland are usually sufficient to "burn it off" during the day, but it remains over the sea, returning inland overnight, with most of the foggy periods occurring around dawn when temperatures are at their lowest. To the annoyance of holidaymakers, summer afternoon sea breezes may carry the sea fog just over the coast giving cold damp conditions on the beaches, while only a short distance inland there is glorious sunshine. Thicker haars may sometimes give rise to drizzle, especially on meeting rising ground, and can be rather persistent in the low lying coastal areas, but usually in the form of low cloud rather than fog.

During the period 1951 to 1960 Kinloss had fog on about 18 days each year and an average duration of 65 hours of fog per annum. Of these there were 14 hours with thick fog — i.e. with visibility less than 200 m (660 ft). However, fog is more frequent both eastwards and westwards along the coast from Kinloss.

In moist airstreams cloud caps due to orographic uplift are common on the higher hills, especially overnight and in conditions of frontal rain. This hill fog can occur with winds from any direction, but is more widespread and forms at a lower level with winds from the exposed sector between north and east. The resulting high humidity and reduction in sunshine greatly affect growth in these upland areas. The higher the hills, the more persistent is the cloud cover, and short-term records from the Cairngorm indicate that on average fog occurs there on about one day in three in most months and that in some months the average frequency may be as high as two days in three. This would indicate that hill walkers at these levels may encounter foggy conditions for several days at a time.

## THUNDER

The coastal area of the Moray Firth has fewer thunderstorms than anywhere else in the British Isles, having on average only 3 or 4 days with thunderstorms per year, while many places in England have between 15 and 20 days with thunder. The storms are most likely in summer, when sea breezes often keep the temperatures near the coast below that necessary for the formation of thunderstorms, and they develop mostly in the inland parts of the District. The water levels in the lower reaches of the rivers can rise unexpectedly due to these sudden downpours in the hills.

# 3

# PLANT LIFE

Miss M. McCALLUM WEBSTER

## HISTORY

There is very little evidence of the study of plant life in the District until the middle of the 18th century.

The earliest collection appears to have been made in 1794 by A. Cooper Esq., advocate to the Earl of Macduff, owner at that time of Innes House, Urquhart. His small collection of pressed specimens, together with a list of some 300 plants, is to be found in the Museum at Elgin and purports to have been collected in the policies of Innes House. There must be some doubt, however, whether the plants listed are truly wild and whether they were all collected there, for there are no data slips attached to the specimens. Furthermore, some of the plants on the list are certainly garden plants and must have been introduced, while others are doubtfully native to North Scotland. Nonetheless this is a very valuable collection and must rank as one of the oldest in Scotland.

About this time James Brodie of Brodie (1744-1824) collected plants, chiefly from the environs of Brodie House, as Brodie Castle was then named, but also from other parts of Scotland. As he, too, failed to write adequate information on his herbarium sheets it cannot be assumed that all the plants he collected came from Brodie. His collection is in the herbarium of the Royal Botanic Gardens, Edinburgh, with duplicate specimens at the British Museum, Kew and other institutions. One interesting note on his specimen of whin reads "rare in the Highlands"; this is certainly not applicable now. James Brodie was a friend of many well known botanists of his day. One of them, Sir W. J. Hooker, who later became Director of the Royal Botanic Gardens at Kew, visited Brodie on several occasions in search of plants, notably the rare wintergreens, for illustrations in his Flora Londonensis.

James Hoy, gardener at Gordon Castle, was also interested in wild plants and was the finder, along with Brodie, of the rare and beautiful One-flowered Wintergreen *(Moneses uniflora)* in the year 1792.

Early in the 19th century field work continued with great enthusiasm. W. A. Stables, factor at Cawdor, and the Rev. George Gordon, minister at Birnie, were most prominent, the former making a large collection of pressed specimens, most of which are to be found in the herbaria at Edinburgh and the University, Aberdeen. Other notable botanists included William Brand, Rev. J. Brichan, Rev. G. Wilson of Alves, Dr. J. G. Innes, Forres, and Dr. Keith, Forres, whose collection of plants is supposed to be the comprehensive collection of specimens in the Falconer Museum at Forres, but here again there are neither data nor names on the sheets.

Towards the end of the century some notable botanists from the south, including E. S. Marshall, W. A. Shoolbred and G. C. Druce, visited the area and recorded many of the critical genera, so adding extensively to the numbers of plants already known to occur in the District.

Interest continued in the 20th century. Alex. MacGregor, schoolmaster at Forres, James Burgess, schoolmaster at Dyke, and members of the Moray Field Club made many interesting records. In recent years under the stimulus of the Distribution Map Scheme, inaugurated by the Botanical Society of the British Isles, the aim of which is to record plants on 10 km (6.2 miles) squares, many new and hitherto unrecorded plants have been added to the lists, chiefly by Roland Richter, George Shepherd, Alan J. Souter and Mary McCallum Webster. New records are being found even now in this well botanized region.

As well as extensive field work, there are several publications on the flora, the earliest work being Alex. Murray's *Northern Flora Pt. 1,* 1836. This was followed by the Rev. G. Gordon's *Collectanea for a Flora of Moray,* 1839; George Dickie's *Botanists Guide to the counties of Aberdeen, Banff and Kincardine,* 1860; W. G. Craib's *Flora of Banffshire,* 1912; James Burgess's *Flora of Moray,* 1935. In manuscript is a "Flora of Moray and Nairn" by Mary McCallum Webster based on the old botanical county boundaries defined by H. C. Watson. Several papers have appeared in various periodicals, especially on the varied flora of the Culbin Sands. The best known are

*The Flora of the Culbin Sands* by D. Patton and E. J. A. Stewart, 1912 and 1923, and *The Check List of the Culbin State Forest* by Mary McCallum Webster, 1968, which contains a list of over 550 flowering plants and a list of lichens and mosses by R. Richter.

## PLANT LIFE

The flora of Moray comprises over 850 native and 300 introduced and well-established species. The area is also extremely rich in bryophytes. Mosses, lichens, liverworts and fungi abound. Seaweeds, however, have been little studied by local naturalists.

The great variety of plant life is due to the wide diversity of habitat within the District, particularly in the very rich valleys of the Spey and the Findhorn, which, together with the upper reaches of the Deveron and the limestone areas by the river Avon, contain about 80% of the total flora. These rivers or their tributaries have their sources in the high mountains or open moorland with acid lochs. Down river they reach deciduous woodlands and in the case of the Findhorn, steep rocky gorges. In their valleys, towards the coast, occur rich arable lands, wet meadows and shingle banks on which lodge many alpine plants washed down from the hills.

With district boundaries redefined to include the high mountains of upper Banffshire, Moray can now boast a more extensive arctic-alpine flora than hitherto, when it had to rely on a few such plants found in the flushes of the Cromdale hills and those already mentioned carried down by the rivers. The rich limestones of Inchrory, known as the Inchrory Marl, have added many species to the list, as have the limestone areas at Tomintoul. The serpentine outcrops of the Cabrach, although interesting to botanists, show few plants not found elsewhere.

The woodlands of the uplands are mostly birch and pine, the latter now generally planted. In the middle reaches of the rivers the native woods are of alder, willow and birch, with ash and hazel on the limestone outcrops. Each species of tree has its own ecology and ground flora, the deciduous trees having particularly rich plant associations. The Findhorn gorges are especially noted for the large variety of ferns, mosses, lichen and fungi.

The arable land known as the Laich of Moray is probably the most fertile in the North-East. Besides growing good crops it

E

abounds in colourful weeds, mostly annuals, as for instance, Redleg, Corn Marigold, Dai Nettle, Poppy, Wild Mustard and Wild Radish. Very local now but still to be found is the Cornflower and very rare indeed, the Corncockle. Two pernicious weeds, the perennial Couch grass and the annual Wild Oat, infest many of the fields.

The life of plants, alpine or otherwise, on the shingle banks is generally short owing to disturbances caused by the great spates. Nevertheless the new banks colonize so quickly that they are always among our floristically most colourful areas.

In addition to the river valleys Moray has a diverse and interesting coast with areas of special note including the Culbin State Forest, the marshes behind the shingle banks at the Leen, Garmouth (once the outlet of the river Spey) and the sea cliffs at Covesea and Cullen.

Throughout the remaining areas of Moray large tracts fall into the category of blanket bog moorland. These areas are very acid and are dominated by Heather and Deer-grass with few ancillary species. Where water gathers in pools and lochans a small number of different plants, mostly aquatics, may be added. Here the main hope of variety of species lies in the bogs and flushes which have become richer due to the deposition of mineral salts.

Many of the plants found in Moray can be termed rare. Sometimes they are locally plentiful but only to be found in one or two sites. Others may be rare plants scattered over the District but nowhere plentiful. In the former category the following can be included: Shining Cranesbill *(Geranium lucidum)*, Bloody Cranesbill *(G. sanguineum)*, Rough Clover *(Trifolium scabrum)*, Knotted Clover *(T. striatum)*, Wild Liquorice *(Astragalus glycyphyllos)*, Tufted Saxifrage *(Saxifraga cespitosa)*, Narrow-leaved Water-parsnip *(Berula erecta)*, Pellitory-of-the-wall *(Parietaria judaica)*, Bog Pimpernel *(Anagallis tenella)*, Gromwell *(Lithospermum officinale)*, Skull-cap *(Scutellaria galericulata)*, Lesser Water-plantain *(Baldellia ranunculoides)* and Herb Paris *(Paris quadrifolia)*.

It is worthwhile commenting in more detail on the interesting individual species which are to be found in some of the broad habitats already outlined.

## The Coastal Belt

In the west of Moray the coastline consists of high sand dunes containing a limited number of plants. Here the dominant plant is Sea Marram *(Ammophila arenaria)*, a grass with long underground roots that bind the sand, and leaves that roll up to prevent evaporation. It is accompanied by two other species of grass, both glaucous-green in colour, one Lyme Grass *(Elymus arenarius)* is rather similar, but more robust than Sea Marram, while the other Sand Couch Grass *(Agropyron junceiforme)* is much shorter, seldom reaching over 30 cm (1 ft) in height, and can be recognized by the long distant spikelets on the flowering stem. Like Marram, both have binding roots and are termed zerophytes, (plants tolerant of dry places). In that they can grow where salt concentration is high, they are also termed halophytes.

In the sheltered pockets among these tall dunes, other halophytes maintain their ground. Many of these have long tap roots and, frequently, fleshy leaves. In this category are Sea Rocket *(Cakile maritima)*, Sea Purslane *(Honkyena peploides)* and Prickly Saltwort *(Salsola kali)*.

Other plants which cannot strictly be termed halophytes also become established on these dry dunes, notably Stinking Willie *(Senecio jacobaea)*, so named after the Duke of Cumberland who was supposed to have introduced the weed to the north in the nosebags of his horses at the time of the battle of Culloden. Groundsel *(S. vulgaris)*, Spear Thistle *(Cirsium vulgare)*, Whin *(Ulex europaeus)*, Broom *(Sarothamnus scoparius)*, and occasionally, as on the old Bar of Culbin, Hogweed *(Heracleum)* and Grant Hogweed *(H. mantegazzianum)*, Lady's Bedstraw *(Galium verum)* and Restharrow *(Ononis repens)* also occur.

Two mosses, *Tortula ruraliformis* and *Brachythecium albicans* are also fairly common in such sites.

Between the outer perimeter of the dry dunes and the land proper lies an area of fixed dune, often inundated by high spring tides. This has a close turf of fine-leaved grasses, mostly Common Bent *(Agrostis tenuis)*, Fiorin *(A. stolonifera)*, Sea Poa *(Puccinellia maritima)* and Creeping Fescue *(Festuca rubra)*. Large areas are colonised by Crowberry *(Empetrum nigrum)* with its heath-like leaves and round, black, bitter berries. In more open places grow two plants which are easily recognized by their form of growth. Baltic Rush *(Juncus balticus)* and Sand Sedge *(Carex arenaria)* have long creeping underground roots which send up tufts of new shoots at regular intervals, making long straight lines through the dunes. Here also are many attractive small plants such as the pink-flowered Sand Centaury *(Centaurium littorale)*, the lilac-flowered Field Gentian *(Gentianella campestris)*, the white starry-flowered Knotted Pearlwort *(Sagina nodosa)* and the early flowering and abundant Sea Pink *(Armeria maritima)*. Interesting, though less colourful, are several very early flowering members of the Chickweed family and the rare Early Forget-me-not *(Myosotis ramossissima)*.

Wet dune slacks, due to draining and planting by the Forestry Commission, are becoming scarcer, but in the Culbin Forest there still remain a few areas that are reasonably damp. Here survive Bogbean *(Manyanthes trifoliata)*, Ragged Robin *(Lychnis flosos-cuculi)*, Grass of Parnassus *(Parnassia palustris)*, several of the bog-loving orchids and the Marsh Cinquefoil *(Potentilla palustris)* with its dark maroon-coloured flowers. The encroachment of Iris and Common Bent grass is fast drying up these damp places. At the Buckie Loch, Culbin, are some good colonies of the two small ferns, Moonwort *(Botrychium lunaria)* and the very rare Adder's Tongue *(Ophioglossum vulgare)*. The former is also to be found by roadsides, on mountain ledges and grassy banks, but in Moray the latter has only been recorded apart from Culbin, at Burghead where it has not been seen in recent years.

There are very few salt marshes along the coast. Small areas between the Bar and the Forest of Culbin, the south and east verges of the Findhorn Estuary and a small area at the mouth of the Spey maintain a limited saltmarsh flora. This consists chiefly of Glasswort *(Salicornia europaea)*, Scurvy-grass *(Cochlearia officinalis)*, Sea Blite *(Suaeda maritima)*, Sea Milkwort *(Glaux maritima)* and Sea Aster *(Aster tripolium)*. The sea Milkwort, a pretty little plant with bunches of pink flowers must contain honey of a toxic quality, for I have seen something in the region of 300 bumble bees lying dead among the blooms in the space of one square metre. All these plants grow on the short turf and must be subjected to much salt water.

Deeper pools among the turf have many rushes and sedges round their borders, the most interesting being Sea Rush *(Juncus maritimus),* Sea Club-rush *(Scirpus maritimus),* One-glumed Spike-rush *(Eleocharis uniglumis)* and Narrow Blysmus *(Blysmus rufus).* None of these plants can be called common elsewhere in Scotland.

The cliffs are mostly grass covered and not steep except for a small area of sheer rock at Covesea and between Findochty and Cullen. The sward of the cliff tops has an abundance of the showy Meadow Saxifrage *(Saxifraga granulata)* in early spring; not quite so common and flowering later with its clusters of deep purple pea flowers is the Purple Milk-vetch *(Astragalus danicus).* On ledges will be found, very sparingly, Cowslips *(Primula veris).* Very common in certain areas of these cliffs are an abundance of Primroses *(Primula vulgaris)* and Wild Hyacinth *(Endymion non-scriptus).* On the sheer cliff faces little vegetation is to be found but in the damper ledges Scurvy-grass and Red Campion *(Silene dioica)* as well as many mosses and lichens are frequent. In cracks of the cave walls a small stiff-fronded fern Sea Spleenwort *(Asplenium marinum)* is locally plentiful.

There are two large areas of shingle and two smaller ones along the coast line. The largest, between Findhorn and Burghead, is now totally planted with pines and has very little ground vegetation. Whin and Broon are common as are grasses and heather, the most interesting plant being English Stonecrop *(Sedum anglicum)* with its fleshy leaves and pink flowers. It is still to be found in open places. Very rare now, where it was formerly quite common, is the Oyster Plant *(Mertensia maritima),* making large prostrate patches of glaucous-green fleshy leaves and bunches of bell-like light blue flowers. Unfortunately, this beautiful plant is becoming increasingly scarce along our coasts on account of the movement of shingle during heavy storms and, regrettably, owing to its attraction to the visitor.

On the stable parts of the shingle several species of Crache *(Atriplex)* will be seen; their flowers are inconspicuous and green but one member of the family the Frosted Orache *(Atriplex laciniata)* has attractive mealy hastate leaves and red stems. The showy white umbellifer with celery shaped leaves, Scotch Lovage *(Ligustum scoticum),* which does not grow south of Northumberland, is common. It is not confined to shingle being equally happy on dry sand dunes and in crevices of rocks.

About the houses in the coastal villages occur some uncommon plants such as Flixweed *(Descurania sophia),* a feathery-leaved crucifer some 50 cm (20 in) in height. Its small dingy yellow flowers are followed by spreading narrow pods on thin stems. Small Mallow *(Malva neglecta)* occurs round the boat house at Findhorn and the Tree Mallow *(Lavatera arborea)* was formerly quite common on the sea wall at the approach to the village, but now seems to have taken refuge in some of the cottage gardens. Maiden Pink, *(Dianthus deltoides)* known until quite recently, and a strange looking annual thistle with very small pale flowers and a continuously spinous stem, the Slender Thistle *(Carduus tenuiflorus)* are to be found. Tree Lupin *(Lupinus arboreus)* with its pale, yellow, scented flowers and the Duke of Argyll's Teaplant *(Lycium chinense)* are well established round the village. Farther to the east, as at Lossiemouth, grows Danish Scurvy-grass *(Cochlearia danica)* distinguished from the other members of its family by its stalked ivy-shaped leaves. In an old quarry occurs Milk-vetch *(Astragalus glycyphyllos)* with its large greenish white pea flowers.

## Woodlands

Moray is among the most wooded Districts in Scotland. The woodland is divided between deciduous and pine woods many of which are planted. The Caledonian Forest, apart from a few old Scots Pine here and there, has long since disappeared. The deciduous woods contain much native birch, alder, ash and oak, with planted trees of beech and sycamore both of which regenerate naturally. The leaf litter of these trees produces a far richer flora than that found in the pine woods.

With few exceptions the flowers found beneath trees are early flowering in order to utilise the light allowed to penetrate before full foliage occurs. Wood Anemone *(Anemone nemorosa),* Dog Violet *(Viola riviniana),* Lesser Celandine *(Ranunculus ficaria)* and Wood Sorrel *(Oxalis acetosella)* are in full flower by April. In May these are soon followed by Large Bittercress *(Cardamine amara)* — similar to the well-known lilac-coloured Lady's Smock but with a larger white flower and the sweet smelling Woodruff *(Galium odoratum).* In such woods, too, grow many ferns, some most delicate, as, for instance, Beech Fern *(Thelypteris phegopteris)* and Oak Fern *(Gymnocarpium dryopteris).* The Oak Fern is one of the most beautiful of our ferns: the stems are black, about 20 cm (8 in) in height and the ternate fronds are rolled up in little balls just before opening. They remain a light yellow-green until they are mature, when they become a dull green.

Only in two stations will be found the Bird's nest Orchid *(Neottia nidus-avis)*, a plant totally devoid of chlorophyll, so that its pale brown stems and flower spike is very difficult to distinguish from the brown withered leaves among which it grows.

At first glance the pine woods appear to have few flowers of note, but when the trees reach a certain height and the canopy becomes less dense, light is able to penetrate, and in the damper places many beautiful plants are to be seen. The Culbin Forest can boast (but this is exceptional) over 550 species of plants. This includes the flora of the dune areas but not the mosses and lichens. Fungi are abundant and in mid September even the amateur can add over 100 species between the edge of the forest and the sea.

In the older plantations where some moisture is retained, the more notable plants are: Creeping Lady's Tresses *(Goodyera repens)*, a small white-flowered orchid with dark green leaves, Lesser Wintergreen *(Pyrola minor)*, resembling a pink Lily-of-the-Valley with roundish shining leaves, Serrated Wintergreen *(Orthilia secunda)* with a one-sided flowering stem of little green bells, and the most beautiful member of our native flora, the One-flowered Wintergreen *(Moneses uniflora)* with small roundish basal leaves and a single stem, topped by a wide open flower of 5 waxy white petals, a lime-green ovary, style and stigma, and orange anthers. Here too, can be found the Coral-root Orchid *(Corallorhiza trifida)* equally at home growing in the damper dune slacks below willows, or in open slacks. It is a very inconspicuous plant, being colourless except for the dark brown markings on the corolla. It is named after the resemblance of the root to a piece of coral. Another inconspicuous plant is the Lesser Twayblade *(Listera cordata)*, a member of the Orchid family with small brownish flowers and two tiny opposite leaves near the base of the stem.

The pine wood mosses are numerous: *Hyphum cupressiforme, Hylocomium splendens, Pseudoscleropodium purum, Plagio-thecium undulatum* (strikingly pale with slightly branched fronds) and the less common *Ptilium crista-castrensis,* a feathery moss, yellow green at the top of the branches. In wetter places another feathery moss *Thuidium tamariscinum* is found; in dry places *Polytrichum formosum* is common. Many species of lichen are found, on trees and on the ground. Of the latter the largest number of species belong to the *genus Cladonia,* two of which are most attractive when closely observed in that they have bright red tops to their fruiting spore cases.

Farther inland where the woods are damper, the ground flora usually consists of large swards of Blaeberry *(Vaccinium myrtillus)* and Cowberry *(V. vitis-idaea)* both with edible fruits, the former blue-black when ripe and sweet tasting, the latter bright red and very bitter. Cowberry is often made into jelly, earning it the misnomer of "Cranberry" in Scotland. If the sward is not too dense the Wintergreens and Creeping Ladies' Tresses will find a foothold. The Intermediate Wintergreen *(Pyrola media),* the most common, is distinguished in the field by the style and stigma protruding well beyond the edge of the petals. (In P. minor they are enclosed by the petals). Pine woods are also the habitat of one of the plants most sought after by botanists, the beautiful little Twinflower *(Linnaea borealis).* This is very difficult to locate unless it is in flower. Its small rounded leaves are very similar to those of Blaeberry with which it nearly always associates. Its long creeping stems are hidden in the undergrowth, but the two bell-like flowers on erect stems of 5 to 7.5 cm (2 to 3 in) are quite easy to see. Linnaeus, the 17th century Swedish naturalist, after whom the plant was named, is said to have looked inside the flower and 'marvelled'. Indeed, I would advise others to do the same for the deep pink markings and the white hairs inside the corolla are quite exquisite.

Birch woods, being more open, tend to have fewer flowers. The dominant plant is generally the grass Common Bent *(Agrostis tenuis),* but some are carpeted with the white, starry-flowered Chickweed Wintergreen *(Trientalis europaea).* This, a very common plant in Moray is also to be found on open moorland and in pine woods. Other plants under birch are Common Cowwheat *(Melampyrum pratense)* and its deep yellow variety *(var. hians),* Hairy Woodrush *(Luzula pilosa)* and Great Woodrush *(L. sylvatica),* the latter often dominant in deciduous woods, suffocating young trees and excluding all other vegetation.

*Hedgerows and Waste Ground*

Due to continual cutting very few species now remain on the

verges of the main roads but, in the uplands, waysides can still be quite colourful with different species of wild flowers. By the main roads the common plants are Wild Chervil *(Anthriscus sylvestris)* a very decorative white umbellifer, the coarser Hogweed *(Heracleum sphondylium)* and several species of thistle. In the upland and moorland areas and on the minor roads in the lowlands many flowers can find a habitat along the verges. Garlic Mustard *(Alliaria petiolata)* with large kidney-shaped leaves and small white four-petalled flowers — the whole plant smelling strongly of garlic when crushed — is common. So too, is Heather *(Calluna vulgaris)*, Tuberous Comfrey *(Symphytum tuberosum)*, Bluebell *(Campanula rotundifolia)*, Lady's Bedstraw *(Galium verum)*, Horse Gowans *(Leucanthemum vulgare)* and Knapweed *(Centaurea nigrum)* as well as many small species. The wild roses hybridize freely and it is difficult to find a true species except for the Burnet Rose *(Rosa pimpinellifolia)* which, although common in Nairn District, is not so common in Moray.

As waste ground often merges into the hedgerows it is difficult to divide species found in these places into separate categories. Both very often include introduced species which may or may not maintain their ground for more than a year or two. For example, waste places left by road widening may be covered with Poppies and Wild Mustard for the first year but twelve months later can be quite overgrown with rank grasses.

Transient introduced species include Long Prickly-headed Poppy *(Papaver argemone)*, Common Melilot *(Melilotus Officinalis)* and While Melilot *(M. alba)*. Perennials such as the White Campion *(Silene alba)* and Lucerne *(Medicago sativa)* have strong roots and may maintain their ground for many years.

Large areas, especially where fire has taken place, can be taken over by Rosebay Willow-herb *(Epilobium angustifolium)* with its tall spikes of purple-red flowers, and by two mosses both of a striking red colour. *Ceratdon purpurescens* and *Funaria hygrometrica*. Gravelly floors of quarries and river shingles are invaded by the New Zealand Willow-herb *(Epilobium brunnescens)* with tiny opposite leaves and pale pink flowers on elongated stalks of about 7.5 cm (3 in) in height.

*Lochs and Bogs*

As habitats for plants, lochs and bogs can be divided into the alkaline and acid types, the former having a far richer flora than the latter. Spynie and Gilston lochs fall into the first category and are rich in species. Lochindorb, Loch Avon and Loch Builg and many small lochans throughout Moray belong to the second group, and are chiefly surrounded by rushes and sedges. They have, however, a few aquatic species and White Water-lily *(Nymphaea alba)* can occasionally be found.

Spynie Loch is surrounded by extensive marshes and is visited by many waterfowl. These are often the cause of the introduction of alien species, the seeds of which become lodged in the webbed feet of the birds. Two plants not native to North Scotland occur near Spynie. One, the Fringed Water-Lily *(Nymphoides peltata)*, although not a true water-lily, is very similar to the Least Yellow Water-Lily at first glance, but can be distinguished by the long fringes on the margins of the petals. The other is the spectacular Flowering Rush *(Botumus umbellatus)*, a tall plant with a large umbel of pink flowers. Neither of these two plants have been recorded for the vicinity in the old floras although the Flowering Rush occurred in one of the Brodie ponds many years ago. Both may have been introduced by man. Quite common in the bogs round the loch is a rare umbellifer in its only known station in the north, the Narrow-leaved Parsnip *(Berula erecta)*. Also, in its northernmost known station is an aquatic, Horn-wort *(Ceratophyllum demersum)*, which, though not seen recently in Spynie, has been discovered in one of the small pools at Gilston, nearby. Many other plants are to be found in the bogs, but the margins of Spynie are now a dense thicket of Reed Grass *(Phragmites australis)* which has pushed out all the smaller plants.

The acid lochs are either shallow and edged with stones or deep and peaty with, perhaps, a pondweed or two. At the shallow edges a small member of the plantain family is to be found forming a dark green turf. It is far-creeping, making rosettes of cylindrical linear leaves which become new plants at each node. This is shore-weed *(Littorella uniflora)*. It grows underwater as well, but flowers out of water being conspicuous only for its pale straw-coloured anthers on filiform stalks, which are readily seen especially when the wind is blowing. Water Lobelia *(Lobelia dortmanna)* is also frequently found in the shallow edges. This plant has the same habit, and its leaves are very similar to Shore-weed, except that they are blunt topped.

The flowers are a pale lilac in colour on a single reddish stem.
Bottle Sedge *(Carex rostrata)*, which has conspicuous,
glaucous-green grass-like leaves is very common in deeper water
on the margins of the acid lochs and also makes large patches
in the moorland bogs. It is often accompanied by Bogbean
*(Menyanthes trifoliata)*, Marsh Cinquefoil *(Potentilla palustris)*
and Lesser Spearwort *(Ranunculus flammula)*, the latter most
variable, especially in the mountain areas.

In the deeper water of Lochindorb will be found Quillwort
*(Isoetes lacustris)*, a stiff, dark, green-leaved near relative of the
fern family. It has spore cases buried at the base of the leaves
which are frequently washed up on the shores of the loch in late
summer along with several species of pondweed.

Acid moorland bogs are often covered with Bog Asphodel
*(Narthecium ossifragum)*, very noticeable not only for its spikes
of starry yellow flowers but for the beautiful apricot colour
of the plant in autumn. Here too, are found two small
insectivorous plants which catch small flies on their leaves.
Butterwort *(Pinguicula vulgaris)* has a flat rosette of sticky
yellow green leaves and a simple stem with violet coloured
flower, and Common Sundew *(Drosera rotundifolia)* with a rosette
of round red leaves covered with sticky glandular hairs, has
flowers that are small and white. Heath Spotted Orchid
*(Dactylorhiza maculata, subspericetorum)* is locally abundant. It
has solid stems with spotted leaves and is very variable in the
colour markings of its pale pink flowers.

With their white fluffy heads when in fruit, two common
species of Cottongrass are among the most spectacular of our
bog plants. Hare's-tail Cottongrass grows in tussocks and has a
single head, while Common Cotton-grass which grows in wetter
peaty pools has long creeping stems and several heads.

*Moorland*

In central Moray there are extensive areas of moorland
where few flowers are to be found. Two such areas are Dava
Moor and the Moss of Bednawinney. Dominated as these tracts
are by Heather *(Calluna vulgaris)* and Deergrass *(Trichophorum
cespitosum)*, a rush-like plant that turns a rich orange-red in
autumn, the smaller plants have difficulty in finding a foothold.
Among the more robust which do occur are the Bearberry
*(Arctostaphylos uva-ursi)*, a prostrate evergreen with shiny, dark

green leaves. The bunches of pink-rimmed, white, bellshaped flowers are replaced later on by deep red berries. Other strong growing plants which manage to compete are Cowberry *(Vaccinium vitis-idaea)*, Crowberry *(Empetrum hermaphroditum)*, with black bitter fruits, Bell Heather *(Erica cinera)* and the pink flowered Cross-leaved Heath *(E. tetralix)*. Among the smaller moorland plants Heath Bedstraw *(Galium saxatile)*, Heath Milkwort *(Polygala serpyllifolia)*, Lousewort *(Pedicularis sylvatica)* and, frequently, a small shrub-like plant with long spines and yellow pea flowers Petty Whin *(Genista angelica)*, are to be found.

Juniper *(Juniperus communis)* is scattered throughout the District. It appears to be tolerant of most soils but is never abundant. Bracken *(Pteridium aquilinum)* colonizes large tracts but is never dominant on the moors. The same applies to the fragrant-leaved Bog Myrtle, locally abundant in wet places. It is a dwarf shrub of from 60 to 90 cm (2 to 3 ft) and has rust-red male catkins in early spring before the leaves appear.

*Mountains*

With the recent changes of District boundaries Moray has acquired a mountain flora. The low limestone hills with their escarpment of cliffs at Inchrory provide many flowers not seen eleswhere: A single tree of the rare Whitebeam *(Sorbus rupicola)* still exists, but only just, on the cliffs above the Lodge. Nearby on the grassy hillside grows Spignel *(Meum athamanticum)*, a dark-green aromatic, feathery-leaved umbellifer, while on the same slope is Common Fleabane *(Erigeron acer)* in its only station in Northern Scotland. Here, too, are many orchids and an abundance of both Rock Rose *(Helianthemum chamaecistus)*, Mountain Pansy *(Viola lutea)* and Quaking Grass *(Briza media)*. The handsome Globeflower *(Trollius europaeus)*, locally known as Butter Balls and becoming rather rare in the lowlands, is fairly frequent here and is also to be found at quite high altitudes on mountain ledges. Among the rocks and boulders below the escarpment are many ferns. Holly Fern *(Polystichum lonchitis);* (Plate 6), with its prickly fronds, and the little Green Spleenwort *(Asplenium viride)* are common. Beech and Oak Ferns, the delicate Brittle Bladder Fern *(Cystopteris fragilis)* and several species of Dryopteris are also found here.

Higher on the rocky escarpment Stone Bramble *(Rubus saxatilis)* is common. It differs from the other brambles in that it has long trailing, red coloured stems without prickles, straw-berry-like leaves and clusters of erect greenish-white flowers, followed by shining red fruits. Wood Vetch *(Vicia sylvatica)* is occasionally found. It too is long trailing and has clusters of rather large pale lilac flowers. Many different species of that confusing genus, Hieracium, grow on the rock ledges. Some have stem leaves, some not and all have large yellow dandelion-like flowers. They are best left to the expert to name.

By the Builg burn is an abundance of the very rare Varie-gated Horsetail *(Equisetum variegatum)*. It has stiff dark green simple stems with black rings round the sheaths and small black, pointed cones. In Moray it has only been recorded at this site, and in the gorge of the Water of Ailnach.

On the slopes of the high mountains the interesting habitats for plants are by the sides of the burns and in the many flushes which occur. Here will grow the Alpine Bistort *(Polygonum viviparum)*, named after the viper (the only snake to produce young already formed) the little red bulbils beneath the pale pink flowers of this plant will proliferate vegetatively and fall off as ready-made plants i.e. no seed is produced.

Sometimes, in quantity, will grow the Scottish Asphodel *(Tofeldia pussila)*, a small white-flowered version of Bog Asphodel, Chickweed Willow-herb *(Epilobium alsinefolium)* and Alpine Willowherb *(E. annagallidifolium)*. All three plants are less than 10 cm (4 in) in height, the Alpine Willowherb normally being much shorter. Other small flowers of such places include Hairy Stonecrop *(Sedum villosum)* a pretty, succulent plant with pink flowers and pink-tinged leaves, Starry Saxifrage *(Saxifraga stellaris)* which has white flowers with yellow spots at the base of the petals and another Saxifrage, Yellow Saxifrage *(S. aizoides)*.

Of the many different species of dandelion (140) now listed in the British Flora there is a very common one found on wet mountain slopes, *Taraxacum faeroense*. It is recognised by its purple leaf stalks, leaves with only two or three lobes and erect bracts on the flower heads. On the high rock ledges of Ben Avon some very rare species of this genus have been recorded.

Below the very high cliff ledges where the arctic-alpines are chiefly found steep screes are often encountered. Surprisingly, many plants are able to maintain a foothold here. Alpine Rock-cress *(Cardaminopsis petraea)*, Alpine Lady's Mantle *(Alchemilla alpina)*, Alpine Cudweed *(Gnaphalium supinum)* and the Spiked

Woodrush *(Luzula spicata)* with its drooping head of small brownish flowers, are some of the more frequent.

The cliff ledges may be very rich in flora and often carry lowland plants such as Water Avens *(Geum rivale)*, Red Campion *(Silene dioica)* and Angelica *(Angelica sylvestris)*. On the higher ledges out of reach of grazing sheep and deer, several species of small willows are common, the Downy Willow *(Salix lapponum)* with long silvery leaves and the Myrtle Willow *(S. myrsinites)* with ovate dark-green shining leaves being the most frequent. The Dwarf Willow *(S. herbacea)* only 2.5 cm (1 in) or so high grows mostly on the bare tops of the hills. Willows, as a family, are most variable and hybridise freely.

The alpines and arctic-alpines are many and colourful. The Purple Saxifrage *(Saxifraga oppositifolia)* will flower as soon as the snow disappears, often as early as the end of February. Found trailing over wet rocks, it is a beautiful plant with very small dark-green leaves and large purple flowers. The Moss Campion *(Silene acaulis)* forms flat mats. It has long tap roots and the flowers may be deep pink to white in colour. It seldom reaches more than 5 cm (2 in) in height. Very rare is the mountain Aven *(Dryas octopetala)*. It is well known as a plant of rockeries with its small oak-like leaves, dark green above and silver grey beneath and has large white flowers and fluffy seed heads.

Other rarities are Alpine Saxifrage *(Saxifraga nivalis)* with a clustered head of rather dingy flowers, and Tufted Saxifrage *(S. cespitosa)*. On the other hand the Mossy Saxifrage *(S. hypnoides)*, many forms of which are seen in gardens, is frequent. In the wild state it has a large white flower.

Mosses abound, a common one being *Amphidium mougetii* which makes swelling tufts in the wet cracks of vertical cliff faces.

On the dry wind-swept tops of the mountains few species can survive. A grey-coloured moss *Rhacomitrum lanuginosum* is often dominant. It is accompanied by Rigid Sedge *(Carex bigelowii)* and the tiny-leaved, prostrate shrub, Mountain Azalea *(Loiseleuria procumbens)* which is studded with deep pink flowers in early June. There will also be a few small plants of the Dwarf Willow and the Alpine Cudweed, but little else.

The Clubmoss family, several species of which are conspicuous at high altitudes, are common at lower levels. Most of them descend to c. 300 m (1000 ft) as at Dava Moor; the

Stag's-horn *(Lycopodium clavatum)* comes down to sea level as at Culbin. Except for the Alpine and Fir Clubmoss few survive above 915 m (3000 ft).

*Introduced Species*

Besides the native plants, Moray, in common with other Districts, has a considerable number of introduced species generally classified as aliens. They can be introduced in a variety of ways. Many have been deliberately planted in gardens, become invasive and have been thrown out, to become established on river banks or waste ground. One such, The Giant Hogweed *(Heracleum mantegazzianum)*, has now become so common as to rank as a pest. It was introduced by the first Lord Leven at Glenferness House as a "curio" and has now invaded river banks from the Deveron to the Findhorn. The foliage is so dense that no other plant can survive underneath it. As the poisonous hairs on the stems can cause great irritation and blisters it is best to treat it with respect. Another plant was introduced in the same way — "a nice one for the rockery"; it is the Slender Speedwell *(Veronica filiformis)*. With bright pale-blue flowers and small roundish leaves it creeps extensively, forming large patches on lawns and short grassland. Bishop Weed was also brought in by man. The Alpine Dock *(Rumex alpinus)*, locally known as Butter Blades, was brought in by the Dutch and used by crofters to wrap up their butter. It is still found on several roadsides and near old buildings. Another source of introduced species comes from foreign grain, chiefly from distilleries, and some interesting plants have been found on the river shingles. Until recently railway yards could always be relied on to produce a rew foreign plants but nowadays more freight goes by road. Flour Mill yards may also harbour a few strange plants. Oxford Ragwort *(Senecio squalidus)* has reached its northernmost limit at Forres station. As many of these plants do not produce seed the possibilities of introducing pests by this means is remote. If seed is produced it is often not viable as the climate in the north is less favourable than in the south.

Several medicinal plants are still to be found. Among the ruins of Kinloss Abbey there are several plants of Deadly Nightshade *(Atropa bella-donna)* with its deep maroon-coloured flowers and deadly poisonous black berries; at Milton Brodie is Birthwort *(Aristolochia clematitis)* introduced by the monks from Fountains Abbey. Caraway *(Carum carvi),* used for flavouring cheese, is still found by old farm buildings. Certain species were once extensively planted for their berries to augment the native diet of pheasants. Examples of these that are often met with are Oregon Grape *(Mahonia aquifolia), Gaultheria shallon* and the Canadian Raspberry *(Rubus spectabilis).* The latter is conspicuous for its early flowering, large, purple-red flowers and raspberry-like fruits at first yellow, turning red to deep purple when fully ripe.

Introduced in the early part of the 20th century and to be found in most of the policies of the larger estates were the double flowered Meadow Saxifrage *(Saxifraga granulata),* a woodrush *(Luzula luzuloides)* and a tall grass, *(Poa chaixii).* Masterwort *(Peucedanum ostruthium),* Blue Comfrey *(Symphytum uplandicum),* once used as a fodder, Yellow Figwort *(Scrophularia vernalis)* and the White Butterbur *(Petasites albus)* are also well established. An interesting annual of the borage family *(Amsinckia intermedia),* resembling a Bugloss but with small yellow flowers, has in recent years become a pest in the fields at the farm of Wester Coltfield, Alves. There are many more that could be included in this category of plants.

*Lost Species*

Many of the plants named in the old floras are not now to be found. Modern agricultural methods have reduced or eliminated the once plentiful weeds, some of which were undoubtedly of attractive appearance. Drainage, close afforestation, cultivation and the replacement of hedgerows by wire fences reduce the areas available for wild plants; the filling-in of pools and quarries, the widening of roads and modern developments all take their toll. This is the price paid for progress.

Too little thought, however, is given to some aspects of this destruction. Selective weed killers on grass verges, for instance, seem to eliminate the herbs and leave the coarse grasses which can obscure the vision of the motorist as badly as ever. Unused ground is not necessarily *waste* ground and is a valuable refuge for native plants.

Awareness that short-term convenience must not lead to the careless extinction of species must be taken into consideration by all. Moray has an unequalled natural heritage. Let us not throw it away.

# 4

# BIRD LIFE

## JOHN EDELSTEN

People are becoming increasingly concerned about conservation matters and care of the environment. This is to some extent enlightened self-interest. When birds are killed by pollution or toxic chemicals, man, who shares the environment with all creatures, must himself be at risk.

The study of birds has become particularly popular and a vast amount of field work was put into the British Trust for Ornithology's Atlas project 1968-1972. A total of 127 breeding species was recorded in this period, with a further 7 species summering and possibly breeding. These records form the nucleus of the first section of the chapter which describes the distribution of the breeding birds. Six main types of habitat are described and the breeding birds are grouped under these headings. Woodlands, which are the most important habitats for birds, are split into four sub-headings: young trees, conifer plantations, birch woods and other broadleaved woodlands. There is, of course, considerable overlap, particularly with those species which are common and widely distributed.

The second section of the chapter describes passage migrants and winter visitors and is divided into four groups of related species. This section has been compiled from the local records of the Scottish Ornithologists' Club. A further 54 species could be listed in this section making a total of 188 recorded in Moray in recent years. However, certain omissions have had to be made to keep the account within reasonable proportions. The distribution of certain extreme rarities has been omitted in the interest of security. Other rarities have been included and readers are reminded that it is an offence under the 1967 Protection of Birds Act wilfully to disturb rare birds at their nests.

It is hoped that this method of treatment will give a clearer picture of the pattern of distribution of birds in Moray than would the customary species list. Further particulars of any

F

species can be obtained from the Bird Report published annually in *Scottish Birds.*

## BREEDING BIRDS

*The Arctic-alpine Zone*

The summits of Ben Macdui, 1,313 m (4,296 ft) and Cairngorm, 1,248 m (4084 ft) mark the southern tip of Moray. The arctic-alpine zone extends from these summits down to about 1,000 metres (3300 ft) depending on the degree of exposure. Much of this hill country is covered in snow during winter and the Ptarmigan, the only resident species, moves to lower ground in severe weather, returning in spring to breed in sheltered corries or amongst boulders on the exposed ridges.

Two species of wader breed regularly on the hills. The Golden Plover returns in early March to its breeding haunts which range from 1,130 m (3,700 ft) on Ben Avon down to 250 m (800 ft) on the moors north of Keith. The Dunlin returns much later to the hills. It has a more restricted range in the hills and also breeds at sea level in the Findhorn area.

The Snowy Owl has been seen summering on the Cairngorms and on moorland in west Moray; it has also wintered on moorland in Strathspey.

*Heather Moorland*

The typical bird of this zone is the Red Grouse. The moors are well keepered and produce some of the best bags in the country.

A few Golden Eagles and Peregrines are tolerated by enlightened keepers and would be more widely distributed if it were not for persecution. Their breeding cliffs are shared by Kestrels and Ravens. The Kestrel is the most common bird of prey in Moray, but the Raven is mainly restricted to moorland, though a pair has been seen near Forres.

The Merlin, the smallest of the falcons, is thinly distributed in moorland areas and feeds largely on meadow Pipits, the commonest species in this zone. The Meadow Pipit also has to put up with the attentions of the Cuckoo which arrives in May, and whose voice is one of the typical sounds on the moors in spring.

Another familiar voice is that of the Curlew which spends winter on the coast and returns in spring to make its nest among the heather or in rushes. The Snipe also nests in moorland bogs and the drumming of the male is another common sound in spring.

Two typical small birds of the open moorland are the Twite and the Ring Ouzel. The Twite, or Mountain Linnet, is more widely distributed than was previously thought, but is nowhere common. The Ring Ouzel is one of the first migrants to return to the moorland, nesting in heather banks or juniper bushes on the hillside.

Three species of gull breed amongst the heather, the Common Gull being the most numerous. There are several colonies of Lesser Black-backed and a few colonies of Herring Gull. There is a mixed colony of the three species on the Balloch Hill near Keith and it is interesting to see how the birds have adapted to the change in habitat due to trees being planted on the hill. Most of the Herring Gulls nest in a plantation of spruce trees which are now over 3 m (10 ft) high. Farther up the hill where the other two species nest, the ground has recently been ploughed and planted with young trees; it will be interesting to see if these birds, too, will adapt to a woodland habitat.

*Woodlands*

(i) Young Trees

Young conifer plantations add variety to the rather restricted range of birds found on heather moorland. The Short-eared Owl can be seen during the day hunting for voles which live in the plantations. Another predatory species, the Hen Harrier, is increasing its range in spite of persecution, thanks to the spread of conifer plantations. It preys upon small birds which live in the young trees.

The range of species is limited when the trees are small, the most typical bird being the Whinchat, but as the trees grow the number of species increases as more characteristic woodland varieties move into the plantations. Most common are the Chaffinch and Robin, but Blue Tit, Coal Tit and Bullfinch are also found amongst young trees in situations where they must have difficulty finding suitable nesting sites.

(ii) Conifer Plantations

Conifer Plantations of varying age and size cover a great deal of Moray. Although not noted for a variety of bird life they contain some of our most interesting species.

Tawny Owls are found in most woods and Long-eared Owls in a few localities; both breed in crows' nests. The crows in Moray are mainly hybrid Hooded/Carrion with some pure Carrion. The Rooks breed commonly in conifer plantations; in winter they flock together at night to roost in very large numbers. The roost in the conifer plantation at Tarryblake near Keith holds over 10,000 Rooks as well as many Jackdaws. The other resident member of the crow family, the Magpie, is fairly common in the eastern part of the District, but becomes more uncommon towards the west.

The smallest British bird, the Goldcrest, is common in conifer plantations. The numbers are augmented in winter by immigration from northern Europe. The Coal Tit is also very common. The Crested Tit is more of a rarity and its range is largely restricted to the woods of Strathspey. It is no longer found in its former haunts at Knock and Cullen, and there are now only a few near Fochabers. It occurs in the woods on the coast west of the Spey and visits bird tables at Lossiemouth in winter. There are small numbers in the woods near Forres.

The Capercaillie is to be found in mature pinewoods throughout Moray. Blackcock prefer woods with open spaces where they can hold their 'leks' or display grounds.

The Crossbill is thinly distributed in the west of Moray and there are a few records from Keith, Dufftown, Glenlivet and Cabrach in the east. The populations are augmented from time to time by irruptions of Continental birds in the early summer. The populations tend to fluctuate as trees are cut.

Tree felling also affects the number of heronries. Many Herons breed in small numbers or even single pairs, but there is still a heronry of 30 pairs at Ballindalloch.

The Redpoll and Siskin both breed in conifer plantations and appear to be increasing. The Siskin which visits bird tables in winter and sometimes in summer is attracted to the red net bags of peanuts put out for tits.

Two birds of prey breed in conifer plantations. The Sparrowhawk is fairly common and appears to be increasing. The Buzzard is well distributed in the west of Moray but becomes scarcer farther east.

(iii) Birch Woods

The birch woods which line the valleys of the hill glens are perhaps the most attractive of the Moray woodlands. A typical bird of the birch woods is the Tree Pipit, a species which may be found down to the coast near Cullen.

Several species of thrush breed in birch woods, the most typical being the Mistle Thrush whose song is one of the first voices to welcome spring back to the glens. The Song Thrush and Blackbird are common in birch woods and other woodland habitats. Two Scandinavian thrushes have recently started to colonise Scotland. The Redwing has been recorded on three occasions in Moray, the Fieldfare once.

Some birch woods contain a high proportion of dead or dying trees, which provide nesting places for the Redstart and Great Spotted Woodpecker (Plate 7).

(iv)   Broadleaf Woodlands

These make up only a small proportion of the extensive woodlands of Moray and the acreage is becoming smaller each year. However, there are still some extensive woods of oak and beech in the valleys of the Spey and Findhorn and near Elgin. These add variety to the birdlife of the District.

The warblers are typical woodland birds. By far the commonest is the Willow Warbler which nests round the edges of woods and in gardens and young conifer plantations. The related Chiffchaff is much less common but is increasing and is found in oakwoods, policies with rhododendrons and in young spruce plantations. The Wood Warbler is much more specialised and is seen in a few oak woods. The Blackcap and Garden Warbler, too, are scarce. Singing Blackcaps have been recorded in a few places in the coastal belt west of Elgin and probably breed in small numbers. They also occur in small numbers in winter and visit bird tables in the Elgin area. The Garden Warbler has bred in a garden near Kinloss and probably breeds in one or two woodlands near the coast.

Tits are also typical woodland birds. The Blue Tit is the commonest with a wide distribution including young plantations on the moors and nest boxes put up in town gardens. The Long-tailed Tit is less common but widely distributed, being found in a variety of woodlands including upland birch woods. The Great Tit is also common. Tits form into flocks at the end of the breeding season, roaming the woods and visiting garden bird tables.

Other typical woodland birds are the Treecreeper and the

Spotted Flycatcher. The Pied Flycatcher is scarce and has been known to breed in only one place on the Spey.

## Rivers and Lochs

The Goosander and Merganser, two fish-eating ducks, are fairly common in spite of shooting, the Goosander being more typical of hill burns, whilst the Merganser is commoner by estuaries and on the coast. The two most typical ducks are the Mallard and Teal which breed by rivers and lochs. Other ducks breeding by lochs include Tufted Duck, Wigeon, which is found in western Moray, and the Shoveler, Pochard and Pintail which are rather scarce.

Other common water birds found on lochs include the Coot, Moorhen and Little Grebe. The Great Crested Grebe reaches the northern limit of its range in Moray; it used to breed on Spynie and is still seen occasionally. The Slavonian Grebe is very scarce. The Water Rail has been heard calling near Elgin and is seen in the winter on the Findhorn and Spey estuaries.

Several species of waders are associated with rivers and lochs, the Common Sandpiper being the most abundant. The Redshank and Greenshank also occur, the latter being confined to one or two places in South Moray.

Of the passerines the Dipper is the most typical river bird; it is found from the coast right up to the hill burn at the head of the glens and even on to the open moorland. The Grey Wagtail, perhaps our most handsome bird, has a similar distribution. The Pied Wagtail is common on river banks as well as in drier places. The Reed Bunting and Sedge Warbler are also found in a variety of habitats but most typically in reeds and bushes bordering rivers and lochs.

## Farmland

Modern farming methods do not encourage birds to nest in arable land, but the Corn Bunting which has a very late breeding season manages to breed in cornfields. The Skylark and Lapwing are common on rough grazing land and the Corncrake is still heard in one or two places near Forres.

Hedgerows and shelter belts near farms hold a variety of small birds including Wren, Robin, Dunnock, Chaffinch, Greenfinch and Yellowhammer. The Goldfinch appears to be increasing though there has been only one breeding record.

The Woodpigeon is very common especially in winter when flocks of continental birds visit this country. By contrast, the Stock Dove, once a common bird in Moray, is now much reduced in numbers. The Collared Dove, unknown until the late fifties, has increased rapidly in lowland areas. A flock of 328 was counted at Covesea in 1972.

Disused farm buildings provide nest sites for Jackdaws and Starlings. Swallows build their nests on beams inside the buildings; House Martins plaster their nests on the walls outside. Barn Owls breed in a few places where they are not disturbed.

Partridges and Pheasants are common on farmland. The Red-legged Partridge has been introduced and can be seen near Cullen. The Quail is occasionally heard near Elgin and Forres.

## The Coast

The cliffs near Portknockie and at Covesea hold colonies of Kittiwakes with a few Fulmars and Shags. The herring Gull and Lesser Black-backed Gull breed along the coast but are also found on moors inland. There used to be a colony of Lesser Black-backed Gulls at the mouth of the Spey which, unfortunately, has been practically wiped out by constant disturbance. A few pairs breed along the shingle towards Lossiemouth.

Rock Pipit and Stonechat are resident on the coast throughout the year. The former occurs wherever there are cliffs, walls or harbours in which it can build its nest; the latter, which frequents gorse bushes along the cliff tops, is at present fairly numerous as a result of successive mild winters.

The Common Tern, a summer visitor, breeds along the coast, on the Spey islands and on shingle banks higher upstream. There is a small colony near Cabrach on the upper reaches of the Deveron. The Arctic Tern breeds only on the coast, sometimes in mixed colonies with the Common Tern. Our smallest tern, the Little Tern, is confined to a few pairs in the Findhorn area. It has a late breeding season which extends into the holiday period and so its breeding grounds are subject to constant disturbance. It seems unlikely that it will survive much longer. The Sandwich Tern used to breed on the Old Findhorn Bar but no longer breeds regularly in Moray. It is hoped that with the creation of a National Nature Reserve in the Findhorn area these sea birds will be given the protection they need to become established on a firm basis.

Three species of duck breed on the coast. The Shelduck is common, the following counts of early Spring flocks being some guide to the size of the breeding populations: Speymouth 25, Lossiemouth 31 and Findhorn 121. A small number of Mergansers breed in the Spey estuary and in the Findhorn area, a few Eiders on the coast near Findhorn.

### PASSAGE MIGRANTS AND WINTER VISITORS

Bird migration can best be observed on the coast. Newly arrived migrants tend to settle on the coast to feed and rest before continuing their voyages. The coastline is an important migration route for some birds. Certain sea birds do not come ashore at all but their movements can be observed from vantage points along the coast. The coast of the Moray Firth attracts many migrating birds, particularly in late summer and autumn. It is the first land fall for many birds arriving from Scandinavia and the north. The estuaries of the Findhorn, Lossie and Spey provide good resting and feeding areas for waders and wildfowl; many remain during the winter, returning north to their breeding grounds in spring.

*Waders*

Young birds of many species of wader disperse rapidly after fledging. Flocks of waders such as Dunlin and Common Sandpiper appear on the coast as early as June; these flocks contain a high proportion of young birds. The Common Sandpiper is a passage migrant which has passed on south by September. Other passage migrants are the Grey Plover, which occurs in flocks of up to 21, Whimbrel (71), Curlew Sandpiper (26), Little Stint (12), and small numbers of Ruffs, Spotted Redshank, Black-tailed Godwit, and Green and Wood Sandpipers. The best place to see these birds is in the Findhorn area but they may also be observed in the estuaries of the Spey and Lossie.

Other waders may stay on throughout winter though the peak numbers are usually in autumn; the commonest is the Oystercatcher (Plate 8) with flocks of several thousand at the end of August. Some indication of the origin of these birds is given by the recovery near Cullen of a bird which had been

ringed as a chick on Fair Isle. Flocks of 2,000 Redshank can
be seen at Findhorn, and several hundred each of Curlew,
Lapwing, and Bar-tailed Godwit. There is an important winter
roost at Buckpool with a few hundred each of Dunlin, Turn-
stone and Knot, whilst at Portessie there is a roost of 300
Purple Sandpiper. Also in the Buckie area, by the Gollachy
Burn, may be found the Jack Snipe. One or two Greenshank
winter at Findhorn, although the bird is largely a passage
migrant.

*Sea Birds*

At the same time as the passage of waders moves along the
Moray coast, a massive migration of sea birds is taking place
offshore. Some of the birds may roost on the shore or on rocks.
Others remain at sea, but can be watched from various vantage
points such as the Old Findhorn Bar, Burghead, and the mouth
of the Spey. Sea birds are present off the coast throughout
winter, but are generally difficult to see except when they come
close to the shore following shoals of sprats, or when they are
driven inshore by gales.

One of the first signs of this sea bird movement is the arrival
on the coast of large flocks of gulls. Hundreds of Great Black-
backed Gulls, which breed in Moray only in small numbers,
may be seen on the sea or roosting on rocks or shingle bars.
Migrating gulls are attracted by floodwater: several thousand
Common and Black-headed Gulls were seen on the floods near
Kinloss in August 1970. Kittiwakes, numbering thousands, have
been seen along the coast while migrating during bad weather in
autumn. The Glaucous and Iceland Gulls are regular winter
visitors from the north but only in small numbers.

Flocks of migrating Common and Arctic Terns numbering
over 500 can be observed at Speymouth in August. Smaller flocks
of Sandwich Terns are seen at Findhorn; both Black Tern and
Roseate Tern are occasionally noted. All these species have
migrated south by the middle of October.

Three species of skua occur offshore on autumn migration.
The Arctic Skua is the commonest, often harrying migrating
terns from the end of July until October. The Great Skua is
seen in smaller numbers and has also been recorded in winter.
One bird which had been colour-ringed on Foula was observed
at Findhorn. The Pomarine Skua is seen in small numbers from

October to December. Gannets appear regularly offshore during winter, occasionally in flocks of several hundreds, when there are shoals of sprats in the Firth.

Four species of diver have been noted in the autumn and winter months: the Red-throated is commonest, a flock of 46 having been seen in Spey Bay in November 1973. Small numbers of Black-throated and Great Northern Divers have been seen and there are two records of the rare White-billed Diver, one of which frequented Buckie harbour for several weeks, attracting bird watchers from all over Scotland.

Cormorants are common, particularly in autumn, when flocks of 100 white bellied juvenile birds roost on rocks near Findochty. Large flocks of juvenile Shags and Black Guillemots are seen in small numbers off the coast each winter and one or two Little Auks are usually found dead on the shore.

*Wildfowl*

At Loch Spynie there is a wintering flock of Grey Lag Geese numbering several hundred; they are occasionally joined by a few Barnacle Geese. Grey Lag and Pink-footed Geese are frequently seen on spring and autumn passage at several places along the coast. Brent Geese may be viewed on passage in the Buckie area and at Findhorn where the largest flock numbering 47 was recorded in September. The Whooper Swan is another passage migrant, though occasionally birds spend the winter at Speymouth. There has also been a record of a summer bird.

Burghead Bay holds huge winter flocks of sea duck: Common Scoter (12,000), Velvet Scoter (2,000), Long-tailed Duck (1,000), Scaup (400), Widgeon (500) and Goldeneye (250). Smaller numbers are found at other places along the coast. There is a winter flock of 200 Eider off Covesea. Small numbers of Gadwall are seen in winter on Loch Spynie and at Gordon Castle, Fochabers. Flocks of Mallard and Teal roost on the sea or come ashore in quiet coves.

*Land Birds*

Large flocks of Fieldfares and Redwings arrive in October and November and many remain here for the winter. Large numbers of Starlings, too, visit Moray in winter; there is a roost of 10,000 at Spynie. Snow Buntings are found in flocks of up to 200 along the shore. The Brambling is a regular winter visitor in flocks of up to 50; a migrating flock of 400 was recorded in early May 1973, near Cabrach.

Flocks of Siskins (up to 70 birds) and Redpolls (up to 150) are found in coastal woodlands during the winter. Large flocks of mixed finches including Chaffinch, Greenfinch and Twite roam the countryside in winter, feeding in stubble and by stackyards. Many of these birds are thought to have come from the continent.

Waxwings are regular winter visitors to certain gardens along the coast. Some years the numbers reach "invasion" proportions as in 1965/6 when over 2,000 birds were reported from the Moray faunal area. Small numbers of Great Grey Shrike are regular winter visitors from the north; occasionally one will stay over the winter period.

Spring migration is a good time for rarities, particularly when east winds blow them off their normal migration routes and they lose their way. Records in the past few years include White Stork, Alpine Swift, Hoopoe, Wryneck, Red-backed Shrike and Black Redstart.

# 5

# OTHER WILD LIFE

## ROLAND RICHTER

### BATS

The only truly flying mammals, bats, have acquired several peculiar bodily features, the chief of which is, of course, the wing. This is an expanse of skin, reaching from the tips of the fingers to the ankles of the foot, continuing around the tip of the tail, thus surrounding the whole body except for the head and neck. Bats have long been famous for their ability to find their way, avoid obstacles and capture insects in the dark. We now know that they do this by echo-location (not "radar"). From the bat's mouth high-pitched squeals are emitted and reflected by any object in the way; this echo is then picked up by the animal's ear.

All British bats hibernate during winter. The mating season is usually during the autumn but fertilization does not take place until spring of next year. The single young is carried by its mother for several days on her aerial hunts.

### Pipistrelle Bat

This is our smallest and commonest bat. It is found throughout the area and is usually abundant. It spends the day and the winter under the roofs of buildings, emerging during the evening. Not uncommonly it can be seen flying in full daylight and even during mild spells in the winter.

### Long-eared Bat

Though less numerous than the Pipistrelle, this species is common in our area, frequenting similar places but, being more strictly nocturnal, it is less often seen. The ears, from which it takes its name, are so long that, when the animal bends back its head, it can touch the base of its tail with the tip of its ears! It is also peculiar (among bats) for mating in spring as frequently as in the autumn.

*Daubenton's Bat*

It is doubtful whether this species occurs in the area at the present time. There are two records from the end of the last century, one from Cromdale, the other from Spey Bay. There may be others of which the writer is not aware.

*Noctule*

H.N. Southern (Handbook of British Mammals) states: "Has been recorded as far North as Morayshire". This record cannot be traced but it seems certain the Noctule is not an established member of our fauna.

INSECTIVORES

*Common Shrew*

This is one of our commonest mammals. It is not often seen alive, as it confines most of its activities to the runways it makes among grass and litter. It is much more often noticed in the autumn lying dead by the roadside, for at that season the whole of the adult population dies. Only the young of the year survive the coming winter. Almost wholly carnivorous, shrews are voracious hunters, on the move both day and night searching for insects, worms and carrion. Their high-pitched, twittering voice can be heard from under the grass in hedgebanks and roadsides. Owls appear to be the shrews' chief enemies. Mammals, such as cats, may kill them but seem to be reluctant to eat them owing to their musky odour.

*Pygmy Shrew*

This is our smallest mammal, of average weight 3.5 g (⅛ oz). It is even more widespread than the common species and has been seen on the summit of the highest Scottish mountains but it is not, on the whole, as abundant. Its habits are similar as is its short life span.

*Water Shrew*

This, our largest shrew, has become adapted to an amphibious life. It is more handsomely coloured than our other shrews, being very dark above and white below. Special "swimming hairs" on tail and feet facilitate smimming and diving. Though often found away from water, much of its hunting is done at the bottom of some burn or pond where it catches water insects, tadpoles and the like. Its breeding habits and life span are similar to those of other shrews.

## Mole

Moles are found all over the Moray area, except on the highest hills, and where the soil is either too shallow to allow burrowing, or too sandy to support the runs. They are most abundant on pasture land where mole hills, that is earth displaced by burrowing, are often troublesome to the farmer. Moles live almost entirely underground, for which life they are uniquely adapted, especially with their peculiar digging "hands" and the structure of their fur. Moles feed on any animal matter they can find, with earthworms forming a large part of their diet. For such a subterranean animal it is surprising how often its bones turn up in Tawny Owl's pellets. Other predatory birds and mammals also take their toll.

## Hedgehog

The hedgehog is found all over the area wherever there is some shelter in the shape of hedges or shrubs, and is often common in gardens and parkland. It avoids bare open pastures and moors and does not ascend high on the hills. Dense forest without shrubby undergrowth also carries a low population. If it were not such a familiar animal, the hedgehog would attract great crowds in a zoo, for it is a peculiar creature. The spines, which are really outsize hairs, cover the upper part of the body except for the face, but the latter can be guarded by lowering the head and pointing the front spines forward. If danger persists the animal rolls up into a ball, spines bristling in all directions. This does not, alas, save it from the motor car and the dead, battered hedgehog on the road is a more familiar sight than a live one. Like that of other insectivores, the hedgehog's diet consists of invertebrates of many kinds, though mice and lizards may also be taken. There is much controversy over the question as to whether hedgehogs will kill adders. In any case, they are not likely to be a major enemy of that reptile. There seems little reliable evidence that the hedgehog is injurious to game interests. Apart from bats, the hedgehog is the only truly hibernating mammal of this area.

## RODENTS

### Red Squirrel

After near-extinction in Scotland in the late 18th century, red squirrels were re-introduced from England and have spread again to cover most of the country. They are now common in all the major pine forests in our area. Most of the squirrels are clearly of the British form, recognised by their tails, cream-coloured in summer, but some dark-tailed specimens suggest admixture of continental stock. The latter has been introduced a few times in the past, though not in Moray. The American Grey Squirrel has not (yet?) penetrated into our part of the country, a blessing, as it has proved a pest in many parts where it has established itself. However, red squirrels may also do damage to conifers by barking the young shoots of the trees. A diurnal animal, the squirrel is more often seen than most other rodents. Pine cones, stripped of all scales except the uppermost, also give conclusive evidence of its presence. Its spherical nest ("drey") in the trees is also conspicuous, though often mistaken for a bird's nest.

### Bank Vole

Although spread over the whole of the area, excepting the mountain tops, this species is absent or scarce on very exposed ground, such as moors and open pasture. It requires more shelter than the field vole. This may take the form of rank vegetation, banks and walls, but more especially the cover afforded by woodland. In plantations it may become a major pest. Bank voles are better climbers than field voles; the damage they do may extend much higher up the trees than that caused by field voles.

### Field Vole (or Short-tailed Vole)

This animal is often called the Field Mouse. As that is also commonly applied to the Wood Mouse (a true, long-tailed mouse) it can be misleading.

Apart from dense woodland and the mountain tops, the field vole is found in every part of the area. Its density is highest in plantations and permanent pasture, much less so on arable land. Numbers may increase to plague proportions in some years, to be followed by a "crash" when the population drops to a very low level. This is, however, a less common occurrence in our part of Scotland than in some others. Even at a normal population level, damage to agricultural and forestry interests can be considerable.

Like the bank vole, the field vole is one of the principal foods of many predatory birds and mammals, buzzards, kestrels and owls, stoats, weasels and foxes all taking their toll.

## Water Vole

This is the "Water Rat" of popular parlance, but it is a true vole. It is a very inoffensive animal, one of the few rodents that does not do any appreciable damage to human interests. In our part of the country, and indeed over most of Britain, the species is confined to the edges of still or running water. Although it ascends quite high in the hills along the courses of burns and drainage ditches, it is much more common on the lower ground. It is numerous in the Laich of Moray. A black form, a very handsome animal, it is not unusual in the area and is much more prevalent than in the south.

The water vole feeds largely on aquatic vegetation and is a strong swimmer and diver. It burrows in the banks at the water's edge, one tunnel at least opening under water for a quick and silent escape.

## Wood Mouse (Long-tailed Field Mouse)

Woods, gardens and shrubberies almost invariably harbour this common mouse but, as its alternative name suggests, it is often found on arable land, where it may do much damage to cereal crops. This is the species responsible for the overnight disappearance of newly planted peas in a garden. It will not only occupy sheds and outhouses, but will invade our homes in the winter months, leaving again in spring. It is then often confused with the House Mouse which is a smaller and greyer animal. Although not normally inhabitants of the high hills, some instances of wood mice living in mountain bothies have been recorded.

A peculiar feature of this species (though it shares it with some other rodents, none of them Scottish) is the ease with which the skin of its tail strips off when grasped. This is perhaps a means of escape from enemies, but it leads to the loss of the exposed portion of the tail.

## House Mouse

A very common and destructive associate of man, the house mouse was introduced into this country in early historic or prehistoric times — much earlier than the two rats. Although best known where it shares our homes, it is all too numerous in fields and gardens. It probably does more damage in corn stacks than in buildings. It will attack almost any kind of human food whether animal or vegetable, and it contaminates more than it eats, leaving behind a most unpleasant smell.

## Harvest Mouse

There have been a few isolated records of this species in Banff in the latter half of the last century. It seems likely that they were due to accidental introduction. The harvest mouse is certainly not established in this area.

## Brown Rat

Rats are undoubtedly the most destructive of our mammals. Normally they inhabit buildings in towns, villages and farms but will spread to almost any kind of cultivated or natural habitat. Being excellent swimmers they establish themselves along rivers and canals; they also infest woodlands, hedgebanks and the like. It is likely that many of these "outdoor" rats return to buildings for the winter, but one can come across them at any season far away from human habitation. The damage they cause is largely due to the wide range of food they will accept. Almost everything, alive or dead, will be taken, grain or root crops, stored meat or pheasants' eggs. Rats, like most small rodents, are prolific breeders, which makes control more difficult. A black form is occasionally met with, and has been erroneously recorded as the Black Rat, a species not found in our area.

### LAGOMORPHS — THE HARE ORDER

## Rabbit

Rabbits were introduced into this country from the Mediterranean area and it seems amazing that they could adapt so well to the harsher climate of Northern Scotland. Before the advent of myxomatosis, the rabbit had been a serious pest of agriculture. The disease, which lasted for several years, caused a spectacular decrease in numbers. When rabbit density reaches

G

a certain point, myxomatosis appears again, but it is unlikely that we shall see again the level of infestation and damage we knew in the past.

### Brown Hare

Hares differ from rabbits in a number of ways. They are longer-legged, longer-eared animals. Their young are born above ground, covered with fur and with their eyes open. Brown hares are found all over the lower ground, ascending on the hills to where heather takes over from pasture. They prefer open fields and extensive woodlands to the broken ground favoured by the rabbit, and the habitats of the two show little overlap. The hare does not burrow but lies out in the open in a depression ("form") which perfectly fits the outline of its body.

Several litters may be born in the course of the year but the hare is not as prolific as the rabbit. Both hares and rabbits practise a peculiar form of "birth control". Some of the embryos carried by the mother may be destroyed and absorbed before birth, so that the numbers born are lower than the numbers conceived. Hares are not affected by myxomatosis.

### Blue (Mountain) Hare

Where the brown hare leaves off in the hills, the blue hare takes over. Like several other Scottish animals and plants, the blue hare is a relic of the Ice Age. After retreat of the ice such species survived where the climate was sufficiently arctic to suit their needs. At the present time the blue hare is confined to the higher levels, chiefly within the area dominated by heather moor, though some ascend to the summits of the mountains.

During the winter months, blue hares assume a dazzling white pelage. This may help them to escape the notice of predators in the snow-bound arctic, but in our climate it is more likely to have the opposite effect. During severe weather, they may descend into farmland and do much damage. On the other hand, they now form an article of export to continental countries where hares are a prized dish.

#### CARNIVORES — THE BEASTS OF PREY

### Fox

During the last few decades foxes have increased here as they have in most parts of this country, and now they occur in every type of habitat, high or low, open or forested. Their earths are usually placed where there is some kind of shelter, such as a bank, wall, boulder, etc.

There is great variety as to the animals taken as prey, according to habitat and season. Rabbits, hares and voles predominate, but the fox's depredations on game, poultry and lambs cannot, unfortunately, be disregarded. Whether the control measures taken at present repay their cost is a much debated question.

## Wild Cat

The wild cat has always been established in the Highland areas of Scotland. In the last 30 years or so there has been an increase in numbers, with considerable colonization of lower ground, especially in forest areas, even Culbin.

Although the Scottish Wild Cat is not now regarded as a species distinct from the domestic cat, it is not the race from which the latter has descended, and there are differences in anatomy and appearance which make identification possible in most cases. Intermediates occur, but rarely, and may be hybrids between the two forms. The wild cat hunts mainly at night and is not often seen. Its main food consists of small mammals up to the size of a hare, but grouse are taken on the moors, and the cat thus comes in conflict with the gamekeeper. Poultry and lambs are occasionally killed as well.

## Badger

This is our largest carnivorous mammal. It occurs mainly in the wooded valleys of the larger rivers. Densities are nowhere high but there are fair-sized populations along the Deveron, Spey and Findhorn. The badger also inhabits the forests of Culbin and Pitgaveney in Moray. The animal is rarely seen as it is wary of man and strictly nocturnal in its habits.

In spite of its membership of the weasel family, the badger is not a fierce hunter, being content with slow-moving prey such as insects, worms and small mammals. Much vegetable food is also taken. Occasional "rogue" individuals may raid hen coops, but on the whole the badger is not injurious to human interests. Contrary to popular belief, the badger does not hibernate during winter months.

## Otter

Otters frequent most of our larger lochs and rivers, and tracks have been seen along the seashore between Findhorn and Nairn. Shy and retiring, they usually avoid the immediate vicinity of human settlements. It was therefore surprising when, in the middle of the 1950s, a pair bred successfully for several years in an ornamental pond in the grounds of Gordonstoun School, much to the delight of the students who used to watch them disporting themselves in the water in the evenings.

Although coarse fish such as eels form the major part of the otter's diet, game fish are commonly taken. In view of the small numbers of otters, it is doubtful whether they make any impact on the fish population. Frogs and toads are taken in their spawning season. Some otters regularly hunt on land, preying on mammals and birds.

## Stoat and Weasel

Both stoats and weasels show great catholicity in their choice of habitat. Gardens and fields, woods and moors are all acceptable. Some individuals venture high up on the hills. Being diurnal in their movements, they are more often noticed than our other predatory mammals. The stoat can be told by the black tip to its tail, and its coat changes to white in the autumn. Both species feed mostly on small mammals, the weasel being so slender that it can follow a mouse into its burrow. Eggs and chicks of gamebirds, as well as poultry, are taken when available.

The weasel has two litters a year; the stoat has one, the young being born ten months after mating.

## American Mink

Mink, escaped from fur farms, have settled in several parts of Britain and Europe. They are firmly established along the upper reaches of the River Isla, in Glenlivet, and possibly elsewhere. They are reluctant to leave the vicinity of water, though they are not as aquatic as the otter. Too little is as yet known of their feeding habits in this country to assess their possible economic impact.

## Grey Seal and Common Seal

Both species of British seal are frequently seen around the

coast of Moray. The grey seal breeds elsewhere. The common
seal at times bears its young on the rocks from Burghead
eastwards to the Aberdeen border. These are isolated occurrences
and do not represent regular breeding colonies. Both species may
take salmon from nets, destroying the latter in the process, but
the chief culprit is the common seal whose main food is flatfish.

## DEER — THE CLOVEN-HOOFED ORDER

### Red Deer

Red deer are inhabitants of the higher hills; they are
particularly numerous on the Cairngorm range. As they move
to lower levels in winter, they come into serious conflict with
the farmer. On the other hand, venison is an important article
of export on some highland estates. A few herds are established
at quite low levels: on the Dava Moor a sizeable group exists at
an elevation of about 250 m (800 ft). A small band of half a
dozen has lived for many years in the forest of Pitgaveney
near Lossiemouth.

### Roe Deer

A forest dweller, the roe is absent from the highest
mountains. It does not form large herds but lives in small
groups at all seasons. This enables it to inhabit quite small
patches of woodland, such as the grounds of some country
houses. If tolerated, it will become quite tame and easy to
observe.

Roe deer can do extensive damage to young plantations of
conifer by stripping the bark off young trees when cleaning
their antlers (not "horns") of velvet. Extensive — and expensive!
The roe is becoming increasingly appreciated as a sporting game,
as it always has been abroad.

### Sika Deer and Fallow Deer

Both these species have been introduced in the past in a
few selected spots. A small group of fallow deer still occupy
woods near Fochabers. In 1965 a single specimen of sika was
observed near Loch na Bo.

## REPTILES

There are only three species of reptiles in Scotland and

all of them occur in Moray: the Adder, the Common Lizard and the Slow Worm. Reports of Grass Snakes in Scotland are to be viewed with suspicion.

### Adder

Adders, which are found mainly on heathland and in young conifer plantations, avoid farmland and dense forest. Their habitat is similar to that of the lizard which is considered to be their main food although small mammals and fledgling birds are also taken. The poison is used to immobilize prey as well as in self defence. Cases of adder bite are fortunately rare. The adder usually retreats at the approach of man; it is perhaps worth noting that its fangs cannot penetrate a leather or rubber boot. A doctor should be contacted as soon as possible; none of the do-it-yourself remedies is really effective.

### Common Lizard

This is our commonest reptile, whose typical habitat is heather, dry grassy banks, and open patches in woods. It is more often heard scuttling into the undergrowth than actually seen. Keep still and it will soon come out again. The male may be identified by its bright orange underside. To catch a lizard, you will have to grab it by the body as the tail readily breaks off. It will grow again but not to its former length and beauty. Lizards are strictly diurnal and require the heat of the sun to become fully active.

### Slow Worm

A legless lizard, the slow worm is often mistaken for a snake. It appears to be rare, but its nocturnal habits make its observation difficult. It feeds on worms, caterpillars and other slow-moving creatures. Like the common lizard, it may shed its tail when handled. The tail does not grow again; only a new point is added to the stump.

The writer has definite records only for the Spey and Findhorn Valleys, but the species is probably more widely distributed.

### AMPHIBIANS

### Frog and Toad

Both frog and toad are common and widely distributed. The

toad does not extend so far up in the hills as does the frog but in low-lying areas it appears to be the more numerous. Frogs fluctuate greatly in numbers: a sharp frost during the spawning season may wipe out many eggs and adults. Toads are less affected by this hazard. On the higher hills, frog tadpoles may hibernate in the larval state, completing their development a year later.

## Newts

There are three species of newt in Britain and they all occur in Moray. Two of them are, however, very rare. The Smooth, or Common, Newt occurs in two pools in Moray, and the Crested Newt also is found in one of these. Both pools are threatened by drainage. On the contrary, the third species, the Palmated Newt, is very common and extends over the whole region, from sea level to high in the hills. It will breed in tiny accumulations of water, such as tractor ruts, as well as in ponds and ditches.

### FRESHWATER FISHES

Moray is famed for its salmon rivers with trout abundant in loch, river and burn. Sea trout, though more like salmon in habits, are now regarded as a form of the Brown Trout. The American Rainbow Trout is being increasingly introduced into many lochs. It tolerates higher temperatures, is easier to breed and manage but it is, in the author's view, much inferior as a table fish. A fourth member of the salmon family, the Char, is said to inhabit Loch Builg.

Eels, spawned in the Sargasso Sea, ascend our rivers after a three year journey, and make their way into lochs and ponds, even travelling overland if need be. After ten to fifteen years, they will again cross the Atlantic, to spawn and die.

The Stickleback (or Brandie) is perhaps our commonest fish. It is best known for the remarkable habits of the male, which builds a nest like a bird, entices some females to lay, but hatches and cares for the brood by himself.

There are Pike and Perch in many lochs. Often they were introduced by man but both are probably native to the area. Roach, imported from the south, have been living for at least eighty years in a pond at Gordonstoun, which is perhaps a tribute to our pleasant climate. Minnows, probably introduced, occur in the Deveron.

The curious little Brook Lamprey can be seen in spring in many of our fast-flowing burns. It has neither jaws nor limbs, and is not a fish, though a true vertebrate. After spending several years in the larval state underneath the gravel it matures suddenly, spawns, and dies. Unlike its cousin, the Sea Lamprey, it does not seem to attack fish, nor take any other food, in the state of maturity.

### The Invertebrate Animals

It is obviously impossible to deal adequately with the vast numbers of invertebrate species in a short chapter. The writer will, therefore, confine himself to a few selected forms which, for some reason or another, appear to him of special interest. They are grouped by habitat rather than by their natural relationships. Scientific names will be used in this section, for few of these animals are well enough known to have English names. Butterflies and moths are an exception.

When Ice Age conditions gave way to a milder climate, some of the inhabitants of this country did not die out but found a refuge in the high hills where summers remained relatively cold, thus giving the arctic element of our fauna. A spider *(Arctosa alpigena)* is found under stones in the Cairngorm range. Outside Scotland, it is only known in Greenland. The Black Mountain Moth, the Northern Rustic and the Mountain Ringlet Butterfly have long been known in the same mountains. Four species of truly arctic water beetles inhabit lochans and pools, descending to 270 m (900 ft) on Dava Moor.

At lower levels, heather moors dominate large tracts of country. Heather is the most important food of the Red Grouse, and the depredations of theHeather Beetle *(Lochmaea Suturalis)* can lead to serious financial loss. In spring, the magnificent males of the Emperor Moth can be seen flying low over the heath in bright sunshine, seeking out the females sitting quietly on the stems. Later on, they are replaced by the Scottish Eggar Moth, equally large and nearly as beautiful. Less enjoyable are the hordes of vicious bloodsuckers headed by midges *(Culicoides species)* and mosquitoes *(Aedes punctor)* with a generous sprinkling of clegs *(Haematopota)*.

Pine forests harbour a rich insect fauna but most species

are rather small and of interest mainly to the specialist. One of the exceptions is the Pine Looper moth whose larvae feed on the needles of the Scots Pine. The damage may be so serious that aerial spraying with insecticides becomes the only remedy.

The large hills built by the Red Wood Ant are conspicuous in many forests. These ants are assiduous killers of insects, yet their nests are the natural home of a number of insects which are tolerated and even encouraged by the ants. The large, metallic green Rose Chafer *(Cetonia cuprea)* spends its larval life feeding on decaying needles in the depths of an anthill. The adult beetle may be seen feeding on the blossom of rowans in June. It is rare, and is known to the writer to occur in Moray in Darnaway Forest only. The Robber Fly *(Laphria flava)* pounces upon and kills beetles up to its own size — a strange diet for a fly. It is not uncommon in the coastal forests but is rarer inland.

Where birch is interspersed with the pines, one of Britain's rarest and most beautiful moths, the Kentish Glory, can still be seen early in the spring. In spite of its name, it appears to be confined to Scotland. It is known, for example, in Culbin Forest.

Freshwater insects of numerous species live in our lochs, pools and streams; others favour more peculiar habitats. Two water beetles *(Hydroporus ferrugineas* and *Hydroporus longulus)* live in underground trickles beneath the soil; another *(Ochthebius lejolisi)*, occurs only in rock pools just above the high tide mark.

One of the most curious inhabitants of lochs and ponds is the famous Water Spider *(Argyroneta aquatica)*, the only true spider that spends its life under the surface, where it spins a silken bell which it fills with air, carried down bubble by bubble from the surface. In this "diving bell" it lives, and there it rears its young.

HISTORICAL

# 6

# THE EARLY PEOPLES

## Miss A. HENSHALL

In this section it is intended to sketch the history of man's occupation from the early third millennium to about 600 B.C., the beginning of the Early Iron Age in Scotland. About 3000 B.C., or perhaps even earlier, the first neolithic immigrants arrived in the area. They had probably moved north from the eastern coastlands of Scotland and England, but beyond that their origins are obscure and probably mixed. These people practised farming, having herds and flocks of cattle and sheep, and probably also pigs, and growing barley and wheat. They also supplemented their supplies by hunting game. They came to a virtually untouched land at a time when the climate was warmer than today: the land was almost entirely covered by forest, or by scrub in the high areas or on the very poor soils. The only people they encountered were a few bands of nomadic mesolithic hunters and fishers, whose forebears had been in the area for upwards of a thousand years. The presence of these shadowy peoples in the area is indicated by finds of their characteristic tiny worked flints (microliths) from the Culbin Sands, and a fine bone fish spearhead with four recurved points along one side, said to have been found in a peat bog in Glen Avon, presumably somewhere above Tomintoul.

The essential tool of the neolithic farming communities was the axe with a stone or flint head, used for clearing the forest to provide grazing for their beasts and to make small fields for their crops, to work wood for building and many other purposes such as tool handles, traps, and containers. Knives, scrapers for preparing skins, and arrowheads (at this time always leaf-shaped) for hunting, were made from flint. Fortunately the only considerable Scottish source of flint, in Buchan, was not far away. This flint is distinctive in colour, being ginger-brown or red, and was used extensively, though grey and buff flint was also employed, probably from small nodules found along the coasts. Axeheads and flints are the commonest relics from this period, and casual finds are not uncommon, coming from almost all parts of the region. Pottery was made too, probably by the women, and the standard was very high. The vessels have round bases, and are either more or less hemispherical in shape, or have concave out-turned necks forming graceful shallow bowls. The wide range of objects made of organic materials, such as wood, bark, skin, horn, and bone, hardly ever survive.

There are a number of habitation sites known in the region, recognised by the quantities of flint waste for making tools, the finished flints, and sometimes axe-heads and remains of hearths. Some of these sites, judging by the forms of the arrowheads and knives, span a long time into the second millennium, perhaps having been re-occupied several times. Flint-working sites have been identified in upland areas such as Lochindorb (NH 9736) and the Cabrach (NJ 3826), and at the other extreme on the Culbin Sands and Findhorn Sands, and also on more fertile but still light sandy soils, at Rothiemay (NJ 5548, 5646) and in the parish of Urquhart. Here, at Kennieshillock (NJ 302607), besides abundant flints and axes picked up over several acres, there were found great numbers of pits up to 3.66 m (12 ft) in diameter; similar finds were made at Wallfield (NJ 294652) (but no pits), Longhill (NJ 274627) where there were also sherds of neolithic pottery, and again at nearby Meft (NJ 268639). The pits were probably for storing grain from successive harvests, and were subsequently filled with domestic rubbish. The best known site of this type, at Easterton of Roseisle (about NJ 144650), produced two stone-lined pits filled with wood ash and charcoal and many sherds of pottery (Fig 8-1) there were also scattered flints and axe-heads in the area. Today there is nothing to be seen at these places, and indeed careful excavation of neolithic occupation sites in Britain has seldom produced convincing remains of houses which seem to have been slight structures leaving no wall foundations nor post holes of wooden uprights.

Visible structures of this period do remain, however, in the form of artificial mounds. In eastern and southern Britain the characteristic monument of the early neolithic peoples are great long mounds averaging about 45.7 m (150 ft in length) and sometimes 3 m (10 ft) high, wider and higher towards one end, built of earth, or turves, or particularly in the north, of stones. Although they generally, but not always, contain a few burials placed in a relatively small structure within the mound, the real purpose of the mounds is obscure but must be regarded as ritual rather than functional. Within the region there is a rather mutilated long mound at Torrieclearack (NJ 445647), and a probable second example at Bank of Roseisle (NJ 149670), whilst other examples probably await recognition. A very unusual site has recently been excavated by H. A. W. Burl at Boghead near Fochabers (NJ 359592, Plate 9). This was a round mound 17 m (56 ft) in diameter, made up of a central low mound of sand and heaps of stones at its edge, all covered by a deep layer of sand. A central pit was also filled with sand. At least nine skeletons were found in the mound, one contemporary with its building, the rest inserted later but probably neolithic. The mound had been built on an old habitation site. A great

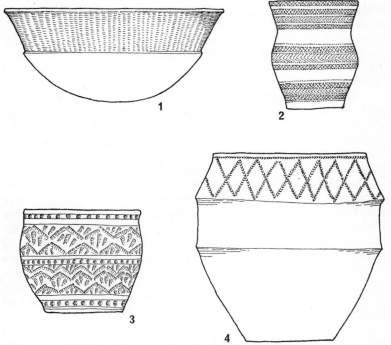

Fig. 8 Prehistoric Pottery — 1 Fluted bowl from Easterton of Roseisle; 2 Beaker from Acres, Knockando; 3 Food Vessel from Kenny's Hillock; 4 Cinerary Urn from Foulford Bridge.

many sherds of pottery, and some flints, were found in and under occupants of the site.

Little is known about the later third millennium in the region; indeed at present only a certain number of distinctive flints and a few other stray finds, such as the fine facetted macehead from Kennieshillock (NJ 304617), and the knobbed stone ball with incised spiral design from near Elgin, and the stone ball and perforated stone axe-hammer found together near Tomintoul (NJ 1618), can be assigned confidently to this period.

A little before 2000 BC there arrived along the east coast of England and Scotland the first of several waves of immigrants, known as the Beaker people from their distinctive pottery (Fig. 8-2), tall narrow flat-based vases generally decorated from lip to base. These new peoples came direct from the Rhineland and coastal areas of the Netherlands and West Germany. They were distinguished physically and culturally from the native population, though probably their economy was not radically different. The next five hundred years saw a gradual adaptation and fusion between the two groups, and this is a time of relatively intense settlement in our region.

There are about twenty recorded Beakers, probably all from graves. Their distribution is along the coastal lowlands and up the major river valleys such as the Deveron and the Spey. The earliest Beakers are represented by only two unlocalised pots from the District of Banff. About two centuries later there were new arrivals from the Rhine delta, and most of the Beakers in the region were made by the descendants of these people during the period to 1500 BC. Besides their pottery, the Beaker people brought other new forms of artifacts to Britain, notably barbed-and-tanged arrowheads, flint stone wristguards for archers' use, and the first rare metal ornaments and small knives. The arrowheads have been found in considerable numbers in the region, particularly in the Culbin Sands, and their appearance at flint-working sites probably indicates occupation at this time as well as earlier. One wristguard has been found in the region. (Metalwork will be described later.)

The Beaker people introduced a new burial rite. Their dead were normally laid crouched on one side in a stone cist built in a pit below ground level. A great number of cist burials have been found in the region, of which sixteen have been accompanied by a Beaker. Some cists have not contained a pot or other distinctive relic, and so are not closely datable.

Later in the period we are considering there appeared a new form of pot, the Food Vessel (Fig 8-3); it is flat-based, of a more squat form, lavishly but often coarsely decorated, and of a thicker and more gritty friable ware. It is the result of a mingling of the late neolithic and Beaker potting traditions, presumably representing a merging of the two peoples involved. The burial rite of the makers of Food Vessels was the same, except that whereas cremation is rare with Beaker burials, it is rather more common with Food Vessels. At least nine Food Vessels have been found in the District, and probably considerably more, for old accounts of discoveries speak of "urns" which from their sizes and descriptions must be either Beakers or Food Vessels.

From about 1600 BC a certain number of richer graves appear. In our region these are mainly female graves, the woman buried with her elaborate necklace of jet, the strings of barrel-shaped beads held apart by flat plates patterned by dots made by fine shallow borings originally probably inlaid with a white substance. No less than nine necklaces have been found, some much worn and incomplete when buried. The finest (Plate 11) comes from a cist at Burgie Lodge Farm (NJ 090606) which also held a Food Vessel; and indeed several other necklaces were associated with Food Vessels. Rich male graves might have a bronze dagger with the corpse, but only one such grave has been discovered in the area, the unusual burial at Bishopmill, Elgin (NJ 220635). The cist, found in 1864, was 1.8 m (6 ft) long. As no bones were seen it may be assumed the burial was an inhumation, laid at full length, equipped with a fine grooved dagger now sadly broken and corroded; the body had been placed on or covered by a hairy animal skin which partly survived and was thought to be from an ox. Another exceptional cist burial had a pair of gold earrings, found at Orbliston (NJ 301585) near Fochabers in 1863.

Cist graves are quite often grouped together, presumably the cemetery of one or more homesteads, and it must often happen that only one or two cists out of a greater number are discovered and recorded. Single cists or grouped cists (not including those in burial mounds) have been recorded from thirty-three sites. The largest cemetery in Moray, at Burgie (NJ 090606),

H

was revealed over many years during sand quarrying. The first cists were probably found before 1723, the most recent in 1914; the finds included at least four Food Vessels and three jet necklaces. The side stone of one cist had been worn by sharpening an axe-head.

Towards the end of the period cremation became the predominant rite, and in the later second millennium, the exclusive rite. This gave rise to the making of Cinerary Urns (Fig 8-4) and three of the four types which occur in Scotland are known in the area. They are all large heavy vessels with narrow bases and wide mouths, developed from different classes of late neolithic domestic pottery which had already been influenced by Beaker forms and decoration. The Cinerary Urns were made specially to contain cremated bodies, unlike Beakers and Food Vessels which had a domestic use. Cinerary Urns were sometimes placed in a cist, but frequently were inverted in a hole in the ground, or in a burial mound.

In the District over seventy round burial mounds have been recorded, though a third of them are now totally destroyed. Mostly they are cairns, built of stone, but a few barrows, built of earth, are known, and a few mounds are a mixture of the two materials. Unlike the earlier long mounds, these were built specifically for burial purposes, though doubtless with strong ritual elements in their construction procedures and subsequent cult significance. In this connection it is of interest that parts of three Beakers had been placed in a small pit just outside the much earlier Boghead mound already mentioned, and a small cist with a cremation was inserted into the top of the mound.

Many of the cairns have been conspicuous features of the landscape since they were built set on the crests of hills: indeed several have been used as boundary markers from at least the medieval period and probably earlier (e.g. the Kist Cairn, Moyness (NH 971531) on the District boundary, near Dava Station (NJ 010390) on the parish boundary, the Monks' Cairn (NJ 500500) near Keith, on the boundary of lands owned by Kinloss Abbey). The cairns range from about 29.6 m (97 ft) to 3 m (10 ft) in diameter, the average being about 15-10 m (50-30 ft). The few relatively well preserved cairns range up to 2.0 m or even 3.8 m (6 ft 6 in to 12 ft) high. Some had their edges defined by a kerb of boulders, today often partly or wholly obscured. Two or three cairns have a low circular platform extending beyond the edge of the mound. Sometimes cairns have been built in groups of two to four.

At least twenty-two of the cairns are known to have contained cists for burials, and it may be presumed most of the others did too. None the less, many more cist burials were without a burial mound over them than with one, and it is difficult to understand the factors which governed the building of mounds. No burial mound in the area has been scientifically excavated, so there are no precise details of their structure available. In other parts of the country cairns and barrows may cover one central cist, either below or on the old ground surface; or there may be several cists in the mound, some at least inserted later; and some mounds may have been enlarged for the later burials. Burials were also made in or under mounds without cists, particularly cremations with or without Cinerary Urns. Near Dava Station (NJ 010390) a small cairn was found to contain two cists, one nearly central at ground level (presumably the primary burial), the other higher and to one side (presumably secondary): one contained a cremation. Two cists were also found in the cairn at Easter Lyne (NJ 1628), one with an inhumation .

Two interesting burial mounds briefly investigated last century, indicate the complexities which can be hidden within the rough exterior. The barrow known as The Law at Wallfield (NJ 294652) was 3.7 m (12 ft) high at the time of excavation in 1885, and 18.3 m (60 ft) in diameter. There was a central cist containing an inhumation accompanied by a Beaker and five curved pieces of worked bone pierced at one end for suspension resembling "the incisors of a large dog or wolf". Around the cist was a wall of boulders 0.9-1.2 m (3-4 ft) thick, and about 0.76 m (2 ft 6 in) high. Outside this was a second circle of smaller stones. Kenny's Hillock (NJ 300605), after which Kennieshillock farm is named, has been destroyed. It covered two pits 1.5 m (5 ft) deep, filled in with stones. In the bottom of one was a layer of "ashes" 5 cm (2 in) deep with a broken Food Vessel, covered by a flagstone; in the bottom of the other was a cist containing a Food Vessel and a flint, and the in-filling containing much charcoal. There were no recognisable bones.

A group of cairns by Foulford Bridge (NJ 490653, 492656) near Cullen, may be selected from among others for mention. They have been casually explored and now remain much mutilated. One produced a cist with an "urn" and bones; another a Cinerary Urn and two smaller "urns" found before 1820; another produced an "urn" near the centre, and two cists each with a broken "urn". Outside the edge of this last cairn were two cremations, one contained in a small Cinerary Urn, set upright, the other in a normal sized Cinerary Urn inverted on a slab; a barbed-and-tanged arrowhead and a bone pin were with one or other of the cremations.

Relatively few Cinerary Urns have been recorded in Moray, though many more must have been found: their survival rate is lower than other funerary vessels as they are easily broken into small pieces even when carefully handled; they are generally unprotected by a cist, and if complete they are too large to be attractive objects to a casual finder. In our area only one has certainly been found in a cist. Several have been found in the Culbin Sands, but the only known group was found at Buckie in 1884 (in a railway cutting, precise location not known), comprising four urns all inverted over the bones they contained. By about 1000 BC the evidence provided by burials comes to an end, for graves certainly dating between then and the Early Christian period are rare in Scotland and unknown in our area.

Besides the long and the round mounds, there are other monuments still to be seen in the countryside, the various types of circular enclosures built for ceremonial or ritual purposes, between them probably spanning the later third millennium and most of the second millennium. In Quarry Wood (NJ 185630) near Elgin there is an earthwork which appears to be the only henge in the District, about midway between the Aberdeenshire examples and those on the Black Isle. Essentially henges consist of a circular bank and ditch, the bank being on the outside (unlike a fort), with one or two gaps providing entrances. Inside there may have been stone or timber structures, or burials, or nothing. The henge in Quarry Wood is today in an unplanted area within a conifer forest, badly overgrown and difficult to examine. The enclosed area is slightly oval, about 47 m (154 ft) by 43 m (141 ft), surrounded by a segmented ditch averaging 3 m (10 ft) wide, and an external bank. There is one entrance on the west side, and inside two boulders may possibly be the remains of a stone circle. There are only thirteen examples of henges with stone circles inside them in the whole of Britain.

Circles of standing stones are also found widespread in

Britain, excluding the east and southeast of England, and are about ten times as numerous as henges. There were once twenty-four stone circles in the area, but half of these have been totally destroyed, or so badly damaged that no useful information can be had from them. The variety of types amongst the remaining circles is fascinating. Two appear to be simple settings of standing stones without any internal feature. At Thorax (NJ 582549), near Cornhill, the circle is complete with a rather irregular setting 8 m (26 ft) in greatest diameter, the tallest stones 1.65 m (5 ft 5 in) high. An outlying stone 17.6 m (58 ft) to the west of the circle is almost buried. The circle at Knock of Alves (NJ 162627) is in an inconspicuous position just south of the A 96 to the west of Elgin. Today six rough boulders remain of what was probably an eight stone circle with a diameter of about 10 m (33 ft), the tallest stone 1.3 m (4 ft 3 in) high. An outlying stone to the west is probably a natural boulder.

The region lies between two areas each of which contains a distinctive and impressive class of monument incorporating stone circles — to the west are the Clava cairns and to the east are the Recumbent Stone Circles. The Clava cairns are centred around Beauly, Inverness and the upper valley of the Nairn with a few in the middle reaches of Strath Spey. The monuments consist of a circle of standing stones, graded in height with the tallest in the SW quadrant of the compass, and within the circle a cairn edged by a kerb similarly graded in height. The cairns are of two types. Either they contain a round burial chamber (once roofed) with an entrance passage, or they are in the form of a ring of cairn stones with an open circular central space. The Clava chambered cairns belong to a class of funerary structure, the passage-graves, found widespread and in considerable numbers (but without stone circles) in western and northern Scotland and Ireland, although they are not precisely like any other group of passage-graves, and their origin and date are both uncertain: they probably belong towards the end of the third millennium. The ring-cairns also belong to a class of monument known to be widespread in its distribution in northern Britain (without stone circles), but which has not been comprehensively studied: they probably belong in the main to the earier centuries of the second millennium, but there must be a chronological overlap between passage-graves and ring-cairns in the Clava-type cairns. One simple ring-cairn at least existed in the region, at Gownie

(NJ 2842). When excavated in 1890 the kerb was found to be 12.2 m (40 ft) in diameter, and the inner area 1.5 m (5 ft) in diameter. It contained a partly burnt burial, with cremated bones and sherds of plain pottery above. The Clava-type cairns thus consist of a unique combination of two types of monument otherwise found separately, stone circles and burial cairns, the latter being of two distinct types.

At the confluence of the Avon and the Spey there is a most interesting group of monuments. At Lagmore there is a Clava-type passage-grave (Plate 10, NJ 176358), four impressive stones of the circle surviving, together with a fifth fallen stone and the stump of a sixth. Within the circle most of the circuit of the kerb can be seen, with the entrance to the low lintelled passage on the South side. In the centre of the cairn, amongst the stony debris, the south side of the roofless chamber can be made out. In a field below this cairn there is a more ruined site (NJ 179359), the remains of a slightly larger circle with five surviving stones, which today stand on the edge of a very low mound with a slightly dished centre, probably the last vestiges of a ring-cairn. Near Ballindalloch Station, about 1.6 km (1 mile) away to the NW, there was once a stone circle (NJ 170364), whilst less than a mile away to the NE across the Avon at Marionburgh (NJ 183364) are considerable remains of what is almost certainly a Clava-type ring-cairn with five upright and four prone slabs and a more clearly defined cairn than at the second Lagmore site. About a mile from Marionburgh, on the other side of the Spey is a fifth site, at Pitchroy (NJ 178382), of which only two stones now remain.

The recumbent stone circles belong mainly to Aberdeenshire, and in some ways resemble the Clava cairns to which they are certainly related, though exactly how is not at all clear. They probably date to the first half of the second millennium. They consist of a circle of stones, graduated in height to a tall pair set in the SW quadrant to flank a large prone slab lying between them, the distinctive feature of these sites. Within the circle was a low cairn, often irregularly circular, and sometimes with an ill-defined open central area. At these sites the circle is the dominant feature and the cairn very subsidiary. None the less the sites were used for burials, as of course were the Clava cairns, normally by cremation, and artifacts are seldom included with them. The only certain recumbent stone circle in the area is at

Mains of Rothiemay (NJ 550487), which was dismantled except for the four upright stones and huge recumbent stone which still remained when the work was stopped.

Another specialised type of stone circle is a small setting of four stones, really a square or rectangle rather than a circle, and which normally contains a burial. A good example is to be seen at Templestone (NJ 068569) with the tallest stone to the SW side. On the Browland, (NJ 339647) near Garmouth, a more ruined site has probably been of this type.

There are a few single standing stones in the region, which are likely to be prehistoric, but such stones can be put up at almost any period, as boundary markers or even as rubbing stones for cattle. One or two of the stones are alleged to be the last survivors of stone circles.

Another expression of ritual activity survives in the form of cup-marked stones, though what was the object of the rites is quite unknown. Cup-marks are hemispherical hollows, up to 10 cm (3 in) in diameter, which were pecked out of flat stone surfaces, generally in groups, but seemingly in random arrangements. Sometimes the cups are joined by pecked grooves, and sometimes they are surrounded by one or more concentric grooves. The markings occur on stones incorporated into cairns, more generally as parts of a cist, on natural rock surfaces or loose stones, on stones of Clava cairns, on simple stone circles, and in profusion on selected uprights or recumbents at recumbent stone circles.

At Roseisle (NJ 145680) there are seven exposed outcrops on the floor of a little dry valley, two of them cupmarked, one profusely with some of the cups ringed; a similar rock with forty-four cupmarks was formerly to be seen on Roseisle Hill (NJ 1467). A large block of sandstone found at Clackmarras (NJ 246584), but now preserved at Blackhills (NJ 270586), has one face covered by cupmarks. A number of other cupmarked slabs have been found in Moray, one (NJ 585551) near the stone circle at Thorax (NJ 582549) already mentioned and which itself has twenty-two cupmarks on the tallest stone. Two of the stone circles of the Lagmore group had cupmarked stones, of which one survives at the lower Lagmore site (NJ 179359). The Mains of Rothiemay (NJ 550487) recumbent stone is well known for the profuse cup-marking, also found on the stone to the east. Cupmarked stones have thrice been recorded in cairns in the region; at Carsewell (NJ 1362) there were thirty-seven cups on both sides of the end stone of a cist; at Greenloan (NJ 3933) eleven cupmarked stones were found a century ago mainly in one cairn and perhaps parts of cists or a kerb; at Leakin (NJ 164420) a cupmarked slab is probably a cist cover.

About 1700 BC a great technological abvance was established in Scotland with the production of metal (bronze) edge tools, though a few small bronze objects had been imported before this. At first casting was in primitive one-piece open moulds carved from sandstone, and it is surprising how many of these moulds have been found in NE Scotland, especially as the nearest source of copper was west of Inverness or in Angus. But already within the conventional Early Bronze Age (about 1700-1500 BC) techniques improved and closed two-piece moulds were used with consequently more sophisticated forms being cast. The main tool was the flat or flanged axehead, and many examples have been found in the region. Other metal objects of the period are rare: an unusual discovery at Sluie (NJ 006519) was a cist, probably with an inhumation, which contained a halberd (a large dagger-like blade which was attached at right-angles to a long shaft as a weapon) together with two flat axes; the dagger from Bishopmill and the gold ear-rings from Orbliston have already been mentioned. Lastly there is a gold ornament or lunula, a crescent-shaped collar made from beaten gold, also found at or near Orbliston (NJ 3058). Altogether the evidence of the metal finds reinforces the deduction that Moray was prosperous during the first half of the second millennium. After this the picture changes. During the Middle Bronze Age (about 1500-900 BC) a wider range of bronze objects was produced, including weapons. But relatively few of these objects have been recorded in the District, only a few of the axeheads of improved design, half a dozen spearheads, and a spearhead mould from the Culbin Sands. The one spectacular find of this period was the hoard of neck ornaments, or torcs, made of beaten strips of gold twisted spirally: the hoard was found in 1857 near The Law of Wallfield (NJ 295651) and consisted of at least thirty-six torcs in all.

Recent excavation of a midden in the Culbin Sands (NJ 991623), by J. M. Coles and J. J. Taylor, has produced the only occupation site certainly of this time. The site had been used temporarily on two occasions, dated by radiocarbon to between

1400 and 1100 BC. Refuse from the midden showed that cattle, sheep and pigs were present, there was a small amount of grain, and shellfood from the shore 1 km (c. ½ mile) away augmented the diet. Another midden in the Sands investigated in 1908 produced pieces of a pot similar to the sherds recovered from the first site, of coarse undecorated tub-like pots.

From about 1000 BC there was a very gradual worsening of the climate which continued until the 5th century BC. This must have affected the livelihood and welfare of the people, and particularly the upland marginal areas where slowly it became impossible to raise grain crops, and there must have been a shift to stock-raising as the basis of the economy. There are areas of moorland hillslopes on which it is possible to trace field boundaries, small cairns which are field clearance for ploughing, and occasionally larger cairns which may have been for burials; at least some of these areas of primitive agriculture may have been occupied in the second or earlier first millennium, and have never been ploughed again. Examples which may be mentioned tentatively are near Dava Station (NJ 012390) (the cairn has been noted already), and near Beachans, N of Dava (NJ 032463-035467).

There is one important but typical occupation site of the Late Bronze Age which was thoroughly excavated by Miss S. Benton in 1929, and it proved to be exceptionally rich in finds: the "Sculptor's Cave" at Covesea (NJ 175707), on the shore of the Firth. The cave is 27.5 m (90 ft) long by 12 m (40 ft) wide, but when it was inhabited access was only possible at low tide. Although there had been lengthy occupation judging by the debris of fires and quantity of finds, the place suggests a refuge rather than a home. Pottery similar to that from the Culbin Sands middens was still being made, and a variety of bone tools, mainly awls and spatulas for leatherworking, and a needle, were found. Ten pieces of so-called ring-money, small penannular rings of bronze, most of them covered by gold foil, and five penannular bronze bracelets, were personal ornaments, the ring-money and one of the bracelets being ultimately of Irish origin, the other bracelets being imports from NW Europe. The last items date the occupation of the cave to the 7th century BC. The cave was occupied a second time in the Roman period. Two other caves at Covesea are said to have been used in the Late Bronze Age, and a cave at both Findochty and at Cullen

(NJ 488679, 519677) have been reported to contain ancient material and may or may not belong to this period.

Other finds of bronze ornaments in NE Scotland witness to contact with NW Europe in the 7th century, and indeed some archaeologists would interpret these as evidence of immigrants coming to settle in this part of Scotland. In our area a hoard of bronzes from Auchtertyre (NJ 178568) included seven armlets like those from Covesea, together with spearheads and a socketed axe, the typical tool of the Late Bronze Age. The only other hoard from the region, from Cullerne House (NJ 047638), included, besides a socketed axe and two spearheads, two less usual objects, a razor and a curved knife, probably a woodworker's tool. Otherwise the material remains of the Late Bronze Age amount to little more than a dozen socketed axes, fourteen spearheads (indicative of increasingly troubled times), three swords and two large penannular gold ornaments from Cromdale (exact find-spot unknown) and Upper Dallochy (NJ 363626).

APPENDIX

*List of Sites with Worthwhile Visible Remains*

Note: Mention of a site does not imply right of access, and permission to visit should be sought.

1 Auchorachan. Standing Stone (NJ 209278)
The stone is 1.7m (5ft 6in) high, the base packed round with stones. It is said to have been moved by a tenant long ago, who, on being "troubled", replaced it.

2 Roseisle. Cupmarked outcrop (NJ 145680)
About seven outcrops of rock occur in a small dry valley, of which two are cupmarked on their horizontal surfaces. One of them bears seven cups, but the other measuring about 4.0 by 2.3m (13ft by 7ft 6in) has at least thirty-three cups, some with rings.

3 Binn Hill. Cairn (NJ 301653)
The cairn is in a forestry plantation. It is 10.5m (35ft) in diameter, with the remains of a boulder kerb, and about 1.5m (5ft) high though the centre is hollowed presumably due to former investigations. A stone 5.0m (17ft) from the cairn may be deliberately set.

4 Bishop Croft. Cairn (NJ 175396)
The cairn is about 10.5m (35ft) in diameter and about 1m (3ft 4in) high, with several stones of the kerb visible on the W side. The N and E sides have been damaged.

5 Blackhills House. Cupmarked stone (NJ 270586)
The stone, found at Clackmarras (NJ 246584), is preserved under cover in the grounds of Blackhills House. The stone is 1.5m (4ft 9in) high, but is said to have been reduced. One face is covered with cupmarks. Two other faces bear carvings, a crescent and a double spiral, which are probably not ancient. Clackmarras (see Blackhills House).

6 Coleburn. Standing stone (NJ 243547)
The stone is 1.4m (4ft 7in) in height, but has evidently once been taller, and is 0.6m (2ft) wide.

7 'The Sculptor's Cave', Covesea. Inhabited cave (NJ 175707)
A natural cave with two entrances, inhabited in the Late Bronze Age and again in the Roman Iron Age. Excavated in 1929, when two occupation layers with many finds were investigated (see p. 107). Most of the finds are in the National Museum of Antiquities of Scotland, some in the Elgin Museum. Incised Pictish symbols of the Early Christian period on the walls.

8 Culvie Hill. Cairn (NJ 580546)
The cairn is well preserved, placed in a prominent position on a small ridge. The diameter is about 10m (33ft) and it is 1.2m (4ft) high.

9 The Doune of Dalmore. Stone circle with ring-cairn (NJ 185308)
Four stones of the stone circle remain, but one of them has fallen. The diameter of the circle is 15.85m (52ft), the tallest stone 1.52m (5ft) high. Within the circle is a ring-cairn with some kerb stones surviving.

10 'Carn na Ciste', East Auchavich. Cairn (NJ 245207)
Set on a false crest, the cairn measures about 20m (66ft) in diameter
and about 0.9m (3ft) high.

11 'The Monks' Cairn', Garrowood. Cairn (NJ 500500)
The cairn, in a wood, is a heather covered mound of earth and
stones measuring about 9.0m (30ft) in diameter. It is about 1.5m
(5ft) in maximum height, with a flat top hollowed in the centre,
probably due to an unrecorded excavation last century or earlier.

12 Hill of Cairns. Cairn (NJ569505)
Of the three cairns which once stood here, one survives, a prominent
mound 10.5m (35ft) in diameter and 1.5m (5ft) high, now in a conifer
wood.

13 'The Deil's Stanes' or 'The Nine Stanes', Innesmill. Stone Circle
(NJ 289640)
Five upright stones remain of an unusually large circle with a
diameter of about 36.6m (120ft), the tallest stone 1.83m (6ft) high.
This has probably been a recumbent stone circle for the stones are
graduated in height, the largest to the S, and there is an old reference
to an "altar" (? recumbent stone).

14 Inverugie. Cairn (NJ 154686)
The cairn supports a stand of trees. It is 16m (53ft) in diameter
and 2.0m (6ft 6in) high. The flat top has a small depression in the
centre, probably the result of investigations in 1859 when a cist was
found.

15 'The Camus Stone', Inverugie. Standing stone (NJ 152683)
An irregular broad block of schist, 1.75m (5ft 9in) high, from which
several pieces have split away in the past. The stone bears a cup and
ring mark.

16 Knock of Alves. Stone circle (NJ 162627)
Six boulders set in a circle, probably consisting of eight stones
originally, overall diameter about 10m (33ft). The tallest stone is 1.3m
(4ft 3in) high. An outlying stone to the W is probably a natural
boulder.

17 Lagmore. Clava-type passage-grave (NJ 176358)
A cairn with an almost complete kerb 12.8m (42ft) in diameter,
contains a roofless circular chamber, and entrance passage on the
S side complete with slightly displaced lintels. The cairn now spreads
beyond the kerb. Four stones of the circle remain round the cairn,
with the stump of a fifth, and a sixth fallen stone. The tallest stone
is 2.13m (7ft) high.

18 Lagmore. Stone circle (NJ 179359)
A circle 19.8m (65ft) in diameter, consisting of three standing stones
and two fallen stones, one of which is covered with cupmarks. The
largest (prone) slab is 3.2m (10ft 6in) long. Within the circle a slight
mound with central hollow suggests the site has been a Clava-type
ring-cairn, or, less likely, a passage-grave.

19 Leakin. Cairn and cupmarked stone (NJ 164420)
The cairn measures about 14 by 16m (46 by 53ft), with a few kerb

stones visible on the N and S sides. It remains about 1.1m (3ft 8in) high, but was once higher. Near the centre a flat rectangular slab is partly exposed, ? part of a cist, with at least twenty cupmarks to be seen.

20 Loch of Blairs. Cist (NJ 019554)
Short cist found in a sand quarry in 1931, still preserved in situ with its coverstone. It contained a cremation and sherds of a Food Vessel, the latter now in the National Museum of Antiquities of Scotland.

21 Mains of Rothiemay. Recumbent stone circle (NJ 550487)
Four standing stones and the recumbent stone (without the flanking stones) remain, forming the incomplete W half of an irregular circle with diameters of about 23.5 to 25.3m (77 to 83ft). The tallest stone is 1.9m (6ft 3in) high, and the massive recumbent stone is 4.37m (14ft 4in) long. There are seven cupmarks on the outer face of one of the uprights, twelve on the upper face of the recumbent stone, and a great number, four with rings, on the inner face of the same stone.

22 Marionburgh. Clava-type ring-cairn
Five standing stones set on a circle of 22.86m (75ft) diameter, the tallest 2.74m (9ft) high, one incorporated in a wall; also a sixth stone leaning acutely but its base probably in position, and two more fallen stones. Within the circle is a ring of cairn material, the edges not clearly defined. About 9.14m (30ft) to the SE of the largest stone are two contiguous upright slabs, perhaps part of another monument, now destroyed.

23 'St Marnan's Chair', Marnoch Church. Standing stone (NJ 597502)
This impressive stone stands within the churchyard. It measures 2.54m (8ft 4in) tall. It has been suggested that it was the flanker of a recumbent stone. Another smaller stone outside the churchyard to the N is not in its original position.

24 Quarry Wood. Henge (NJ 185630)
The site is greatly overgrown and partly planted with conifers. The external bank and internal segmented ditch enclose a slightly oval area measuring 47m (154ft) by 43m (141ft). There is an entrance on the W side. Two boulders near the side of the enclosed space may be remains of a stonecircle.

25 Tarrieclerack. Long mound (NJ 445647)
The mound, much disturbed and now overgrown, lies with its long axis almost E and W. The length is about 37m (121ft), with a maximum height of 1.83m (6ft). The greater width and height is towards the W end, which is unusual but not unknown among long mounds.

26 Templestone. Stone circle (NJ 068569)
A setting of four stones in a square, a small and late type of stone circle sometimes referred to as a "four poster". The tallest stone, to the SW, is 1.4m (4ft 7in) high, the greatest diameter of the setting only 3.96m (13ft). Unfortunately it is much overgrown by whins.

27   Thorax. Stone circle (NJ 582549)
     Six stones set in an irregular circle, joined together by a modern wall.
     Twenty-two cupmarks on the tall stone, 1.8m (5ft 11in) high, on the
     NW side. An outlying stone 17.6m (58ft) to the W of the circle,
     almost buried, has six cupmarks on the upper surface.

28   Thorax. Cupmarked stone (NJ 585551)
     About 160m (525ft) NE of the stone circle, a rectangular slab was
     ploughed up in 1964, and now lies at the edge of the field. It bears
     twenty-two cupmarks on one face.

29   'The Law', Wallfield. Barrow (NJ 294652)
     A bowl-shaped barrow, now rather mutilated and covered with whins,
     14m (46ft) in diameter and 2.0m (6ft 6in) high. A platform extending
     beyond the edge of the mound now survives only on the N side, 3.5m
     (12ft) wide and 1.5m (5ft) high. Excavated in 1855 when a central cist
     was found, details p. 106. The Beaker is now in the Elgin Museum.

MUSEUMS.    Finds from the district are mainly to be seen in the
Museum of The Elgin Society, Elgin, in The Falconer Museum, Forres, and
in The National Museum of Antiquities of Scotland. Edinburgh.

# 7

# IRON AGE AND PICTISH MORAY

## ALAN SMALL

The Moray District has considerably fewer monuments of the Iron Age and Pictish periods (Fig 9) than the neighbouring areas of Aberdeen and Banff. This is largely due to the sterner nature of the physical environment over much of the area and in a small part to a considerable lack of field investigation. In fact only one fort, that at Burghead, has been closely examined and the assignment of the other forts in the region to the Iron Age can be no more than a tentative suggestion at the moment. At present, the Iron Age is considered to have commenced between 900 and 700 BC with the arrival of Celtic peoples from the continent, bringing not only iron using techniques, but also a new language and culture involving community territories frequently dominated by one or more substantial fortifications.

It has been postulated that the movement of some of the Celtic invaders was precipitated by the climatic deterioration of the sub-Atlantic with the onset of colder weather conditions, more like what we have today in contrast to the warmer, drier, sub-Boreal period of the late Bronze Age, when settlement could comfortably extend up to the 500 m (1640 ft) contour (cf. the cairns to the south of Tomintoul). The ramifications of this climatic upheaval are well demonstrated with the extension of blanket bog over many of the cairns in the higher parts of the area. As a result of the climatic deterioration and the resultant vegetation changes, Iron Age settlement was thus limited in its habitable areas to the river valleys and the coastal plains and even there conditions were more adverse to settlement than in neighbouring districts. The river valleys are frequently narrow and subject to severe flash floods while the coastal plains had extensive areas under water (for example, the vast extent of the former Loch Spynie described in Chapter 1) and marsh (Ogilvie). Despite these constrictions on settlement, Moray has produced a number of monuments of more than local significance. Within

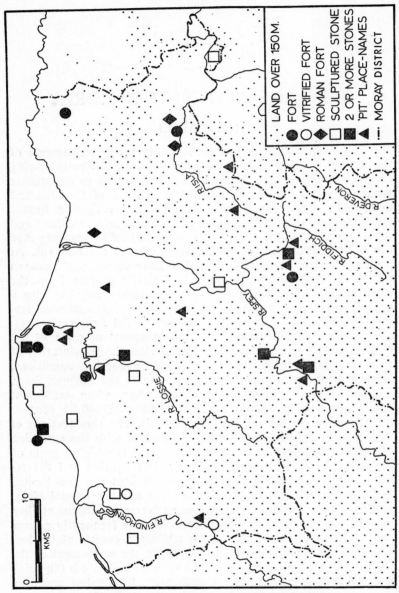

Fig. 9 Moray: Iron Age, Roman and Pictish sties

1. Loch Avon, Cairngorms, looking west; an example of a glacially deepened valley basin. *(Aerofilms Ltd.)*

2. The Bow Fiddle rock, Portnockie

3. Findhorn Bay, showing hooked shingle spit and sandbar

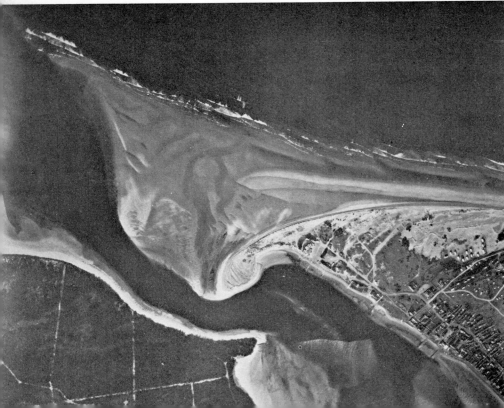

4.  Fochabers, a planned settlement, and the Laich o' Moray. *(Aerofilms Ltd.)*

5. Dwarf Cornel

6. Holly Fern

7. Great Spotted Woodpecker

8. Oyster Catchers

9. Neolithic site, near Fochabers

10. Lagmore Passage Grave, near Ballindalloch

11. Jet Necklace, Burgie, near Elgin (Elgin Museum)

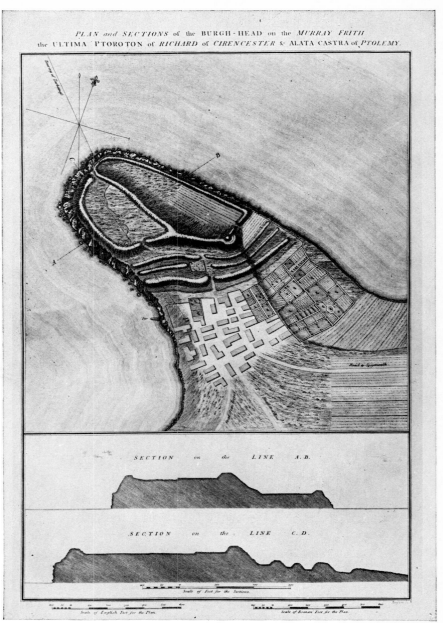

12.  General Roy's plan of Burghead (1793)

13. Burghead
Bulls

14. Rodney Stone, near Brodie
Castle

15. Sueno's Stone, Forres

SUENO'S STONE

THIS GREAT MONOLITH WAS WORKED
BY THE PICTS IN THE 9TH OR 10TH

16.  Duffus Castle

17.  Balvenie Castle, Dufftown

the limits of the environmental restrictions, rich communities existed in Lowland Moray in the Bronze Age (Walker, 1967), as is particularly demonstrated by the find of some gold torcs last century. Unfortunately, most of these are now lost (Scott).

Although the fort at Burghead was constructed in the 4th century A.D. (Small, 1969) in the early part of the Pictish period, its building techniques were introduced to Scotland in the Early Iron Age as had been demonstrated at Finavon, Angus (McKie), Cullykhan in Banffshire (Greig), and Craig Phadrig, Inverness (Small and Cottam) among others. This style of construction is probably representative of the other forts in the area, particularly the Doune of Relugas and Castle Law, Forres, and a brief review of the evidence from Burghead may well serve as a sample of more widespread Iron Age features.

Plate 12 reproduces General Roy's plan of the Fort (Roy, 1793, Pl. 33) before the building of the harbour and the modern planned settlement of Burghead brought about the devastation of the remains in the first decade of the 19th century (Young, 1868). The headland consists of two flat areas, the higher rising to 10 m (33 ft) above the lower lying to the north east which is essentially a raised shoreline, the fossil back-cliff forming a division between the two. Both areas are enclosed by massive ramparts with gateways in the south east. These defences of which there is hardly any trace today, were further strengthened by three parallel ramparts across the neck of the peninsula. During the reconstruction of the village and harbour, in the cemetery, and in the course of the 19th century excavations, a number of small finds were recorded. The most important of these are the symbol stones each showing only a fine, well articulated bull, (Plate 13). Some 25-30 of these are recorded in the literature from Burghead, but only six survive. Other finds include a Roman coin of Otho, fragments of an Early Christian corner post shrine, Anglo-Saxon metalwork, and numerous bronze spears "given away to any English tourist who happened to be passing".

Clearly this is a structure of major importance and consequently it has attracted the attention of excavators on a number of occasions. The most important of these were undertaken by Hugh Young in the late 19th century (Young, 1891, 1893) who suggested that the ramparts of the lower fort were timber-laced structures with regularly placed beams nailed together as in a Gallic Fort. Detailed examination of the north-west rampart of

I

the upper fort in 1967 (Small, 1969) revealed a wall some 9 m (30 ft) thick at the base and still standing over 3 m (9 ft) high under the present turf. Two revetments retained a core of large rounded beach pebbles. Only the lower courses of the outer revetment remained consisting of massive undressed boulders while the inner face of the rampart, on the other hand, was extremely carefully constructed of finely dressed and carefully coursed red sandstone flags. Approximately every metre upwards, the face was set back a few centimetres giving a steplike appearance. Long, well-hewn, planks were intercoursed with the flags at intervals, lying parallel to the face of the wall. Occasionally, and irregularly, transverse planks and logs were set at right angles to the face, though they seldom penetrated more than a metre into the core. At no point where the longitudinal and transverse timbers met was there any evidence of nailing. It was also clear that the transverse timbers had frequently projected from the wall, presumably to act as supports for wooden structures in the fort. There was no evidence to suggest timber buildings ranged along the wall interior, therefore one must postulate the projecting beams being used either to give access to the wall top, or to support a wall walk. At its full height the wall had originally been between 6 and 10 m (20 and 33 ft). Radio carbon dates indicate that this fort was constructed in the 4th century A.D., and other evidence suggests that it was well maintained till its destruction by fire in the 9th century. The ruins were probably re-occupied in the early medieval period.

The construction of the timber laced fort at Burghead is later than all the other examples so far accurately dated in Scotland and Castle Hill, while probably of similar construction, may be as much as 1000 years earlier. These large forts represent the defensive centres of substantial, well organised, communities who must have been acting under strong leadership to organise the labour necessary for such an undertaking. Elsewhere, (Small, 1975) it has been suggested that a hierarchial society may have existed with the large fort dominating a considerable tribal territory with small forts or duns occupied by local chieftains representing a second level of settlement. The Moray District is, however, somewhat lacking in these second level sites at the current state of knowledge. The bulk of the population would have been scattered throughout the territory, inhabiting groups of hut circles in areas where the environment could have provided an adequate food supply. Excavation of hill forts in Scotland frequently reveals a remarkable lack of artifacts, particularly those of a domestic nature. This suggests that they were not used as permanent settlements and the high altitude of some would also make this unlikely. A number of forts have produced substantial quantities of animal bones, particularly of deer, suggesting that hunting played an important part in the economy.

The old view that these forts were constructed by the native population as defences against the Roman advance must be totally rejected. Forts not only exist in many areas of Scotland that the Romans never reached, but radio carbon dating techniques have also confirmed that many were constructed long before the Roman era. Each must therefore be viewed as the defensive centre of a native group against a neighbouring tribe. Different tribes would have gained political ascendancy at different times and as a result new forts would be constructed, accounting for the wide range of dates attributable to these structures. The politically troubled nature of these times is confirmed by the fact that a large number of forts show signs of destruction and one or more periods of reconstruction. The most spectacular evidence of destruction is seen in the vitrified forts, where as a result of firing under attack, or accidental burning or natural catastrophe, the timbers in the lacing of the wall were ignited. As the timbers in the wall burnt out, the vents in the dry stone wall created an effect like a blast furnace giving very high temperatures in the core of the wall. Field evidence suggests that temperatures in the range of 1250°C were obtained. Rocks which have a lower melting point than the temperature of the burning wall will melt while those with a high melting point will tend to crack and shatter. As the core of the wall is usually made up of a wide variety of rock types, both situations occur in any wall which has reached a high temperature with the melted rock tending to fuse together the shattered portions of unmelted rock. Clearly this process would have resulted in the collapse of the walls and therefore vitrification cannot be interpreted either as a design feature or as an indication of a peculiar class of fort. Clunie Hill, Forres, and the Doune of Relugas, both show signs of vitrification but neither has been closely investigated.

As a very rough approximation, each cubic metre of timber-laced wall represents ten man hours of work in the surface collection of the stone, cutting of timber, and construction of the wall. Burghead therefore represents at least 110,000 man hours work. In other words it is within the scope of a hundred men in four months, or two hundred in two months. Allowing for women and children, and the incapacitated as well as the food providers, one can suggest that the fort at Burghead is perhaps indicative of a territory serving about five hundred people. Until accurate dates are established for other forts in the area it is impossible to suggest the extent of the territory.

The distribution map, Fig. 9, demonstrates the importance of the coastal lowland in the Iron Age. There is practically no penetration of the Highland part of the District with the exception of the fort on Little Conval near Dufftown, representing penetration into the interior by the river valleys. The Doune of Relugas may represent a similar tendency in the Findhorn Valley but the upper part of that valley has much less potential for settlement than the well drained fluvioglacial deposits lying along the Spey and its tributaries. Furthermore the Spey is the only major routeway through the interior, ultimately providing a link with Tayside by way of Drumochter Pass. The Findhorn Valley on the other hand has a high and difficult watershed crossing to the Great Glen. Within the coastal strip the Laich of Moray would appear to have been the most attractive area with three forts — Burghead, Quarry Wood (Elgin), Kineddar, and a small defensive structure to the west of Arthur's Bridge. No trace of a fort exists at Kineddar today but accounts of the Medieval Castle at Kineddar describe earthen ramparts surrounding the building. These ramparts were cast into their respective ditches during agricultural improvements at the beginning of the 18th century when the labourers expressed astonishment at the amount of ashes and oak charcoal which they contained. This is clearly suggestive of a timber laced fort on this site and is particularly important since there may mave been sequent, if not continuous, occupation of this site from the time the fort was constructed through to the medieval stone built castle, since a Class 1 Pictish symbol stone and fourteen Class 111 fragments are recorded nearby. The river mouths of the Spey and Findhorn, both of which have had considerable and dramatic changes of course within historic times, were studiously avoided. The Laich forts must be seen in relation to the environment of Iron Age times when Loch Spynie and its neighbours would have made the ridge from Burghead to Roseisle and Covesea an almost insular feature. The Laich with the fertile soils and mild climate would have been an ideal environment for the Iron Age economy which probably had animal husbandry as its basis. A fair amount of grain was also grown and the diet supplemented by hunting and fishing.

As a result of air reconnaisance, (St. Joseph, 1969, 1973), knowledge of Roman activity in northern Scotland is continually expanding and the location of three Roman temporary camps in Moray have now been positively identified. The full extent of the camp at Bellie which covers at least 10 hectares (25 acres) has not yet been established and it can only be tentatively assigned to the Flavian period, perhaps representing one section of Agricola's army during the sixth campaign. The camp at Auchinhove in the Pass of Grange is also of small size encompassing just over 10 hectares (25 acres). It has distinctive gates of the so-called "Stracathro type" which may distinguish it as part of a separate series from the Bellie camp, though still of Flavian date. The third camp at Muiryfold some 4 km (2½ miles) to the east of Auchinhove is much larger enclosing an area of over 44 hectares (109 acres). This is the most northerly of the series of large temporary camps running northwards from Ardoch in Perthshire which includes Normandykes at Culter, Kintore, and Ythan Wells. This group can be assigned to the Severan Campaigns of the early 3rd century. It is imperative to stress that these camps were of a temporary nature and represent the tangible remains of exploratory and punitive expeditions of the Roman army into the native held territories north of the Antonine Wall. The Roman impact on native society was minimal, and while some of the native fortifications may have been refurbished and utilised against the Roman advances, the net effect on the long term day to day life of the people was of no account. Indeed, as has been demonstrated at Burghead, the techniques of fort building employed in post-Severan times are precisely the same as those developed in the preceding centuries.

Roman coins are recorded from a variety of points in the habitable part of the District, one of the most notable groups coming from the Sculptor's Cave at Covesea. This group included 4th century coins of Constantius. Since Roman coins, glass and other goods probably survived long after the Roman occupation and entered into the trading patterns of the Picts, they do not necessarily indicate a Roman presence in any given area. Indeed, some of the Covesea coins had been drilled and used for personal decoration, still having strands of wire attached when discovered. Similar arguments apply to the Roman glass and metalwork from the Culbin Sands and Lochside, Spynie.

Roman writers refer to the population living north of the Antonine Wall as the Picti or Picts, and in archaeological terms the Pictish period is regarded as running from about A.D. 250 until the arrival of feudalism. Until the last decade, knowledge of this period derived from literary sources, many of doubtful accuracy, and from the carved stones and from place-name evidence. Fortifications, houses, pre-Christian Pictish graves and the associated raw data of archaeology were remarkable for their absence in this period. On the basis of the distribution of carved stones and the Pictish place name *Pit,* both of which are almost entirely located in eastern Scotland north of the Forth/Clyde line, the suggestion has been made that the Picts were a discrete race of people. This view was largely based on the symbolism found on the carved stones which in addition to well articulated, recognisable animals, such as the bulls from Burghead (Plate 13-1,2), and the goose from Easterton of Roseisle, includes grotesque creatures such as the fish monster on the stone from Upper Manbeen and the so-called Pictish elephant which can be seen on the Rodney Stone (Plate 14) at Brodie and also on that from Elgin Cathedral. The corpus of Pictish art also includes a unique series of symbols such as the crescent and V-rod, the mirror and comb, decorated rectangles, etc. The significance of the symbols and the purpose of the stones are the subject of continuing debate. Suggestions range from funerary monuments, to heraldic devices, to territorial markers, or even to indications of marriage contracts.

These carved monuments are usually divided into three classes. The earliest in the sequence have only symbols incised on rough undressed boulders. Two schools of thought exist as to their date — one arguing that they cannot be earlier than A.D. 650, while the other sees no reason why they could not go back as far as the 4th century. Class 11 monuments following chronologically are characterised by symbols standing out in relief from a specially prepared stone. Frequently, elaborately decorated crosses and associated zoomorphic art work cover one side of Class 11 stones as at Brodie and Elgin Cathedral suggesting the establishment of Christianity in the area and the symbiosis of Christian and Pre-Christian motifs. The latest group of stones are distinguished by their having no Pictish symbols. Their designs include a continuation of the hunting and battle scenes sometimes found on Class II stones as well as elaborate allegorical features. Most of the Class 111 monuments in Moray are extremely fragmentary, particularly those from Drainie. However, Sueno's Stone (Plate 15) to the east of Forres is one of the finest of its type in Scotland. The stone towers some 6 m (20 ft) in height and is decorated on all four sides. The front is dominated by a cross, the shaft and side panels of which are covered by fine interlace work, while a panel at the base of the cross shows five figures. The back of the stone is covered with human figures apparently engaged in battle. Rows of armed horsemen fill the top quarter of the stone and are succeeded by foot soldiers with drawn swords, spears and shields. In the central part a heap of severed heads lie below what may be a Celtic bell. Decapitated warriors are stacked up to the left, while armed warriors on the right look on. The macabre sequences continue in the lower panels with further groups of warriors and horsemen along with more headless bodies and detached limbs. The narrow sides of the stone are fully decorated with zoomorphic interlace work. Local tradition maintains that this stone commemorates a battle with the Danes in this area but there is no historical evidence to support this view. Although there is no evidence of any Scandinavian settlement in Moray there are numerous recorded raids and battles and the discovery of weapons and skeletons near the stone in the 18th and early 19th centuries coupled with the warlike scenes on the stone may well have enhanced the speculation.

The coastline at Covesea has numerous caves and a number of these have produced prehistoric relics. The sculptor's Cave is the most well known and was excavated in 1929, (Benton, 1931), producing stratified artifacts from the Bronze Age through to the early centuries A.D. (see Chapter 6). The walls of the cave have incised Pictish symbols including a fish, two crescents and V-rod symbols, the triple vessica as well as geometric designs. The standard of workmanship is of poorer quality than is usually found on the symbol stones but it is impossible to suggest a date for the carving. Miss Benton suggests a top date of 4th century A.D. for the deposits on the cave floor and present thinking would suggest that perhaps this is a little early for Pictish symbols. It is worth noting that there was no evidence produced from the cave floor to suggest Pictish domestic occupation.

The carved stones probably represent a less accurate picture of the distribution of settlement than does the distribution of forts in that many stones probably lie undiscovered, while many others have been destroyed through the ages, notably at the time of the Reformation. However, they are the only indication of settlement which we have for much of the early part of the period and in this area they do indicate a continuity of the patterns which had already been established in the pre-Roman Iron Age. In the first instance, the total number of stones is much lower than in the neighbouring areas of Inverness and Aberdeen, reflecting the continuing environmental difficulties of the District. The core area of settlement is once again the coastal lowlands with the area round the former Loch Spynie dominating the scene. Inland penetration by way of the Spey and its tributaries is clearly demonstrable with the sequence of stones at Arndilly near Rothes, Knockando and the surprising concentration of four Class 1 stones at Inveravon, three of which are said to have come from the foundations of the old church and the most recent being located in the churchyard. Similarly, the Early Christian site at Mortlach (Dufftown) has two recorded stones confirming settlement in the Fiddich Valley. It surely is significant that in any attempted interpretation of the stones in this area that so many of them are associated with sites of early churches, viz: Inveravon, Mortlach, Elgin and Burghead, although in all but the case of Elgin an argument can be made for the stones pre-dating the introduction of the Christian church and the latter establishing itself within existing communities.

The stone at Brodie Castle, originally discovered in the digging of the foundations of the church of Dyke and Moy, is of particular interest as it includes the only example of ogham inscriptions in Moray on both the back and front of the stone. Unfortunately, the inscription is badly defaced. Ogham is an alphabetic script dating from the 4th century used to inscribe stone monuments in either Irish Gaelic or Pictish. The letters are formed by a series of strokes set against or across a line, frequently using the edge of a stone as the line. The final indicator of Pictish settlement which must be considered is the place name evidence. Analysis reveals that the bulk of the place

names in Moray are Gaelic in origin with a small number
attributable to other languages such as Anglo-Saxon and French.
When all the elements assignable to known languages have been
removed, a number of elements remain, the commonest of which
is 'Pit' as in 'Pitgaveny' and 'Pittendreich'. It is assumed that
these elements are the last remnants of the language spoken by
the local population before the arrival of Gaelic and are, therefore, Pictish. Furthermore, since the 'Pit' element is invariably
followed by a Gaelic element it can be suggested that these
names could not have been formed until after the Union of the
Picts and the Scots in the mid 9th century. It has recently been
shown (Cottam and Small, 1975) that the Pit names represent
new late settlement in forest clearings probably by migrants to
eastern Scotland from the south west after the union of the
Picts and the Scots. In Moray, as the map shows, they continue
to obey the long established environmental controls. Some such
as Pitgaveny fall into this pattern around Loch Spynie, while in
the major river valleys a clear relationship to earlier settlements is
also indicated at Pitglassie and Pittyvaich near Mortlach and Pitchroy near Inveravon. Continued use of the lower Findhorn valley
is demonstrated by the name Pitneisk near the Doune of Relugas.

In southern Pictland it has been suggested (Small and
Cottam, 1975) that the broad pattern of settlement changes as
the Pictish period progresses, the phase associated with Class 1
having a dispersed pattern with nucleation developing during
Class 11 and becoming very marked in the time of the Class 111
stones. The number of stones recorded from Moray is too small
to implement the statistical techniques used in Southern Pictland
but similar conclusions do seem to apply. With the exception of
the unique collection of bull stones from Burghead all the
lowland Class 1 stones were single finds suggesting dispersion
of population. Only in the Spey Valley where settlement sites
are constricted by relief do groups of Class 1 stones appear at
one site such as Knockando or Inveravon. The distribution of
Class 111 stones is much less widespread — at our present
state of knowledge limited to four sites at Birnie Churchyard,
Altyre, Drainie (Kineddar Manse) and Burghead. This suggests
a significant degree of nucleation particularly as fourteen Class
111 fragments are recorded from Drainie. Furthermore, three of
these sites have Class 1 stones suggesting continued use of the
same site and each of these three have demonstrable Early

Christian connections. One can therefore argue that the church was probably the nucleating factor.

The identification of the Picts as a discrete race of people arose largely from their identification with the regional, highly symbolised art form characteristic of eastern Scotland north of the Forth in the first millennium A.D. and supported by vestigial remnants of the Pictish language in the same area. The lack of pre-Christian graves, houses, and fortifications was problematic. Modern work has now shown that typical pre-Roman Iron Age forts were still being constructed in the Pictish period as at Burghead, while other forts such as Craig Phadrig at Inverness were reoccupied during the Pictish phase, while at Kineddar a contiguous find of symbol stones and timber laced fort can be postulated. It is only with modern radio carbon dating methods that it has been possible to distinguish that the corpus of forts has a Pictish component and the practice of assigning them all to the pre-Roman Iron Age must be discarded. It follows that the next few years may well produce 'typical Iron Age" hut circles and graves with Pictish radio-carbon dates and ultimately it may be possible to distinguish classificatory types of Pictish pottery from the somewhat amorphous mass of undecorated ware which tends to be labelled Scottish Iron Age. In this context the circumstances of the find of the Class 1 symbol stone at Easterton of Roseisle are particularly apposite (Young, 1895). This stone which has crescent and V-rod, another crescentic symbol and a mirror and comb on one side and the goose and a fish on the other was found as the side slab of an irregular stone cist probably containing one or two crouched burials. This is definitely a secondary use of the stone and the burial must post date the carving on the stone probably by quite a few years. In other words, pre-Roman burial customs certainly continued long into the Pictish period. It now seems clear that since Roman activity had so little impact in this area, pre-Roman Iron Age cultural concepts continued undisturbed into the post Roman era and there is no reason to look for any separate racial characteristics in the Picts or any new invading peoples. The Picts of the literary sources are the direct descendants of the pre Roman population and Pictish art is a local stylised development in eastern Scotland which, although having a clear individuality, has some artistic connections with developments in other parts of Britain and Europe at this time.

# 8

# THE MIDDLE AGES

## RONALD CANT

*Introduction*

The name 'Moray' as applied to the District constituted under this title by the Local Government Act of 1973 represents the third major phase in a change of identity to which there is no parallel elsewhere in Scotland. The earliest reference to Moray or *Muref* is as one of the major regions of the "Pictish confederation" which embraced most of the later Scotland down to the mid 9th century A.D. The region seems to have stretched from the river Spey on the east to considerably beyond the Ness on the west and from the coastlands on the north deep into the Grampian Mountains on the south. Over these territories there was some kind of 'regional king', although the growth of a 'national monarchy' latterly reduced his status to more that of a 'provincial governor' under the title of *mormaer* or earl.

This area, then, was the historic 'Province of Moray'. While its importance in the sphere of civil government declined from the 12th century onwards, in the sphere of ecclesiastical government it proved considerably more enduring. Whether the Bishopric of Moray originated in the 1120's in association with the national monarchy or at an earlier date in association with the local ruling house, it is clear that the boundaries of its diocese were very largely those of the ancient regional kingdom. After the Reformation the limits alike of the episcopal diocese and the presbyterian synod continued the same tradition and have in fact persisted to the present day.

When the Scottish monarchy took over direct control of Moray in 1135 the earldom was annexed to the crown. The chief local officers, under the king, were now the sheriffs whose sheriffdoms or shires comprised much smaller areas, and although the earldom was revived in the form of a regality in 1312 this endured only until 1455. By the time of its final revival in 1562 the Earldom of Moray had little of its earlier significance and finally lost such powers as it retained to the shires with the abolition of 'heritable jurisdictions' in 1747.

Within Moray the centres of the shires were royal castles with associated burghs at Elgin (Plate 19), Nairn, and Inverness. East of the Spey a long strip of country running inland from the coast similarly formed the shire of Banff, having a certain integrity of its own but awkwardly divided for ecclesiastical purposes between the dioceses of Moray and Aberdeen. At a relatively early date Elgin and Forres were conjoined as a single sheriffdom in which the former became the predominant centre, giving the district the name of 'Elginshire'. Next to the west was the small but distinctive shire of Nairn. By contrast 'Inverness-shire' came to include large areas very much farther afield, and although its heart was the western part of the old province, and the southern part retained strong links with the 'laich' country to the north, these wider associations gradually drew Inverness away from Moray towards a different role as 'capital of the Highlands'. With this giant on the west and the sizeable shire of Aberdeen on the east the three smaller units along the Moray Firth formed a group with a character of its own.

When the old shires became 'administrative counties' in 1890 there was already a tendency to speak of 'Elgin-shire' as 'Moray-shire', a practice that was given official recognition in 1919. In 1975, as has been noted, the name 'Moray' was given a still more radical change of meaning when most of the administrative county was joined with most of that of Banff (but excluding the county town and its immediate neighbourhood) to form the new 'Moray District' within the 'Grampian region'. While an extension of Moray east of the Spey is not without precedent, the diocese having commonly included Strathbogie, the great river has usually been accepted as one of the major dividing lines in the historical geography of Scotland. The new Moray draws within its boundaries territories to the east of the Spey more extensive than those which it has retained to the west, although the actual centre of the District remains here in the ancient city and royal burgh of Elgin.

*Early History*

Explanation of the varying significance of the name 'Moray'

is a necessary preliminary to the discussion of its history, especially in the Middle Ages (Fig. 10). Throughout this period, usually accepted as embracing the thousand years or so from around 500 to 1500 A.D., Moray held a uniquely influential position in northern Britain. Having its own intrinsic importance in political and economic terms, it was repeatedly a 'debateable land' between what might be called northern and southern or perhaps 'particularist' and 'centralist' influences. This is seen at

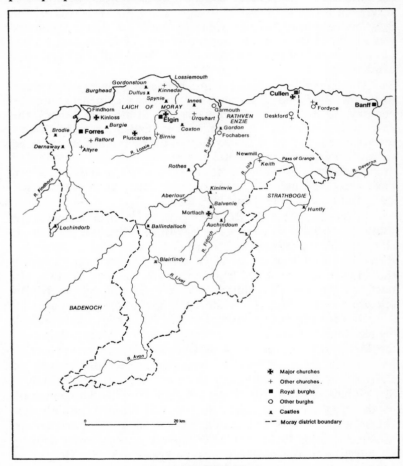

Fig. 10 Medieval Moray

an earlier stage in connection with the Roman attempt, pursued intermittently from 80 to 209 A.D., to incorporate northern Britain within their Empire, an attempt that penetrated no farther than Moray. Indeed, apart from two great advances, under Agricola and Severus, at the beginning and end of this period, Roman power in the north took the form of a limited military occupation falling far short of the Grampian mountain barrier. Even so, vestiges of the two advances beyond this survive in a line of marching camps up to the east bank of the Spey and according to one view the battle of 'Mons Graupius' was fought in the Pass of Grange just east of Keith. Suggestions of Roman penetration west of the Spey still lack decisive confirmation.

The Roman experience is instructive as showing what came to be the chief line of advance for southern influences into the country north of the Grampians, by Strathmore round the eastern end of the mountain barrier and thence north-west towards the lower Spey. It also showed the difficulties encountered by such influences in maintaining themselves at the end of a prolonged chain of communications against strong and determined local resistance unless a base could be found in the area itself and given time to consolidate.

In its last phase (in the 4th century) the Roman power in southern Britain was associated with a Christian church, a church which persisted and expanded under native 'Romano-British' leadership after the withdrawal of Roman forces before the impact of the English invasions in the 5th century. In northern Britain this church was represented by St Ninian operating from a base at Whithorn in Galloway but thought by some to have begun a movement for the conversion of the Pictish peoples much farther to the north-east. In Moray, however, the first certain introduction of Christian influences appears to have come from Ireland by way of the Scottish colony of Dalriada in Argyll. Although the most famous figure here is St Columba of Iona, who has been credited with the conversion of the northern Picts, his influence was almost certainly less extensive, and the foundation of the missionary centre at Mortlach (beside Dufftown) in the late 6th century seems actually to have been the work of his contemporary St Moluag of Lismore. A century later additional centres were established at

Keith and Rafford (south of Forres) by St Maelrubha of Apple-cross.

These missionary centres took the form of simple monasteries closely identified with the life of the local communities in which they were set. The units themselves may quite possibly have been represented by the thanages, baronies, and parishes of later organisation. At this stage most of them were probably of tribal character, under a chief, but in the case of the thanages the corresponding dignitary (thane itself being of later usage) seems to have had something of the character of a royal official. As already noted, the kingdom of Moray covered a wide area west of the Spey and was undoubtedly the strongest of such kingdoms north of the Grampians, although from the 8th century at least the most powerful ruler in the entire Pictish area was based south of the mountain barrier in the Tay valley.

The Celtic church, to which the various local monasteries belonged, while lacking in organic unity, followed approximately similar usages differing somewhat from those elsewhere in western Europe. In the Pictish area there was also a noteworthy cultural unity extending back into pre-Christian times, its most remarkable manifestation being a unique school of monumental sculpture. In Moray the 'Elgin pillar' displays the distinctive Pictish symbols on one face and a Celtic cross on the other, while on 'Sueno's Stone' (Plate 15) at Forres the symbols are replaced by hunting and battle scenes.

By the 8th century Pictish ecclesiastical observances had come more into line with those elsewhere, and in the mid 9th century the place of the chief king of the area was taken by the King of Scots. Employing the same power base as his later Pictish predecessors, he established a closer control over the other ('regional') kings than they had achieved. He also extended the 'episcopal' system that had begun to displace the 'abbatial' in the church as part of the process of assimilation already mentioned and created a 'chief bishop' associated with the Columban centre of Dunkeld and claiming a status perhaps similar to his own as 'High King'. Whether the authority of either was extended effectively north of the Grampians is open to question, but a bishopric may well have been created for Moray by its own king about this time and another based on Mortlach for the territories east of the Spey.

## Coming of the Medieval Order

While all this was happening, however, the relative isolation which the British Isles had enjoyed for some three centuries, and the northern areas for over twice as long, was broken by the Viking invasions. Beginning around 800, they led to large-scale Norwegian settlement in Shetland, Orkney, and the northern mainland. Here a powerful line of local *jarls* emerged whose political influence was carried across the Moray Firth to the territories on its southern shores. Towards the close of the 9th century Jarl Sigurd is said to have established a stronghold here, possibly at Burghead, and although the local rulers regained control of the situation, an attempt by them a century later to carry the conflict north ended in failure. Nevertheless the death of the great Jarl Sigurd the Stout at the battle of Clontarf in 1014 created a power vacuum in which Moray was able to recover and consolidate itself under a *mormaer* or king of exceptional ability, Macbeth.

Few historic characters have been more misunderstood and misrepresented than this famous figure. His replacement of his kinsman Duncan as King of Scots in 1040 arose from Duncan's death in battle, apparently in Moray, at the hands of Jarl Thorfinn Sigurdsson. But according to the convention of 'collateral succession' then accepted Macbeth had an excellent claim to the throne in his own right, as guardian of the interests of his wife's son (representing another collateral claim), and as the man on the spot in a particularly critical situation. If he entered into some kind of accommodation with Thorfinn after his accession this was no more than common prudence, not treachery. All the evidence suggests that he was a strong and effective ruler, familiar with the new ideas of government developing in Europe at this time. He is even said to have visited the Pope in Rome. But in 1054 he was defeated and killed in an invasion of the realm by Duncan's son Malcolm with Northumbrian support.

After the fall of Macbeth his stepson Lulach, who had as good a claim to the Scottish throne as Malcolm, maintained himself for a time in the territories north of the Grampians but in 1057 he too was destroyed by his rival. Even so, his descendants were able to sustain a prolonged rearguard action for a further seventy years against the attempts of King Malcolm III and his

18.  Elgin Cathedral

19. Elgin (early 1950s) with Lady Hill and its castle site in the foreground. *(Aerofilms Ltd.)*

20. Pluscarden Abbey

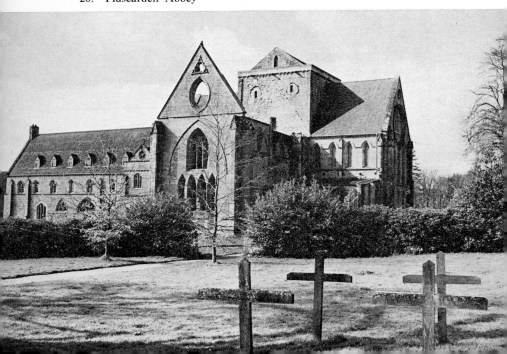

21.   Coxton Tower, near Lhanbryde

22.   Forres Square showing the Tolbooth

23. The Round Square, Gordonstoun

24. Shorthorn Bull: Glamis First Lord

25. Doo'cot, New Elgin

26. Buckie Harbour

27. Houses, gable end to the sea, east of Buckie

28. Tormore Distillery

29. Kynoch's Wool Mill, Keith

30.  Ramsay Macdonald, first Labour Prime Minister

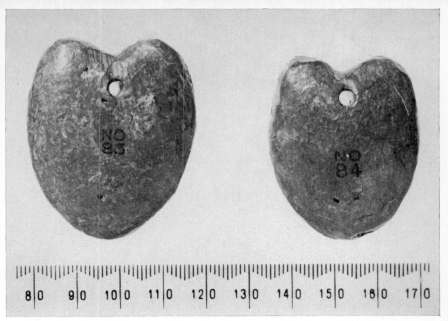

31. Two Lead Hearts: said to have been used in the parish of Forres and neighbourhood for curing heart ailments of children

32. 6d. of George II, from Banffshire, placed in a pail before milking to preserve the milk from witchcraft

Pendant (found on the Culbin Sands) formed of a small quartz pebble in a mount of copper strips

33.   Old Gravestone, Michael Kirk, Gordonstoun

sons to impose the authority of the central monarchy on this recalcitrant province. In 1130, however, King David I defeated Angus of Moray (apparently outside the latter's own territory) and followed this up by a punitive campaign and an initial 'settlement of Moray' in 1135. Despite this, it required a further campaign by his grandson and successor Malcolm IV and a more drastic settlement in 1163 before Moray was brought finally and effectively under the control of the Scottish crown and its way of life irreversibly changed.

The 'new order' introduced into Moray at this time was by now well-established in the more southerly parts of the Scottish kingdom. It conformed to the pattern introduced into England by the Norman Conquest of 1066 and for Moray at least its appearance had something of a similar character since it was imposed by force and with the assistance of families which had earlier participated in the conquest of England and the reorganisation of southern Scotland. A good example is the 'house of Freskin'. Its founder appears to have been a Flemish soldier of fortune who was rewarded for his services to the Scottish crown by an estate in West Lothian. From here the family moved north, obtaining the important lordship of Duffus as the base of what came to be known as 'the house of Moray'. By the 13th century it had become the most influential family in the whole north of Scotland with the main line deeply entrenched in Moray itself, both in church and state, and a branch with a similar position in Sutherland across the firth.

Families of this kind, holding their newly acquired lands as hereditary military *fiefs* from the crown, formed the hard core of the new order. In medieval society political and economic power depended on the tenure of land, and in Moray all the great estates passed to these 'incomers' whose castles dominated local life as they dominated the landscape. The immense 'motte and bailey' fortress of Duffus (Plate 16), still visible in outline beneath a later re-building, gives a good impression of the formidable quality of its early lords. But among great fiefs of this kind many lesser units of the older order survived as thanages, some at least in the hands of their ancient holders, others granted to royal servants likely to be of more reliable disposition in the longer run than some of the greater lords so necessary to the crown in the first stage of the 'settlement'. A further example of 'selective conservatism' on the part of the monarchy was the

K

maintenance of older dues and obligations alongside the new tenurial conditions. Thus while these reforming monarchs were resolved to destroy local independence where it seemed to threaten the integrity of their realm, resolved also to reorganise the structure of government on the new continental pattern, they seem to have been conscious of their position as heirs of a Celtic inheritance and disposed to continue such aspects of it as might be to their advantage.

It must not in any event be thought that the kings depended on the feudal structure alone for control of local life. As we have seen, they had their own officers, especially the sheriffs, based in royal castles in such places as Elgin and Forres. Associated with these castles were royal burghs, in effect 'new towns' established by the crown as centres of trade and industry. The early burgesses were largely drawn from the south and constituted a special element in the development of the new regime. Finally there was the reorganised ecclesiastical order. Whatever may have been the earlier history of the bishopric of Moray, from the 1130's it was closely associated with the monarchy, although it was some time before it acquired a fixed seat. At a local level feudal lords co-operated with king and bishop to establish parish churches in their fiefs. And at Kinloss in 1150 David I founded an abbey of the fashionable Cistercian order with monks brought here from Melrose in the southern borders.

*The Golden Age*

The work of drawing Moray into the fabric of the Scottish kingdom was mainly effected under the rule of Malcolm IV and William (1153-1214). The next two reigns, of Alexander II and Alexander III (1214-86), saw this work consolidated and enriched to a degree that made later generations look back to it as a golden age. It had been the hope of the reforming kings that in reorganising their realm in the way that has been described not only would they increase their own power but establish Scotland as a full participant in the benefits of medieval civilisation, then approaching its peak, and a respected independent member of the European state system. These objectives they largely realised, and among all the various regions of their kingdom it was in Moray that the results were most apparent. Despite its somewhat remote situation, on the north side of a massive mountain range separating it from the heart of the country, the land was fertile and the climate equable. The wide plain between the Spey and the Findhorn, with its twin focal points at Elgin and Forres, was particularly suited to be the setting for a prosperous and well-ordered society with a plentiful supply of fine sandstone for the construction of churches, castles, and other buildings. Royal officials, reinforced at intervals by the personal presence of the king, assured the maintenance of law and order, while there is evidence of a fairly harmonious co-operation between feudatories, burgesses and ecclesiastics from their respective positions within the social and administrative structure.

By general agreement the most notable achievement of the 13th century in Moray was the creation of a proper cathedral church at Elgin as the centre of its religious life. Prior to this the bishops of Moray had moved between Birnie, Kineddar and Spynie. In 1208 authority was given for a cathedral at the last named but by 1224 this was superseded by 'the church of the Holy Trinity beside Elgin'. Even in its first form this was a building of considerable size and architectural distinction (Plate 18). As completed some fifty years later it had become the finest church ever to be built in Scotland. Although smaller than the cathedrals of St Andrews and Glasgow and of only moderate scale when compared with the vast edifices of England and the continent, it reflected the same high standard of design, part-French part-English in inspiration and yet entirely appropriate to its particular setting and purpose. That a building of such quality could be created here in this century is striking confirmation of the level of civilisation attained by Moray at this stage of its history.

After Elgin Cathedral the two most important ecclesiastical foundations in the District were the monasteries of Kinloss and Pluscarden (Plate 20) each with buildings of some size and distinction, Kinloss being mainly romanesque work of the 12th and Pluscarden gothic from the 13th century. Kinloss, as has been seen, belonged to the Cistercian order, well represented elsewhere in Scotland, but Pluscarden reflected the preference of King Alexander II in 1230 for Valliscaulians, a somewhat recondite French order unknown in the British Isles apart from two other rather small houses in Scotland and one in Wales. From about 1136 to 1454 a community of Benedictine monks existed at Urquhart east of Elgin but it was absorbed with Pluscarden under the control of its original mother-house of

Dunfermline and nothing of its buildings remains. In Elgin itself there was an early appearance in 1234 of the preaching brotherhood of Dominicans or Blackfriars but plans to establish Franciscans or Greyfriars here were not fully effective until the 15th century. Hospitals or hospices under religious auspices existed at Elgin (Maison Dieu) and in Rathven and at the east end of 'the Bridge of Spey' opposite Orton.

These foundations are very typical of medieval ecclesiastical organisation and all affected the life of the neighbourhood in some measure but the spiritual well-being of the ordinary Christian was the special concern of the parish church. By the opening of the 13th century the parochial map of Moray had assumed the general form which it has retained ever since. In origin many of the parishes were probably continuations of very much older social units; many again corresponded to baronies of the new feudal system. But although varying considerably in size and character each had a church maintained by the parishioners and served by a parish priest. Almost from the outset, however, parishes were 'appropriated' to monasteries, cathedrals and bishoprics, so that only part of their resources was available for the church fabric and the stipend of the vicar or resident priest. Because of this the typical parish church was a relatively modest building, not only in Moray but throughout Scotland as a whole. But the romanesque (12th century) structure still in use at Birnie near Elgin and the ruined gothic (13th century) example at Altyre near Forres show that they were not devoid of architectural merit. The larger and finer design of Mortlach is explained by its persisting status as a minster or 'mother-church' for its neighbourhood even after its bishop had moved to Aberdeen in the 1130's.

Apart from the churches the most important features in the landscape of 13th century Moray were the castles of the king and feudal lords. In their first form these would be of timber but by the end of the century most had towers and enclosures of stone. While the sites of most of them are well known, as at Elgin and Forres, at Darnaway, Duffus (Plate 16) and Rothes, the structures that survive are replacements of later date. The same is true of lesser country dwellings and the houses of merchants and craftsmen in the burghs, advancing steadily in prosperity and the regulation of their own affairs. Yet from the areas of settlement it is evident that Moray supported a considerable population in conditions of reasonable comfort and security when the whole future of the Scottish kingdom was suddenly placed in doubt in 1290.

## The War of Independence

The crisis of 1290 was caused by the death of the child Queen of Scots, Margaret, sole descendant of King Alexander III who had died in 1286. Although the problem of the succession was resolved by reference of the issue to King Edward I of England, he insisted that he could only adjudicate between the claimants as 'Lord Paramount' of Scotland, and when he selected John Balliol in 1292 the new King of Scots became so as his vassal. By 1295 Edward's interpretation of what this involved, namely, the complete subordination of Scotland to his authority, had provoked the leading men of the country to resistance. In 1296, however, this first attempt to reassert the independence of the Scottish kingdom was crushed in one brief campaign. It is interesting and perhaps significant that when Edward had secured the southern and central parts of the realm and obtained the humiliating submission of King John he considered it advisable to proceed north of the Grampians and give visible evidence of his triumph as far as Elgin. Thereafter he returned south, leaving his subordinates to organise the conquered country as a dependancy of England, but within a year a new movement of resistance had emerged.

This rising of 1297 was remarkable for its wide geographical extent and the way in which it involved all sections of Scottish society, giving it the character of a truly national movement. Particularly noteworthy was the prominent part played in it by Moray and the leadership provided not only here but in the reconstruction of an independent Scottish state by Andrew 'of Moray'. This Andrew was a descendant of the 'house of Freskin' which had come to Moray only a century and a half before as a beneficiary of King David's 'plantation' but had thereafter identified itself so effectively with the life of the region that it could command the general support of the population, whether of more ancient origin, in a crisis of this kind.

The military operations initiated by Andrew of Moray against the English occupation in the spring of 1297 coincided with those begun by William Wallace in the Glasgow area at just this time. There can be little doubt that some liaison existed between them and other 'resistance groups', most obviously through the church, but the northern movement had its own independent impetus. Not only did it include the majority of the feudatories in the area but its forces also comprised burgesses from the towns, assured of the active sympathy of the clergy. Within a short period the whole vital area on the south side of the Moray Firth, from well beyond Inverness on the west to Banff on the east, was free from English control. The two main Scottish groups then joined forces in the heart of the kingdom and won a decisive victory over the main English army of occupation at Stirling Bridge. Unfortunately Andrew of Moray was mortally wounded in the battle, and although he was appointed joint Guardian of the kingdom with Wallace he died before the end of the year.

The brilliant reassertion of Scottish independence in 1297, to which the men of Moray had made so significant a contribution, was followed by a prolonged struggle in which repeated efforts were needed to keep the national cause alive. In 1298 Edward I returned in person to Scotland, defeated Wallace at Falkirk, and re-established a measure of English control, but resistance continued in many parts of the country and it required another supreme personal effort by Edward in 1303-4 to achieve something like the complete domination at which he aimed. Once again his campaign took him north by way of Banff and Elgin as far as Kinloss Abbey before he turned south to complete his conquest.

By 1304 Scotland was indeed a conquered country and in 1305, after the capture and execution of Wallace, Edward made what was intended to be the permanent settlement of its government. Only a year later, however, a new resistance leader appeared in the person of Robert Bruce. If his initial effort to establish himself as king of an independent Scotland aroused only limited support and met with military disaster, after the death of Edward I in 1307 his prospects improved considerably. In the task of rallying and maintaining support for his cause the influence of the Scottish church was of the greatest importance. Among its leaders the significance of Bishop David of Moray (1299-1326) was second only to that of Bishop William Lamberton of St Andrews (1297-1328), both owing their nomination to Scottish guardians during periods of regained independence. Bishop David's leadership in the north was particularly valuable during the years 1306-12 when no one of comparable stature was available in the area. In 1312, however, he was joined by one of King Robert's ablest lieutenants, Thomas Randolph, for whom the Earldom of Moray was revived at this time.

The consequences of this development for Moray in the longer term will be considered in due course. It will be sufficient at this stage to emphasise its significance for the national cause. With the resources of this important region at his disposal the new Earl was enabled to make a particularly effective contribution to the resources available to his king. The Moray contingent featured prominently in the Scottish victory at Bannockburn in 1314 and Earl Randolph remained King Robert's most trusted adviser thereafter. In 1326, two years after the birth of his son and heir David, the King arranged for the Earl of Moray to be Guardian for him should the boy succeed under age. This was in fact what occurred in 1329, but King Robert could at least die with the satisfaction that just a year before he had obtained full recognition by England of his status as lawful ruler of a completely independent Scotland.

*The Later Middle Ages*

Wars of independence inevitably leave an aftermath of problems. But the unsettled condition of Scotland after 1329 was only partly attributable to the War which was actually renewed in quite a serious form in the 1330's and continued intermittently to the end of the Middle Ages. The problems facing the kingdom in this period arose from within as well as from without and in part at least from the policies of the great King Robert himself. The grant of the Earldom of Moray to Thomas Randolph is a good example of the king's over-generous attitude to the great nobles. Not only did it include wide territories but important jurisdiction for the entire earldom, including the royal castles and burghs of Elgin, Forres, and Inverness, was to be held heritably 'as a free regality, together with the four pleas pertaining to our royal crown'. A regality was automatically outwith the jurisdiction of the king's sheriff. The addition of the 'four pleas' meant that it was outwith the jurisdiction of his justiciar, a kind of autonomous principality exempt from all control other than that of the king himself in the last resort.

The earldom of Moray was the extreme case of its kind but, if anomalous, functioned moderately well in itself, and the burghs comprised within it advanced towards self-government much as they would have done under the crown. Indeed, considering the lack of effective royal direction in the period 1329-1424, it was perhaps an advantage for Moray to have its own autonomous government. Paradoxically, the greatest threat to law and order came from a brother of King Robert III, Alexander Stewart, Lord of Badenoch, who descended from his highland fastness to ravage Elgin and Forres in 1390. Among the casualties of this outrage was Elgin Cathedral which had to be extensively re-built thereafter.

Under James I and his successors the crown recovered something of its authority, but the repeated minorities between one reign and the next meant that the exercise of this authority was intermittent. For Moray the great landmark of this period was the conflict of the 1450's between King James II and the house of Douglas which had added this northern earldom to its older possessions in southern Scotland in 1451. After the triumph of the king in 1455 the earldom was once again annexed to the crown and remained so until the close of the Middle Ages.

The destruction of the power of the Douglas earls created a gap in the ranks of the great feudatories which was filled by the rise of the Gordon Earls of Huntly, although James II in advancing them had no intention that they should attain a remotely comparable position. As newcomers to the area, from distant Berwickshire, it was obviously to the interest of the Gordons to co-operate with the crown and in general they tended to do so. Their lands lay mainly to the east of the Spey, in the Enzie and Strathbogie, with others farther afield in Mar and Badenoch, but they chose to be buried in Elgin Cathedral and in considerable style as part of a set policy to establish themselves as the leading family of the north. The powers assigned to the third Earl of Huntly by James IV in 1501, even if temporary, confirmed his position as chief agent of the crown in the entire area beyond the Grampians.

The co-operation existing between the Gordons and the kings of this period extended to other lords. Although James III showed intermittent tendencies towards centralisation, his father and his son were prepared to allow their feudatories considerable independence and even to hold royal offices such as sheriffdoms heritably, provided they recognised the overall authority of the crown. They were also encouraged to create their own 'burghs of barony'. The privileges which these enjoyed were necessarily less than those pertaining to the royal burghs and the new settlements could never hope to rival well-established urban centres like Elgin or Forres, but they held at least some possibility of economic growth. Among creations of this kind were Spynie (1451, under the Bishop of Moray whose principal residence was here), Fordyce (1499, under the Bishop of Aberdeen), and Findhorn (1532, under the Abbot of Kinloss).

The castles from which these lords held sway, whether secular or ecclesiastical, were now substantial stone buildings of some size and even elegance. By far the largest still to be seen is the immense structure of Duffus, a 14th century re-building of the earlier motte and bailey castle. By far the most distinguished architectural feature is the stately hall surviving from this same period at Darnaway. The 15th century bishop's palace at Spynie shows an impressive combination of strength and sophistication. And across the Spey, in central Banffshire, the twin strongholds of Balvenie (Plate 17) and Auchindoun form an interesting contrast, the former evincing a well-developed courtyard plan, the latter a more simple yet formidable tower-house not so different from the Earl of Huntly's principal seat at Bog o' Gight or 'Gordon Castle' to the north.

Within the burghs good stone houses were no longer the rarity they had previously been among the timber-framed dwellings of the merchants and craftsmen, but in the country villages, even those which might rank as burghs of barony, construction was more modest. And in the various settlements, whether urban or rural, it was the churches that continued to display the greatest architectural merit. Of these the finely restored Greyfriars convent at Elgin (1479) is undoubtedly the most impressive but the collegiate church of Cullen is more characteristic of the last medieval phase. A corporate chantry founded by Alexander Ogilvie of that ilk in 1543, it contains his own ornate tomb and a 'sacrament house' the rich carving of which is only rivalled in work of this kind by the example in the other Ogilvie church at nearby Deskford.

The close of the Middle Ages was marked by disorder and disintegration, particularly acute in some of the largest and wealthiest of European kingdoms. By comparison the condition of Scotland was not so unhappy. If its church life stood in serious need of reform, there are indications of fresh vitality within the old structure such as the renaissance enterprises at Kinloss Abbey promoted by Abbot Crystal and the pluralist Bishop Reid with the help of a specially imported Italian scholar Giovanni Ferrari. If the authority of the crown may seem to have been unduly lax and complaisant it was usually strong enough to maintain order while the regalities and baronies were by no means as chaotic and oppressive as has often been supposed, sometimes quite the reverse. In the towns the burgesses pursued their business in reasonable security and commentators on the life of Moray at the end of the Middle Ages are unanimous in emphasising its general well-being.

# 9

# EARLY MODERN TIMES

## RONALD CANT

*The Reformation*

For Scotland the event that marks the end of the Middle Ages and the beginning of modern times more emphatically than any other is the Reformation of 1560. And yet the occurrences of that year were more limited in their effect than has often been supposed. The proceedings of the 'Reformation Parliament' were the work of a group of revolutionaries whose objectives were by no means consistent with each other and whose success had only been made possible by the grudging intervention of Elizabeth of England. Even if the settlement lasted, under it the reformed church was recognised rather than established, the old order of religion was obstructed but not destroyed, and in many parts of the country there were influential elements ready to reverse the situation if opportunity offered.

Prominent in this category was the North-East including Moray. While some of the clergy, lairds and burgesses went over to the side of reform and the traditional religious observances ceased in the cathedral and conventional corporations, Bishop Patrick Hepburn immured himself at Spynie, clearly disapproving of developments although at the same time too cautious to expose himself without adequate military and political support. Such support should in fact have been forthcoming, for the greatest magnate of the north, the fourth Earl of Huntly, remained loyal to the old faith. When it became clear, in 1561, that Queen Mary was to return to Scotland following the death of her husband the French king, he actually proposed that she should land here and use the persisting support for Catholicism to carry through a counter-reformation. Instead, she accepted the advice of her half-brother, Lord James Stewart, to adopt a more moderate policy, remaining a Catholic herself but declining to countenance any 'alteration of the state of religion found standing at her arrival', that is, resulting from the partial settlement of 1560.

The attitude of the Queen, while defensible in a country as deeply divided as Scotland was over the question of religion, disappointed and confused her fellow-Catholics. Huntly in particular was resentful that his advice had been ignored for that of a man who was now to be his territorial rival in his own particular region. This was when the Earldom of Moray was revived for Lord James in 1562. In the autumn of this year Huntly and his sons were responsible for ill-judged acts of defiance at both Aberdeen and Inverness when the Queen made a progress with the new earl in the north. What her intentions or those of the Gordons may have been is not clear, but in the end there was an armed confrontation at Corrichie near Aberdeen in which Huntly met his death. His estates were then forfeited and Moray emerged as the most influential figure alike in the north and in the royal government for the time being.

This situation did not endure for long, Huntly's heir the fifth Earl being restored to his estates but not to his full traditional powers in 1567, and Moray, by then Regent, being assassinated in 1570. The events of 1561-62 can be seen in retrospect as a turning point of major importance. The alienation between the Queen and the most powerful Catholic noble in Scotland destroyed the best prospect for a counter-reformation, and while support for the Queen continued beyond her removal from office in 1567, it rested on a political rather than a religious base. With the triumph of the 'King's Party' (supporting the nominal rule of her young son) in the civil war of 1568-73, the 'Queen's Party' virtually disintegrated and the prolonged Reformation crisis was at an end.

If Scotland at this stage was far from being a completely Protestant country, Protestantism had now an irreversible ascendancy and Catholicism was reduced to a small and steadily dwindling minority. Even so, the activities of the northern 'Catholic earls' (Huntly and Erroll) in the last years of the century caused great alarm among Protestants because of their continuing influence in the area and their association with a possible Spanish invasion. The involvement of Huntly (the sixth Earl) in 1592 in the brutal killing of 'the Bonnie Earl of Moray', son-in-law of the Regent and bright hope of the Protestants, also occasioned widespread horror. But even the Earl's victory over government forces under Argyll at Glenlivet in 1594 could not prevent the collapse of their position thereafter.

In the same year, 1573, in which the civil war ended, Bishop Hepburn of Moray died. But although hostile to reform he had been unable to prevent the gradual replacement of Catholic priests by Protestant ministers in the churches of his diocese, under the direction of Robert Pont as 'commissioner for the plantation of kirks in Moray, Inverness, and Banff' at Elgin. Over a third of these ministers were in fact former priests, and as the reformed church experienced great difficulty in finding qualified candidates for its ministry such men were in a position to command considerable influence. Among the most notable was George Hay, rector of Rathven before the Reformation and minister of this and several adjoining parishes thereafter. The fact that he was a university graduate and socially well-connected increased his assurance and authority. He was Moderator of the General Assembly in 1570 and a member of innumerable commissions concerned with the establishment of Protestantism in the north and farther afield.

When Hay was Moderator, only a handful of ministers, supplemented by 'readers' and 'exhorters', were available for service in the neighbourhood. When he died in 1588 nearly every parish had a minister of its own working with a group of 'elders' as the 'kirk session' of the congregation. At Banff, Elgin, and Forres 'presbyteries' had been established to supervise the churches in the surrounding district, and if the relations between them and the Protestant bishops had become a matter of controversy the reformed church was secure in itself.

*Social Change*

The Reformation most obviously involved religious change but it also had far-reaching social and political implications. These are to be seen at their most idealistic level in the programme worked out for the reformed church in the *First Book of Discipline* of 1560. This envisaged that in each parish the 'congregation' of Christian folk should be a kind of egalitarian society, electing its minister and elders and concerning itself with the well-being of all its members. The young were to be educated, the poor and the old were to be cared for, and all persons, regardless of wealth and influence, were to be under the guidance and 'discipline' of the church. To finance these enterprises the parochial tithes or *teinds* were to be returned from the monasteries and other parts of the medieval ecclesiastical structure to which they had been appropriated and used for the benefit of the locality from which they were drawn.

It proved very hard indeed to secure this simple and laudable end, not so much through the difficulty of dislodging the dignitaries of the old church as because of the competing ambitions of the reformers' political allies, the nobility in particular. While many of them were devout exponents of reform they had reservations about establishing a church of so democratic a character, all the more so when it was to be financed in the manner proposed. Some leading nobles, Lord James Stewart among them, were already in control of monastic properties as 'commendators' or titular abbots and had no wish to lose the economic and political advantages which this gave them. And although the reformers were tactful enough to make no claim on monastic lands this concession did little to reconcile their aristocratic supporters to the return of the teinds. Part of them was indeed allocated to the reformed church in 1562 and rather more in 1567 but most of the remainder, together with the ecclesiastical lands, passed to the nobility.

In Moray, as we have seen, the establishment of the reformed church proceeded slowly and in most parishes it was not until the 1580's that kirk sessions were functioning in the manner envisaged by the *Book of Discipline*. Even then it is doubtful whether much in the way of formal educational provision existed outside the towns. There were also certain areas where the population adhered to the old faith and either through sheer remoteness, as in the glens of upper Banffshire, or by the protection of a powerful local lord, as with Huntly's tenants in the Enzie, were able to hold reform at bay. But even where the new church encountered no such difficulties it proceeded in a more tolerant manner than was usual farther south. And when the controversy over episcopacy and presbyterianism broke out, from 1574 onwards, although there was no opposition to the establishment of presbyteries, there was at the same time little desire to abandon the episcopal system that had operated in the reformed church, in some form, since 1560.

The general effect of the Reformation, then, was to create a new church order but one which fell short in many respects of the ideals of its early promoters. In financial terms the chief beneficiaries from the redistribution of the considerable wealth of the old church were what may be described as 'secular interests'. But the process was complicated by the revival of the monarchy from 1584 onwards under King James VI who used his authority to control the distribution of such church lands as were at his disposal to build up a royalist interest among the feudal aristocracy. In 1589 Pluscarden Priory was confirmed as a barony to its commendator Alexander Seton and in 1601 Edward Bruce received Kinloss Abbey with the greater dignity of 'lord of parliament', both recipients being members of lowland families associated with the crown. In 1590, when the Bishopric of Moray was vacant, James granted most of its lands to Alexander Lindsay as Lord Spynie but after the king's abandonment of the presbyterian experiment of 1592-1600 the lands were restored to the next bishop and the new lord received compensation elsewhere.

Although the nobles were the chief gainers from these changes others might also benefit from them. Long before the Reformation many ecclesiastical lords had begun to 'feu' parts of their estates, that is, to make hereditary grants on payment of a simple annual 'feu-duty'. Kinloss Abbey disposed of considerable areas in this way and the process continued under the new proprietors. Again, within a royal burgh like Elgin ecclesiastical properties were assigned to the town council and although they were intended for educational and charitable purposes this end was quite often secured by feuing. But changes in ownership and the rise of new families might be unconnected with the redistribution of church lands save in so far as this, in association with the spirit of enterprise engendered by both the Reformation and the Renaissance, created a more fluid social and economic situation. And while this might be advantageous in many ways it could also entail suffering for people like the 'kindly tenants' long settled on the Moray estates who found themselves displaced by newcomers prepared to pay a higher rental.

The society that resulted from these changes, although still contained within the traditional feudal structure, was rather more varied in origin, rank, and character of holdings. At its summit were great estates belonging to important national figures like the Earls of Moray and Huntly, who held considerable jurisdictional powers over their tenants as lords of regality and who could influence the political behaviour of their lesser neighbours by 'bonds of manrent' or in other ways. These lesser proprietors, many of them of baronial status, included such families as those of Brodie, Dunbar, and Cumming in the Forres area, Innes to the east of Elgin, Leslie and Grant along the Spey, Ogilvy beyond it, with varieties of Gordon in all parts. But some landowners were merchants, like Thomas Menzies from Aberdeen who built Fordyce Castle in 1592 and quite a few more round Elgin. The small feuars, having complete security of tenure, formed the nucleus of a rural middle class which also included many 'tacksmen' or leaseholders who might retain possession of their holdings for quite prolonged periods and even from one generation to another. Admittedly such persons were still subject to the economic and jurisdictional control of their 'laird' but even this had to take some account of the interests of the social group over which it was exercised.

In sum, then, the conception of Scottish rural life of this period as a combination of autocratic lairds and subservient peasants stands in need of considerable modification. At the same time the notion of the urban communities as islands of democracy is almost more misleading. True, royal burghs like Elgin, Forres, Banff, and Cullen now enjoyed virtually complete autonomy under their own elected provosts, baillies, and other officers. But participation in municipal government was confined to full 'burgesses' and dominated by the merchants. In the course of the 16th century the craftsmen obtained a limited share in the work of their town councils. On the other hand they themselves maintained a strict control of their own craft — in the building trades and the provision of food and clothing — maintaining standards perhaps but also restricting expansion and the adoption of new methods. Despite all this, however, the greater prosperity that came to the burghs allowed of a certain movement within their populations and occasionally a more enlightened attitude on the part of their authorities.

## A Time of Peace

The prosperity of Scotland in the early 17th century derived in great part from the order imposed by the monarchy under James VI. Admittedly the degree of direct control exercised by the royal government was limited and the king's plan of 1587 to introduce 'commissioners and justices' in each shire to maintain law and order was considerably modified when it was put into effect in 1609 so as not to interfere with the jurisdictions of the barons and lords of regality. In this connection it is interesting to observe that under the original scheme the three smaller shires along the Moray Firth were allotted seven commissioners each, the total of twenty-one equalling the figure for the larger shires of Inverness and Aberdeen on either side. But the king, in confirming the traditional prominence of the nobility both in local and central government, made it abundantly clear that this derived from royal grant or royal benevolence, and that no disorder or defiance of his authority would be tolerated. Thus although isolated acts of violence could still occur, like the assault on the minister of Forres in his own church by the laird of Cromarty in 1623, these were exceptional.

This mixture of firmness and flexibility on the part of the monarchy was quite remarkably successful within its limits. The older nobility, some of whom had attempted to overwhelm the king before James had established himself, accepted royal domination in the assurance that it would not seriously threaten their position. Alongside them, but not to an extent that could occasion alarm, rose a few nobility drawn mainly from lairds or younger sons of the old nobility who had rendered service to the crown. Examples of new lordships created out of former ecclesiastical estates in the Moray area have already been given. The most striking case of a local laird being raised to the peerage is that of Sir Walter Ogilvy who became Lord Ogilvy of Deskford in 1615 and Earl of Findlater in 1638. And to maintain the eminence of his family among the northern aristocracy, in 1599 the formerly rebellious Earl of Huntly was elevated to the rank of Marquis. But it was on the new nobility that King James placed greatest reliance in the conduct of his government, as evidenced in the remarkable career of Alexander Seton, commendator of Pluscarden, Lord President of the Court of Session from 1593 to 1605, thereafter Lord Chancellor and Earl of Dunfermline until his death in 1622.

As at other times, it is possible to gather something of the quality of life, at least of the more prosperous members of this society, from the design of their buildings. The great palace of Huntly, just outside the District to the east, reflects the grandeur thought appropriate to the head of the house of Gordon and elaborates the concept of the architectural 'frontispiece' developed slightly earlier at Balvenie by the Stewart Earls of

L

Atholl. At Darnaway the Earls of Moray seem to have lived in comparable style although no construction of this period is extant. But lairds of substance, like the Dunbars of Burgie on the other side of Forres, could also aspire to a residence in the 'palatial' manner, spreading out laterally even if still prudently associated with the defensive verticality of the traditional tower-house.

A similar spaciousness and sophistication may be seen, rather more unexpectedly, in the remodelling of Ballindalloch by its Grant laird in this same year 1602. Deeper into the hill country to the east of the Spey the Huntly outpost of Blairfindy in Glenlivet and the Leslie castle of Kininvie in Glenfiddich show an understandably greater concern for security. But it is surprising to find the most compactly defensive of all tower-houses built by a branch of the Innes family at Coxton (Plate 21) in the Laich just east of Elgin in the early 1600's and still regarded as a desirable home in 1641. The fact that civil war had broken out again by the latter date might explain this conservatism of outlook but at this very time, between 1640 and 1653, Sir Robert Innes of that ilk did not hesitate to build a new mansion in an advanced renaissance style — although by no means ignoring defensive considerations altogether. Its designer was apparently William Aitoun, Master Mason of Heriot's Hospital, Edinburgh, whose influence may perhaps also be seen at Thunderton House, Elgin, the greatest town mansion of this period in Moray.

'Thunderton House' was the name applied at a much later period to the splendid residence developed by Alexander Sutherland, first Lord Duffus (1651), on the site of the old 'King's House'. Interestingly, this family was one of two important offshoots of the Earldom of Sutherland, founded from Moray in 1228, which had returned here. The Sutherlands of Duffus had actually done so in the 15th century, the Gordons of Plewlands or 'Gordonstoun' as recently as the 1630's in the person of Sir Robert Gordon, brother of the twelfth earl, guardian of the thirteenth, and a man of exceptional accomplishment and influence throughout his long life. While Thunderton House was the grandest of the town *ludgings* of the neighbouring aristocracy that were such a feature of the larger burghs, all were of the same solid stone construction that had now become general in urban building. Most of the houses, however, belonged to the merchants and craftsmen of the burgh who conducted their business within them.

If the government of the royal burghs was in the hands of a 'self-perpetuating oligarchy', these officers were jealous guardians of their independence and so formed a useful counterpoise to the domination of local life by the feudatories. Their civic pride (tempered by economy) also inclined them to build tolbooths (Plate 22) which served as court-houses and prisons for the sheriffs, otherwise unprovided with such facilities. And, despite the criticism that can be made of their lethargy and obstructiveness, the authorities of Elgin were responsible for the building of a major bridge over the Lossie in 1630 and in 1633 were already beginning to plan a port at its mouth that developed later in the century into 'Lossiemouth'. This proved to be more successful in the long run than that associated with the old burgh of barony at Findhorn or the newer foundation at Garmouth (1587) by the Innes family. Indeed, burghs of barony as a whole were neither very numerous nor particularly successful in the region in this period.

## A Time of Conflict

When James VI was succeeded by his son Charles I in 1625 Scotland exchanged a ruler of vast experience and understanding for one with little knowledge of what was actually his native land, who really believed in the absolute authority of monarchy which his father had preached but rarely practised, and who was set on using this authority to curtail the traditional influence of the nobility and to make the Scottish church more completely episcopal in government and worship. Despite the strains produced by this policy, nevertheless, there was little hint at the time of the king's visit to Scotland for his coronation in 1633 that by 1638 his regime would have collapsed and that Bishop Guthrie of Moray, so prominent in the ceremonies, would be deposed and excommunicated by a resurgent General Assembly.

Of the attitude of Moray to these events it is difficult to speak with absolute certainty but all the evidence suggests that the area was reasonably content with the modified episcopal polity of the church contrived by James VI. Under this, although effective power rested with the king and the bishops, presbyteries and kirk sessions still functioned and the worship of the parish churches was of the simple type that had prevailed in Scotland since the Reformation. Thus despite some misgivings about more recent royal policy, when the National Covenant was circulated in the spring of 1638 it seems to have aroused no great response in Moray. The area was certainly represented in the Glasgow Assembly at the close of the year but its deposition of Bishop Guthrie remained ineffective for some time.

By 1639 the situation had moved into a fresh context in which the alignment of the various localities of Scotland would be determined not by argument or organisation but by superiority of armed force. Initially, such a superiority was held here by Huntly but he came under attack from the army sent by the Covenanters under Montrose to secure the adherence to their cause of the indifferent or unwilling North-East. The pacific attitude of the Moray area is well represented by the efforts of the Earl of Findlater, 'a man of peaceable temper' believing both in the authority of the crown and the justice of some at least of the Covenanters' demands, who effected a brief truce between Montrose and Huntly. By 1640, however, the Covenanters had won complete control, here as elsewhere in Scotland. Bishop Guthrie was removed from his palace at Spynie (although not by any local force) and with few exceptions his ministers then submitted to the presbyterian church order. An unhappy example of fanaticism on the part of the new regime, in general not unduly oppressive in the area, was the destruction of the rood screen at Elgin Cathedral, as yet intact within the ruined building, but this, while effected with local help, derived from an instruction of the General Assembly.

In 1643 a serious division developed in Scotland over the Solemn League and Covenant by which the Covenanters agreed to assist the Parliamentary opposition to Charles I in England in return for the security of their own regime at home and the assurance of a comparable regime, in church as well as in state, in the other British realms. The agreement was denounced by Montrose who in 1644-45 made a brilliant but ultimately unsuccessful attempt to win back his countrymen in support of the king and the original limited aims of the National Covenant. His campaign took him through Moray where on this occasion he could count on the support of Huntly and the Gordons. But there is little suggestion of any very great enthusiasm otherwise for his cause, rather the reverse after the wanton sacking of Elgin, an atrocity without any of the justification that might be adduced for the ravaging of the lands of Duffus or the burning of Brodie Castle where the owners were at least leading supporters of the other side. When the Covenanters regained control Argyll in turn devastated the Gordon lands in the Enzie, Strathisla, and Strathavon.

In 1649 the troubled career of Charles I came to an end with his trial and execution by his English opponents and it became necessary for the Scottish Covenanters to decide whether to align themselves with the new republican regime or with the deceased king's son. In this situation the crucial factor was the refusal of the English republicans to implement the ecclesiastical obligations of the Solemn League and Covenant. In the 'Engagement' of 1647 Charles I had at least agreed to implement them for a kind of trial period and there was hope that Charles II might be induced to go further and become a 'covenanted King'. This improbable role he finally accepted in 1650 following the failure of a fresh expedition by Montrose on a more purely royalist basis. Thus only a few weeks after his most loyal supporter had passed through Elgin on his way to his execution in Edinburgh — being 'wonderfully cheered', it is pleasant to record, by the kindness of the minister of Duffus — Charles II landed at Garmouth and signed both Covenants.

The regime thus inaugurated lasted little more than a year. By the autumn of 1651 Scotland had been over-run by the English republican forces and in 1653 the country was absorbed in a single British 'commonwealth'. While Scotland was obviously an unwilling partner in this venture and hence placed under a strict military occupation, the English troops and officials behaved moderately well. The destruction of Kinloss Abbey for which they were responsible was to obtain building material for their great citadel at Inverness, most of Fortrose Cathedral being applied to the same purpose, but it was the construction of the fortress rather than the obliteration of these medieval ruins that aroused resentment in the area at the time.

In 1660 Charles II was restored, not as a covenanted king but as an absolute monarch who also controlled the church through a revived episcopal system. An attempt was indeed made to persuade him to agree to a presbyterian settlement but one of the two chief negotiators, James Sharp, a native of Banff, was irresolute and ambitious and emerged from the discussions as Archbishop of St Andrews, thus substantiating the doubts that had been expressed regarding him by one of the few Moray critics of these proceedings, Thomas Urquhart, minister of Essil beside Garmouth. He and a few others were subsequently deprived of their parishes but their efforts to maintain 'conventicles' in rivalry to the official church order met with little response in a region traditionally inclined towards episcopacy and royalism.

*Towards a New Age*

Although the Restoration period tends to be remembered, in southern Scotland at least, for the oppressions of the royal government and the sufferings of the Covenanters who refused to accept its authority, its character was actually rather different. The presbyterian non-conformists, while strongly represented in the south-west and certain other areas, formed a steadily declining minority in the country as a whole and in regions such as Moray and the North-East tended to be outnumbered by the still persisting adherents of the Catholic faith. The polity of the established church was not so very different from what it had been under James VI, a place being found for presbyteries or 'exercises' within its episcopal structure and its congregational life proceeding on the general lines that had prevailed virtually since the reformation.

Thus the regime was more generally acceptable than has sometimes been thought, although the acquiescence which it received arose also from a sheer lessening of the interest in ecclesiastical matters which had so dominated Scottish life since the Reformation. This interest had reached its climax between 1637 and 1651 and seemed to have produced nothing but conflict and failure. If an interest in politics remained, it was beginning to take a more restrained form. But for many Scots such fields of activity as economic enterprise or scientific enquiry seemed to offer prospects more inviting than either politics or religion. As we have seen, this kind of outlook had been characteristic of Moray for some time and one should perhaps be careful not to award it too high a degree of positive merit. The 'moderation' apparent in the reaction of the region to the problems of the preceding age was at least partly due to an inability to view them with the sense of urgent personal involvement apparent elsewhere in Scotland. But it also derived from a humanity which sought to avoid or ameliorate divisions in society over political and religious issues. Of this there is ample evidence beyond the examples that have been mentioned already. Signs of a preoccupation with business affairs are particularly apparent in Elgin. The arcaded buildings that once lined its High Street practically from end to end date from the later 17th century. Almost all were built by merchants and indicate both their prosperity and their awareness of architectural developments elsewhere in Europe. From one of them in the early 18th century William Duff created a highly successful banking business that made him one of the wealthiest men of his day. If the merchants of the preceding period did not attain to quite this degree of affluence they were deeply involved and highly successful in their various enterprises. Such men had clearly too much at stake to run the risks of political or ecclesiastical dissent but to be fair there is little indication of tendencies of this kind on anyone's part in Moray under Charles II or James VII.

This being so, it is perhaps surprising that the Revolution of 1688-90 should have resulted in so many deprivations of parish ministers in the District, especially since active opposition to its establishment had been relatively slight. It suggests that these were in fact men of principle who had supported the old regime from conviction and not from mere acquiescence. Indeed, the respect in which they were held made it difficult for the presbyterians to obtain control of the parish churches when the episcopal incumbents were still supported by their congregations and, as at Elgin, by the municipal authorities. And even when the settlement had been fully implemented, in the early 1700's, the presbyterian establishment had to accept the persistence of a sizeable episcopal church outwith its control. In Moray and the North-East episcopalians and catholics were in fact so numerous that it was beyond the power of the authorities to persecute them even if public opinion had been prepared to sanction this. When suppression came it was because of episcopal and catholic support for the Jacobite cause, as in 1715, and even then was relatively mild by the standards of the 17th century. The heir of the House of Gordon (Dukes since 1684) suffered no more than a short imprisonment for his part in the rising although Lord Duffus was deprived of all his estates and forced into exile, first in Sweden and then in Russia.

The determination of the presbyterian party to root out

recalcitrant episcopalians in Moray after 1690 originated in southern Scotland where the party had suffered severe persecution in the preceding period. But the Revolution Settlement had a positive as well as a negative aspect. As the conscious heirs of the ideals of the early reformers the presbyterian leaders were concerned, among other things, to realise their plans for universal education. Efforts to establish schools in every parish had in fact continued throughout the intervening period, but it was only after a fresh act in 1696 that the project became a reality. These 'parochial schools' led on to the 'grammar schools' that had existed for some time in centres like Elgin, Forres, Banff, and Fordyce, and which prepared promising pupils for the tertiary stage of university education, in this area almost always at King's College, Aberdeen.

The Revolution of 1688 was succeeded by the Union of 1707. By this the Scots agreed to the absorption of their parliament in that of England in return for a share in English trade as members of the new United Kingdom of Great Britain. It is true that the union included safeguards for the continuation of a separate established church, legal system, and form of local government in 'North Britain', but the central feature of the scheme was this straight exchange of political independence for economic advantage. The fact that such an arrangement should have been even remotely acceptable indicates the transformation of the national outlook that had occurred in the preceding period.

That Moray shared in this change is fairly evident. Even if the attitude of the Earl of Seafield in commending the Union as Chancellor cannot be taken as representative, he was probably right in considering that the landowners and burghers of his region were more interested in their own economic concerns than anything else. While the obsession of the former with the 'improvement' of their estates did not become an all-absorbing passion until the post-union period, proprietors like the Gordons of Gordonstoun and quite a few more had begun to think and to act along these lines very much earlier. Indeed, the more the situation is examined the more it becomes apparent that in Moray and elsewhere the conditions that made union possible and which determined the character of Scotland for many years thereafter lay deep in the 17th century.

# 10

# THE 18TH AND 19TH CENTURIES

## DONALD WITHRINGTON

There can hardly have been a period that brought such widespread change in upland and lowland Moray as the 18th and 19th centuries — in the use and appearance of the land, in the style of living of the people, in the relationship between Moray and other parts of Britain. As early as the first years of the 19th century it was being written that "old Moray" had gone: and throughout that century, decade by decade, commentators drew attention to the undeniable distinctiveness and modernity of the times at which they happened to be writing.

No study of these two hundred years can avoid beginning with agriculture. At its beginning the vast majority of Moray folk lived very close to the soil: very few of them indeed did not farm some extent of land, if only to provide a subsistence in food. By the mid-1860's it was estimated that, in 'Elginshire' at least, things had changed: "agricultural pursuits . . . give employment to about half the inhabitants", while the remainder apparently gained a livelihood in commercial and industrial enterprises in villages and towns, both inland and on the coast. This was one of a number of significant changes that accompanied the economic and social reconstruction of Moray within a relatively short historical period: we shall be exploring these changes in this chapter.

The earliest years of the 18th century were indeed years of difficulty. The renowned 'ill-years' of the 1690's brought a time of privation and dearth which affected the parishes in our area very unequally; and these years were followed by a damaging inflation, the threat of national bankruptcy as trade stagnated and widespread vagrancy. The pillaging of lowland parishes and towns, by bands of robber-vagrants from the low country and by hungry highlanders, was widely complained of.

The aftermath of the 1715 rebellion brought little respite to these problems; indeed, after a partial economic recovery in the 1720's and 1730's, there came a series of bad harvests in the early 1740's which were in turn followed by the '45 — a Jacobite rebellion that brought both government and rebel forces through the Moray plain.

*An Age of Improvements*

The period of the 1740's seems to have had two important effects: firstly, after the '45 the traditional raiding of the parishes of the Moray laigh by the highlanders seems to have petered out; secondly, and in the light of the greater security which the end of that raiding brought, a number of Moray landlords were convinced of both the need and the opportunity for improvement on their estates. However, there were many factors which prompted this move towards agricultural reform, and they worked differently and at different speeds in our area: agrarian change, in point of fact, was seldom very sudden and it spread comparatively slowly. The old Statistical Account (OSA) of the 1790's, for instance, indicates that a goodly number of parishes had even then hardly begun on serious improving policies, and at the time the New Statistical Account (NSA) was written in the 1840's improvement was still a quite recent occurrence in several corners.

Local circumstances (including the readiness of the tenantry to co-operate) had always to be taken into account. What is clear from the OSA and NSA reports and from the county agricultural reports of the 1790's and 1810's is that, if the dearth of the 1740's had not convinced both landlords and tenants of the need to do something, then the next threat of famine — in the near-disastrous year of 1782-83 — most certainly did so. In those years, in many parishes, only government aid and the energy of landlords and ministers in obtaining cheap meal saved the inhabitants from starvation. As a result of this near-calamity there was a real beginning to the end of the old-style run-rig farming, and of opposition to consolidation of farm-units, to enclosures and to crop rotation. Another stimulus to improvement was the threat of widespread emigration by tenants (at a time when farm labour was difficult to obtain and when the maintenance of an adequate 'free' workforce was seen as vital

to improving schemes), and this convinced even the most conservative landowners to join the improvers. In 'Elginshire'
and 'Banffshire', indeed, there were good examples of sensible
improvements to follow — especially on the estates of the
earls of Findlater and Gordon. Typical of the economic
philosophies of the later 18th century, both magnates associated
agrarian change with a wide and general economic reconstruction
of their lands: timber plantations were associated with projects
for sawmilling and otherwise working with matured wood; the
introduction of new crops such as flax was accompanied, in
Findlater's case at least, with the provision by him of spinning
wheels to the tenants' wives; the removal of tenants by clearance
and the reduction of pasture by taking common grazings into
cultivation were often related to a sort of magic formula which
was seen as an economic, moral and even spiritual panacea
for later 18th century rural society — namely, the founding
and development of planned villages which would provide local
markets for the produce of the estate and provide employment
and housing for the displaced tenantry.

In 1763 a factor on the Seaforth estates reported (with
reference to upland changes) on the problems which beset an
improving laird: the tenants were very conscious of the in-
security of their situation, they were in no position to share the
landlord's long-term vision and it was they who had to be flexible
in learning new farming techniques or even to change
employments:

> I don't wonder that the present tenants complain of the
> improvements of the hills: 'tis a new thing to them. They
> have not so much room for pasture, their present ideas are
> confined to feeding cattle, but in a few years when they are
> obliged to till more ground and to till it better, less ground
> will maintain their cattle . . . Necessity will first make them
> apply to the raising of corne, and by degrees they'll find the
> advantage of it preferable to pasture and do it of choice.
> Hence it is probable that the tenant will not be hurt and the
> master will have more rent or more tenants. And an increase
> of tenants will give opportunity to form a town and raise
> manufactures.

The North East of Scotland was to provide a host of
instances of outstanding success in promoting new manufacturing
and market villages, with some of the earliest examples in the
counties of Banff and Elgin (later named Moray). A few of the
village settlements in our area pre-dated the mania for founding

villages, but were then — oftener than not — expanded and laid out according to the current fashion. Findhorn, the "port of Forres", was already so active in the 1690's that the magistrates of Elgin determined to found their own port at the mouth of the River Lossie. (Unfortunately for them, by the time that Lossiemouth was established in c. 1703 trade was at its nadir — and the subsequent story of Lossiemouth is one of slow and fitful expansion, in the early 19th century, as a seaside bathing resort rather than as a commercial port, until it took its part in the great explosion of Moray Firth fishing in the later part of that century. When the town, with Branderburgh, was expanded, it followed the highly successful and attractive grid-plan that was so much in favour in the North East.) Burghead, another older settlement, seems to have been rebuilt in the early years of the 19th century. Of the Banffshire fishing stations, Easter Buckie seems to have been first settled c. 1650, Portknockie reputedly dates from 1677, Findochty from 1716, Nether Buckie from 1723, and Portessie from 1727: all were due for expansion and development throughout our period.

Among the more important and eventually successful new village-settlements of the 18th century we find New Keith (c. 1750), soon to be followed by Fife-Keith to its immediate north (as a rival establishment by the earl of Fife to the earl of Findlater's foundation close to the site of an old and decaying village, the so-called Old Keith) — all in a district which also already contained an existing settlement in Newmill. New Keith was a well-known success, as is shown in a report by a general inspector of the Board of Annexed Estates to his masters in 1767:

> My Lord Findlater has, among others equally calculated for the good of the country, carried the plan of erecting villages into execution upon his estate. The surprising effect that it has had in his lordship's village of New Keith, has induced many others to follow his example.

Findlater also founded Rothes in 1766, which, however, remained a residential rather than a manufacturing villiage ("beautiful and picturesque" and somewhat battered in the Moray floods of 1829) until the building of the Grant distillery c. 1840 and its swift expansion thereafter. Especially impressive, even at the time of its establishment, was Fochabers (Plate 4), an attractively laid-out village founded by the duke of Gordon in 1776 — when he cleared away the old haphazardly-grown community from a position close to Gordon Castle and settled its inhabitants in a carefully-planned settlement at a little distance to the south. The grid-plan for Tomintoul was well forward by 1779, while Garmouth and Kingston Port were established as ship-building sites in 1784. Portgordon was laid out in 1797, to take advantage of the expanding fisheries; Hopeman, again with a view to its fishing capabilities, was settled in 1805 (only for it to be written in 1835 that "though regularly built [it] is extremely dirty, and its harbour has been of late allowed to go almost completely to wreck.") But in 1812 Charles Grant of Wester Elchies was much more successful when he planned and built the spacious and attractive village of Charlestown of Aberlour; and this was soon followed by another distillery village and another definite success, the Earl of Fife's founding of Dufftown in 1817. Thereafter, the inhabitants of our area become gradually but increasingly town-dwellers and village-dwellers, bringing about a very distinctive change in life-style for a very substantial portion of the population. The trend is easily seen in the following table (which begins in 1831 because only after then is the necessary information available in the NSA and census returns):

The Morayshire parishes in the early 19th century contained, of course, the already well-established and populous burghs of Elgin and Forres: hence the disparity in Table 6 in the earlier decades, between the Moray and Banffshire returns. What is to be noted here is the way in which the expansion of the Banffshire fisher-towns and distilling sites in the later 19th century brought the counties to an almost identical point by 1901, in those parishes which are within the new Moray District that is.

*Improvements*

The early stimulus to this movement into towns and villages was from the landlords and came directly from their improving policies (see also Chapter 16). In all the improvements which took place, whether quickly or slowly, the landlord was in control. He used the lease directly as an instrument of improvement which could easily support his intentions in law — in his own baronial court (even after 1747 for not all powers were removed from it by the Heritable Jurisdictions Act) and, since the laird was frequently a J.P. as well, in the local quarter-sessions of the justice of the peace. True, landlords could, and too often did,

Table 6

PLACE OF RESIDENCE, 1831 - 1901: TOWN/VILLAGE, RURAL (in percentages)

| | | 1831 | 1841 | 1851 | 1861 | 1871 | 1881 | 1891 | 1901 |
|---|---|---|---|---|---|---|---|---|---|
| Banffshire parishes | Town/Village | 32.5 | 35.4 | 38.1* | 39.8 | 44.7 | 47.8 | 51.3 | 57.0 |
| | Landward | 67.5 | 64.6 | 61.9* | 60.2 | 55.3 | 52.2 | 48.7 | 43.0 |
| Morayshire parishes | Town/Village | 42.9 | 43.1 | 49.0* | 51.8 | 55.9 | 54.7 | 56.8 | 58.0 |
| | Landward | 57.1 | 56.9 | 51.0* | 48.2 | 44.1 | 45.3 | 43.2 | 42.0 |

*The census tables for 1851 do not include returns for all towns and villages: these figures are estimates.

use the lease also to maintain the old feudal services such as bonnage, carriage, thirlage and statute labour on the public roads (such as they were): but, in fact, the close control of their lands did nonetheless promote improvement more successfully than might otherwise have been the case.

It was not until the 18th century itself that the major landlords who were to dominate agrarian reform in Moray and Banffshire — the Gordons, Grants and Duffs, occupying their various lordships, earldoms and dukedoms — really got their hands on substantial areas of the land. Two examples will show what was happening. In Grange in Strathisla there were still, in the early decades of the 18th century, numerous small proprietors who had obtained their parcels of land from the church before or at the Reformation. And Alexander Duff of Braco, progenitor of the earls of Fife, is reported to have said of these minor heritors, in viewing the smoking chimneys of their homes in the strath, that "he would make the smoke of all these houses go through the one vent by and bye": he was so successful in this plan that by 1793 some four-fifths of the parish belonged to the Duffs, with only one small heritage left in the hands of an ancient holder, the remainder having been purchased by the Duke of Gordon. Similarly, in the small parish of Birnie "there were 6 heritors in 1766" but "since that period the Earl of Findlater has purchased all the lands except a croft of about 5 acres", and the new owner "induced his tenants to make considerable improvements in agriculture." Moreover, if these large proprietors were not buying out the older and less wealthy heritors, then they were arranging valuable exchanges of lands with each other, so making it more easy to consolidate their holdings with a view to drainage, enclosure and cropping schemes. In these ways, not least in gaining such a conclusive control of the land itself, these very substantial owners could lead a concerted and astutely-judged movement for improvement: and as they cleared tenants, enclosed fields, built roads and established manufacturing and market villages, they changed the face of the land. Yet improvement did not depend *entirely* on the largest proprietors: there were some smaller lairds who were both pioneering and successful. Of these one of the more obvious examples in Moray is William Young of Burghead, renowned among his contemporaries for reclaiming coastal, sandblown land for a very remunerative agriculture, better known perhaps to us for his later role as a factor on the Sutherland estates (with another Morayan, Patrick Sellar) in the great period of The Clearances there.

By the 1860's it was a common assertion that "perhaps no part of Scotland has been improved so much, in all that pertains to the cultivation of the soil, as this county has been within the past sixty years . . . spirited landlords, enterprising tenants and a Farmers' Society have together brought the cultivation of the soil to a degree of perfection which will bear comparison with that obtained in any other county in the kingdom" (*Moray-shire Described*, p. 7). In wreaking this mighty change, the landlords found help where they could. The Earl of Findlater, for instance, imported at least one Berwickshire man in order to have him instruct local tenants in up-to-date farming methods. The great men were also ready to follow the lead of a number of English commercial companies which came to Moray and Banffshire to exploit the natural resources: such a company opened up the Abernethy/Rothiemurchus forests by floating the timber down the Spey, and helped to found its own or other companies' sawmilling, cartwrighting and shipbuilding interests; there was an early, and none too successful, iron-mining enterprise in upper Banffshire; there was the application of astute business methods in salmon-fishing and curing, and in the shipping of salmon, herring, white fish and shellfish out of the Moray Firth ports to the south, especially to the lucrative London market. Capital, initiative and a spirit of enterprise were all that were needed, it seemed.

The blockade of British ports in the French Revolutionary and Napoleonic Wars also helped to accelerate land-improvements. The restrictions on importing grain — and foreign spirits — pushed corn prices very high and prompted owners to take more and more land into cultivation and to extend the amount that was in arable. In the 1790's and 1800's there was an almost irresistible drive to consolidate farms, to form field systems and to enclose them with turf walls or wooden palings as well as with dykes and hedges. The bad years of 1782-83 had been followed by a substantial emigration to the colonies and to difficulties in replacing tenants on vacant buildings — itself a stimulus to bringing farms into larger units; this brought a scarcity of farm labour which was then made worse by the recruitment of young men into the forces and the militia in

## Table 7

### PARISH POPULATION CHANGES 1755 - 1831

| | 1755 | %± | 1790s | %± | 1801 | %± | 1811 | %± | 1822 | %± | 1831 | %± |
|---|---|---|---|---|---|---|---|---|---|---|---|---|
| Moray District | 47077 | -4 | 45198 | -2 | 44255 | +2 | 45262 | +13 | 51051 | +12 | 57218 | +1 |
| (a) Lowland (21) | 34483 | -5 | 32916 | +1 | 33136 | +2 | 33856 | +14 | 38535 | +12 | 43039 | +3 |
| (b) Highland (9) | 12594 | -2 | 12282 | -9 | 11119 | +3 | 11406 | +10 | 12516 | +13 | 14179 | -4 |
| 'Elginshire' parishes | 27685 | -4 | 26589 | -5 | 25306 | +1 | 25466 | +12 | 28563 | +10 | 31340 | +3 |
| 'Banffshire' parishes | 19392 | -4 | 18609 | +2 | 18949 | +4 | 19796 | +14 | 22488 | +15 | 25878 | -1 |

### PARISH POPULATION CHANGES 1841 - 1901

| | 1841 | %± | 1851 | %± | 1861 | %± | 1871 | %± | 1881 | %± | 1891 | %± | 1901 |
|---|---|---|---|---|---|---|---|---|---|---|---|---|---|
| Moray District | 57951 | +10 | 63874 | +9 | 69795 | +3 | 71623 | +2 | 72948 | +4 | 74875 | +3 | 77816 |
| (a) Lowland (21) | 44297 | +12 | 49406 | +11 | 54773 | +4 | 56812 | +4 | 58904 | +4 | 60977 | +4 | 63447 |
| (b) Highland (9) | 13654 | +6 | 14468 | +4 | 15022 | -1 | 14811 | -5 | 14044 | -1 | 13898 | +3 | 14369 |
| 'Elginshire' parishes | 32278 | +11 | 35835 | +10 | 39275 | +1 | 39699 | +2 | 40618 | -1 | 40396 | +3 | 41541 |
| 'Banffshire' parishes | 25673 | +9 | 28039 | +9 | 30520 | +5 | 31924 | +1 | 32330 | +7 | 34479 | +5 | 36275 |

M

the 1790's. Being scarce and in much demand, farm labour could demand higher and higher wages; and smaller tenants found it increasingly difficult to work their lands for a profit. In turn this led to further amalgamation and still larger farm units, and to an increasingly clear social division between farmer and farm worker. A small plot of land, enough for a potato patch and a cow and a pig perhaps, was all that a cottager needed: he and his family became as dependent on the success of the potato crop as did the farmer on the grain crop (with more and more barley being grown for the widespread illicit distilling before the 1820's and the expanding licensed distilling thereafter). In the 1820's-1840's each met its problems: there were the periodic collapses of the grain market, and poor years of short corn and bad returns, as well as the potato failures of the late 1830's and mid-1840's. By the later 1860's a stronger, more resilient mixed agriculture had been established — not least as dairy produce and increasing supplies of fresh meat were required by a local population that, as we have seen, become more and more concentrated in villages and towns. By 1868 we read that "the breeding and rearing of cattle has now become one of the most important branches of the agricultural industry" while Morayshire was "no less distinguished for the excellence of its sheep than for that of its cattle", as well as maintaining its reputation as a grain area. This mixed economy, and the good local market, enabled the area to survive with fair ease the worst years of the agricultural depression of the late 1870's and 1880's.

*Population Distribution*

How, generally, were these changes reflected in the distribution of population in the 19th century in those parishes which now lie within the bounds of the new Moray District? Was population increasing throughout the area? Let us look at the relevant figures. In Table 7 the parishes have been divided into 'Lowland' and 'Highland' — this latter category comprising nine parishes (Edinkillie and Knockando in Morayshire; Botriphnie, Boharm, Aberlour, Mortlach, Cabrach, Inveravon and Kirkmichael in Banffshire) — and also divided according to the old county boundaries: the percentaged increases or decreases in population are also shown (see also Figure 13).

Note the uniform decrease from 1755 to the OSA returns in the 1790's, when the minister of Mortlach proclaimed the cause as "calamitous eighty-two", forcing widespread emigration abroad and removal to the manufacturing districts of the south: in Alves the minister meanwhile blamed the great scarcity of peat fuel since the mosses there had been worked out. But even where 1782 had not been especially troublesome and where there was plenty of peat available, there was usually still a decrease — because of engrossment of farms, lack of manufactures, the attractions of a military life, and so on. The Lowland/Banffshire increase between the 1790's and 1801 is almost entirely due to the rising fishing villages of Rathven (Buckie, Portessie, Findochty, Portknockie, Portgordon) and to the expansion of Keith. The end of the Napoleonic War brought an emphatic rise in population in all districts, confirming the increased manufacturing and commercial activity of the 1810's and 1820's — spinning and weaving, the knitting of stockings, the bleaching of linens, the milling of flax, hemp and tobacco as well as of grain, shipbuilding (especially in Kingston Port) and sawmilling, quarrying of stone and slate for the building of better houses and the laying down of town and village streets and pavements and the erection of harbours and quays, the quarrying of limestone for burning as fertiliser, increasing trade through the numerous local shops as well as by export from Moray Firth ports, with distant markets, the important sales of salmon and shellfish to the south (even in the early 1840's the Spey fishings in Bellie parish brought in £16,500 p.a. whereas land rentals grossed only £12,500 p.a.)

But by the 1830's spinning and weaving were in decline, there was recession and more emigration — especially from highland parishes such as Boharm or Kirkmichael which suffered clearances, the abolition of subletting of crofts, the suppressing of illicit distilling and smuggling and some bad years for grain and potato crops. (In Birnie, a drop in population between 1831 and 1841 was blamed on a particularly virulent scarlet fever in 1834-35). Thereafter the highland areas were always losing population to the neighbouring lowlands or to the south and overseas: and in the lowland districts population growth depended mainly on the expansion of towns and villages — the later decades of the century saw a boom time in the fishing settlements, especially those in the parishes of Rathven, Duffus and Drainie. The relatively mild climate, good beaches and golf courses, the establishment of fashionable hydropathies such as that at Clunyhill in Forres attracted visitors and long-term residents to coastal and inland resorts alike, more easily reached in the course of the century along vastly improved communications by road and then by rail. Interestingly, we read that in some resort areas goats were kept "for the accommodation of tender people in summer" — perhaps to help their stomachs recover from "taking the waters" in the spas.

If we take the average population of our parishes over the half-century, 1801-51, and compare it with the 1801 figure, then Duffus with its villages of Burghead, Hopeman, Duffus, New Duffus and Portcumming heads the list with an increase of 69 per cent, closely followed by Rathven (the Buckie group of villages) and Aberlour with its quickly-growing village of Charlestown; Elgin, St Andrews, Lhanbryde (a virtual commuter settlement for Elgin) and Dallas rose at the same time by one-third. If we make a similar calculation for the years 1861-1901, again comparing the average with the figure for 1801, then Drainie (Lossiemouth, Branderburgh, Stotfield) shows a population increased three-and-a-half times, Duffus and Rathven a rise of about 290 per cent, Aberlour still holding its place at a two-and-a-half times increase, with Elgin, New Spynie (Bishop-mill) and Keith doubling in size in this later period. Only Dyke and Moy, Rafford and Alves show an absolute loss of population in 1801-1851, and only Dyke and Moy, Rafford and Kirkmichael are on average below their 1801 figures over the period 1861-1901.

*Education*

An increasing population, its readiness to move, the concentration of well-peopled settlements in new districts of a parish, changes in employment, all put old social welfare agencies — for instance, the provision of schooling and parochial relief for the poor — under strain. Add to them the problems of inflation — on the fixed interest returns on investments for the poor and on the virtually fixed incomes of schoolmasters and the difficulties could be severe. Both schooling and poor relief suffered in the later 18th and earlier 19th centuries.

That most perceptive and entertaining writer, author of the admirable General View of the Agriculture of the Counties of Nairn and Moray (London 1813), William Leslie of Balnageith, was minister of St Andrews Lhanbryde from 1783 to 1839 and wrote both the Old and New Statistical Accounts of the parish.

In the 1790's he had this to say about the state of schooling in rural areas:

> It is probable, the ancestors of the present generation of peasants possessed at no period, a much larger stock of knowledge: but since, by the alteration of the times, the salaries of schoolmasters can in no way support a family, that office has fallen altogether into the hands of mere schoolboys, which they abandon as soon as their own education is supposed to be completed, or into that of bankrupt tenants, still less qualified for the duties of it. So that a thicker cloud of ignorance must be settling over the lower ranks of the people, than that which covered their fathers. And while the reputation for learning, which Scotland has so long supported among the nations, must in a short time be lost, those numbers who, by means of that mediocrity of literature acquired in the parish schools, rose from the lowest stations in life to *merit, wealth* and *rank,* must be henceforth chained down, hopeless and inglorious, to the miserable spheres of their humble birth.

Mr Leslie's complaint against the landowners for condoning this situation is muted and restrained in comparison with the anonymous OSA return from Duffus:

> The school here, like those in many other parishes, is neglected; the salary only 7 bolls of barley, and the school fees so small, that nobody thinks it worth their while to accept of it, unless some young lad for a year or two. It seems that the present generation of landholders wish to extirpate learning altogether, in order to introduce ignorance and slavery among the lower class of people, else they would give some encouragement to schoolmasters.

Even in Grange, where the stipend was more than double that of Duffus, the same kind of complaint is found:

> The schoolmasters are frequently changed, owing to the poor encouragement; and the people are, from habit, backward in sending their children to school; they allege, that by the time their children begin to make any progress with a schoolmaster, he is about to remove to a better place or business . . . If the salaries of parochial schoolmasters are not made something better worth the while of a man of liberal education, that most useful institution will soon be abandoned altogether.

Nonetheless, although there may be comments about the low state of education locally, the OSA indicates that a rudimentary education, and normally a good deal more than that, was readily available at low cost throughout the area. The complaints were most frequently about quality rather than availability of schooling, about the restricted curriculum that was taught rather than about lack of any teaching at all. And there were certainly parishes where the school was in good heart (e.g. Keith). The adverse comments we have quoted relate, of course, to parish rather than burgh schools and to schooling for the sons of small tenants and labourers rather than of substantial farmers who could afford to pay boarding fees at a nearby town's public or private grammar school. The major burgh schools, in Elgin and Forres, were well supported (in stipend as well as in pupils), were expanding their curricula into the modern or 'academy' subjects such as French or book-keeping or land mensuration or astronomy or geography — an extension which several of the more active parochial school-masters were also doing — and had a reputation which attracted pupils from a distance (as did some parish schools, e.g. the female school at Dyke which in the late 18th century brought in girls from Caithness).

As incomes rose in the earlier 19th century the numbers of expensive courses in existing schools and the establishment of separate private schools began to increase. A little later, when we have the reports of government enquiries into schooling, made in 1834 and 1838, together with the information from the NSA, it is possible to give a clearer, and probably fairer, picture of the educational situation in Moray. How well schooled was it?

In the late 1830's only two of our thirty parishes had no grammar school at all — Birnie and Dallas: the remaining twenty-eight provided a total of 40. Of these, 32 were official parochial or burgh schools, the 'doubles' being at Pluscarden (Elgin parish) and at Wester Elchies (Knockando); a further 3 grammar schools were supported by agencies such as the General Assembly of the Church or SSPCK (Society in Scotland for the Propagation of Christian Knowledge) — at Burghead (Duffus), Glenlivet (Inveravon) and Deskie (Inveravon). As many as 5 fully-fledged grammar schools were founded on private adventure — Mr G. Crawford's at Elgin; one at Newmills in Alves with a substantial boarding element; the well-known all-boarding school at Calcots (St Andrews) where 27 boys — the sons of heritors and large tenants in the area — were given a full schooling; and two others, one at Bogmoor (Bellie), the other at Moss-side (Rothiemay). Besides these grammar schools there were 56 mixed elementary, one male elementary (or SSPCK school at Archies-town [Knockando]) and 14 female elementary establishments: of these schools, 18 were supported by heritors and/or session and can be designated 'parochial', 16 were supported by the General Assembly or SSPCK and 37 (27 mixed and 10 female) were taught on private adventure.

Even with a total number standing at 71 schools of all kinds, this is probably an underestimate: Drainie is only recorded as having one grammar school, but it is very likely that it supported 3 other schools, Duffus certainly had 2 grammar schools and it may well have had another grammar and 4 female sewing schools, Forres and Elgin doubtless had more schools than the 5 or 7, respectively, of whose existence we are quite sure. All the indications are, indeed, that the area was very well provided with schools in the later 1830's and that they were well utilised.

No doubt one important factor in the improvement in the official parochial schools since the 1790's — all but two now with masters who could teach Latin — was the supplement to parish schoolmasters' salaries by the Dick Bequest, to be obtained however only after a pretty stiff examination. No doubt too the threat of the private academies to their livelihood was a stimulus to the parochial teachers who added French and geography and history, sometimes book-keeping and mensuration, to the standard curriculum. But perhaps this threat was more apparent than real: for a good many of the boarding academies, especially those for females, were "superior" and very expensive and to that extent very exclusive, and concentrated to some degree on would-be gentlemanly and lady-like pursuits, e.g. horseriding, fencing, deportment, Italian, and so on.

It would appear that the Moray District, in both lowland and highland areas — Inveravon had 3 grammar schools, Cabrach one grammar and at least 4 elementary schools, Kirkmichael 2 grammar schools and one other — was, for the time, very well provided in the 1830's and 1840's. In terms of the numbers of schools alone, comparatively little changed after the introduction of the Education (Scotland) Act of 1872 and the era of elected school boards with state backing: in the three cases just mentioned in the early 1890's, Cabrach had 2 public schools, Kirkmichael had 3 and Inveravon provided 4 schools in Glenlivet and 3 in the remainder of the parish. During the 19th century, indeed, it was a mark of Moray and Banffshire that their successful sons — oftener than not making their fortunes in India or the Indies — gave generously towards schoolbuilding, schoolmasters' salaries and bursaries at school and at university for local children: they left monuments to themselves in the fine buildings that were erected out of their monies but they left many more in those (often very poor) children whose lives benefited immeasurably from the free or very cheap school and higher education that they could not have obtained so easily elsewhere.

In comments about the worsening of educational provision in the later 18th century, it is often remarked that it stemmed in part from the break-down of the older, coherent, all but static, parochial society of a century before. This vision of a more idyllic local community in the recent past frequently arises, too, in comment about the changing attitudes to, and by, the poor in the later 18th and early 19th centuries. In particular, just as the ceaseless shifting of farm-labouring groups — taking the opportunity for changing masters in the half-yearly feeing markets which became prominent and important in and after the late 18th century — brought problems of continuing contact with church and school, so too the greater (and increasing) mobility of the poor raised difficulties for the authorities.

*The Poor*

A major problem here was that very few parishes could entirely support even their neediest poor from the parish funds. Many parishes had little or nothing in the way of mortified money and there was, in any case, always the difficulty of finding a secure investment for it. Relief for the poor from church funds relied on the weekly church collections. But, as more and more land came into fewer, socially and politically, greater hands, the main heritors no longer resided in the parish, no longer came regularly to church, no longer gave handsomely in the Sunday collections. During the 18th century, and indeed before then too, the poor were relieved intermittently and to *some* effect from the weekly distributions from the poor's box, but they depended also on the generosity of relatives, neighbours and friends at other times. In a subsistence economy, always liable to the bad harvest years which hit everyone in the locality, the potential poor supported the actual poor. In such a situation local resources might not be able to cope. In 'normal' times, as we read in the OSA return for Birnie, the "aged and infirm must travel beyond the bounds of the parish and implore alms from the charitable".

The support of the deserving through 'wandering' poor always raised problems. Was there enough to aid even the strictly native poor? In fact, the obviously deserving seem to have been well received. But there was another difficulty over the wandering poor — those who were not obviously so deserving, yet settled in the parish. (It was suggested, indeed, that a stiff tax on leather, making it too expensive for these vagrants to obtain shoes would resolve the difficulty!) The Keith minister in the 1790's remarks bitterly about "the great influx of Highlanders who during the summer months range this and neighbouring parishes" and prove "a great encroachment on the truly native poor". But even the temporarily resident highlander was preferable to the 'professional' vagrants, bands of whom might appear and in effect terrorise a neighbourhood. These sorners (to use the old official description of them) were a constant plague in the aftermath of the ill years of the 1690's: we find evidence of their descending on the Moray parishes intermittently throughout the 18th century, oftener than not in times of dearth when food and money were very scarce anyway. They were particularly active and well-organised in the 1820's and 1830's, eventually being driven north as counties to the south organised new-style police forces. In the early 1840's the Knockando minister reports that "the parish is much infested by sturdy beggars and tinkers, especially during the summer season": and in Urquhart, which then had neither J.P. nor constable, it was said that "to give a small matter to vagrants is found to be attended with less trouble and expense" than setting up a police force to deal with them. But by the late 1840's things had improved. A new poor law, state-supported and more stringent, removed some part of the problem: and a small county police force had been set up by then too. There were, of course, vagrants in Moray in the remainder of the century but they were fewer in number and seem to have kept to a 'beat' on which they were recognised and tolerated. Many of the reminiscences of last century retail stories of 'characters' who were in effect vagrants living off their wits and other people's sympathy: they were known and, like the tinkers and other travellers, would always have a tale to tell, some gossip to pass on.

*Conclusion*

There were many other aspects of the changing life of Moray in two centuries of colossal development. For instance, in the early years of the 19th century there was no coach service from Inverness or Elgin to Aberdeen, yet within a space of fifty years, Moray and Banffshire were criss-crossed by turnpike roads and well-made public highways thronged by wheeled traffic and, even more dramatically, had begun on the railway revolution (For details of transport developments see Chapter 16). Again, in the 18th century, much of the trade of our area lay to the north of Scotland and to Holland and was as well supported by the landlords as by the merchants in Elgin and Forres: Forres merchants, indeed, provided a complete shopping service for the inhabitants of eastern Sutherland for it was said that there was no shop in the whole county at that time. By the beginning of the 19th century, the direction of seagoing trade was with the south of Britain — not just with Aberdeen or Leith but with London, and no longer in the hands of the landed groups; and, as direct shipping links were established from the Moray Firth ports, so the coastal parishes could avoid and ignore the Elgin and other old landward markets.

We have seen how in these landward districts there was a growing social distance between landowner and tenant. In the coastal towns too there grew up two communities, very self sufficient and distinct — the fisherfolk and the agricultural commercial population. Indeed, an increasing divisiveness in community life developed apace in the course of the 19th century — wealth brought new social distinctions within the towns, to be reflected in the schools which families used and in the churches they used too, as different sects found growth points in the district; and the growth of a more assertive political party feeling, together with the rapid extension of the franchise, provided further points of division.

It was not only the 'face of the land' that took on a recognisably modern look in these two centuries.

# GENERAL

# 11

# AGRICULTURE AND
# AGRICULTURAL ARCHITECTURE

ISOBEL BROWN and ELIZABETH BEATON

*History*

The earlier history of farming in the Moray District* brings to notice the extreme poverty and simplicity of the lives of those engaged in its pursuit.

Prior to the 18th century, the land was divided into an infield and outfield. The former received all the manure to help produce crops such as oats, bere (a kind of barley) and peas. The infield was cultivated continuously until the crops failed; then it was allowed to lie fallow for one year before being cropped again. Both the outfield and infield were cropped on a basis of shifting agriculture known as the "run-rig" system, whereby the land was divided into rigs or strips allocated in such a way that it was impossible for the tenant to consolidate his holding.

The land was ploughed with the "thrapple plough", drawn by up to six garrons (small light horses). This plough was a primitive construction made of wood apart from the iron share and coulter. It required three people to operate it: two to keep the plough straight and at an adequate depth in the soil and a third walking backwards between the leading beasts. A day's labour with this plough turned over a mere 0.1 hectare (¼ acre). In the second half of the 18th century the lighter two-horse plough was introduced.

Tenants normally rented the land from large landowners or lairds; the tenant in turn could rent land to a sub-tenant. At the foot of this social order was the poor cottar who might have a tiny patch of land of his own amounting to perhaps 0.6 hectares (1½ acres). Rent was paid to the laird mainly in kind by sowing, cutting, gathering, threshing and milling grain, by

*An interesting account of agricultural history may be read in *Commemorating the County of Banff* (see bibliography).

weeding and hoeing and by giving to him quantities of bere, oats, poultry, eggs, pigs, calves, etc. For about eight months of the year tenants and cottars had to work exceptionally long hours, about 15 per day being quite common. For the lairds there were few problems: labour was in abundant supply and wages paid were very low.

Up until the 1780's the land of Moray was unfenced but with fencing came an acceleration of land improvements. By the 1830's a great deal of attention was being paid to artificial fertilisers, e.g. lime was widely used and seaweed was applied to land near the coast. From the middle of the 19th century there was a marked increase in the arable acreage: in the period 1857-70 the amount of arable land in Moray had trebled; few places in Scotland had undergone so much improvement in so short a period. The rapid growth of fishing villages led to a much greater demand for local farm produce whose expansion continued until the general fall in prices in the 1870's, causing great hardship to many families in the area.

In the 19th century reaping of the crop was done by heuk (sickle) or scythe. Grain and straw were separated by the use of a flail, a simple short staff hinged with leather to a handle. The oats were either winnowed in hand riddles or barns were constructed in such a way as to permit a through draught of air carrying the chaff away. Technical advances led to the reaper (back delivery), the binder and the combine harvester which has brought in its wake the grain drier.

*The Land*

The granulites, quartzites and flagstones of Moray do not produce good soils, and where these are the country rocks the land is generally given over to forestry, hill grazing and grouse moor, with little or no population. Farmlands tend to be concentrated on the superficial deposits on the valley floors and on the river terraces and "haughs". This is typical of the lands bordering the Findhorn, the Spey and the Avon. Farther east, apart from the quartzite hilltops, the black schists and limestones provide better soils and farmland is more extensive.

The best soils in the District are in the Laich area, where deposits of silt and clay mark the sites of former lakes and estuaries. One must add that the productivity of the Laich might be as much a factor of climate as of soil. A certain amount of deep draining has to be maintained in the low-lying parts to get the best use of this land, particularly in the old Loch Spynie basin. In parts the soil is light and sandy and considerable soil-blowing can occur in the late spring drought period. Being drought prone a considerable acreage of the area cannot stand too much cropping. Most years a water deficit builds up through summer to around 100 m (4 in) and in extreme years it can reach 180 mm (7 in). By contrast, prolonged rain in the catchment areas of rivers such as the Spey and Findhorn can cause flooding problems along the lowest terraces and coastal lowlands). Extra fertiliser dressings are applied early in the year to counteract the drought, especially on grassland. Not all the land of lower Moray is fertile, and there are many large spreads of fluvio-glacial gravel and areas of old storm beach shingle ridges and blown sand where soils are poor or even non-existent.

*Crops*

On the varied soils of Moray the old pattern of a mixed farming economy still generally persists. Most commonly practised is a six year cropping rotation which includes three years of grass.

However, considerable changes in the pattern of agriculture and the relative importance of crops have taken place during the past fifty years. At the time of writing statistics are available related only to the former county boundaries and those of Moray have been included (Table 8). From these it can be seen that there has been a steady trend towards owner occupation although two-thirds remain tenanted. The number of agricultural units amount to only one-third of the 1912 figure although the average size of a farm unit has almost trebled to c.56 hectares (140 acres), which is well above the average for Scotland. As in other farming counties there is a considerable drop in the number of farm workers employed, a trend that is still continuing. Yet output still goes up because of the increasing mechanisation.

By far the chief crop earlier this century was oats but by the mid 1960's barley had replaced it as the principal cereal. The wheat acreage had increased until 1969 but it is once more on the decline. Barley, when up to the standard required, goes for distilling but in the main is sold for feeding. In the county of Banff in the 1950's up to one-third of the barley crop went to the distilleries. Small acreages of rye used to be grown on the lighter soils. The straw, because of its length, was much sought after

**Table 8**

A SELECTION OF AGRICULTURAL STATISTICS RELATING TO THE COUNTY OF MORAY

| | 1912 | 1938 | 1961 | 1969 | 1972 | Scottish Figures 1972 | Percentage of Scottish Figures for 1972 | 1972 Figures as a Percentage of 1912 Figures |
|---|---|---|---|---|---|---|---|---|
| Acreage of Crops and grass | 98,939 | 95,030 | 91,032 | 92,381 | 90,273 | 4,163,408 | 2.1 | 91.2% |
| Tillage Acreage | 52,675 | 45,329 | 44,547 | 42,925 | 40,171 | 1,449,332 | 2.7 | 76.2% |
| Tillage Acreage as a Percentage of Crops and Grass Acreage | 53.2% | 47.7% | 48.9% | 46.5% | 44.4% | 34.8% | — | — |
| Number of Agricultural Units | 1,715 | 1,449 | 1,041 | 859 | 650 | 37,930 | 1.7 | 37.9% |
| Number of Agricultural Units owned by Occupier | 70 | 230 | 282 | 276 | 225 | 18,019 | — | — |
| Number of Agricultural Units Tenanted. | 1,645 | 1,219 | 759 | 583 | 425 | 19,911 | — | — |
| Percentage Tenanted of Total number of units | 95.9% | 84.1% | 72.9% | 67.9% | 65.3% | 52.4% | — | — |
| Average Size of Unit in acres | 57.7 | 65.6 | 87.4 | 107.5 | 138.8 | 109.7 | — | 240.5% |

**Table 8**—Continued

| | 1912 | 1938 | 1961 | 1969 | 1972 | Scottish Figures 1972 | Percentage of Scottish Figures for 1972 | 1972 Figures as a Percentage of 1912 Figures |
|---|---|---|---|---|---|---|---|---|
| Oat Acreage | 23,588 | 19,455 | 16,850 | 11,622 | 8,706 | 232,978 | 3.7 | 36.9% |
| Barley Acreage | 10,749 | 9,361 | 12,761 | 19,911 | 21,804 | 820,986 | 2.6 | 202.8% |
| Wheat Acreage | 677 | 2,224 | 2,071 | 3,409 | 2,531 | 81,437 | 3.1 | 373.8% |
| Potato Acreage | 1,971 | 1,734 | 3,503 | 1,945 | 1,731 | 90,450 | 1.9 | 87.8% |
| Turnip/Swede Acreage | 14,750 | 10,937 | 7,019 | 3,833 | 3,540 | 136,565 | 2.5 | 24.0% |
| Carrot Acreage | 21 | 104 | 185 | 299 | 249 | 1,947 | 12.7 | 1185.7% |
| Other Vegetable Acreage | — | — | 114 | 174 | 214 | 12,538 | 1.7 | — |
| Small Fruit Acreage | 18 | 30 | 132 | 131 | 157 | 11,358 | 1.3 | 872.2% |
| Total Dairy Animals | 22,331 | 23,311 | 6,283 | 8,557 | 9,076 | 640,933 | 1.4 } 2.0 | 216.6% |
| Total Beef Animals | | | 33,850 | 35,558 | 39,295 | 1,746,722 | 2.2 | |
| Total Sheep | 53,754 | 48,527 | 46,767 | 37,220 | 30,637 | 5,388,741 | 0.5 | 56.9% |
| Total Pigs | 2,426 | 5,190 | 11,507 | 18,015 | 19,260 | 666,074 | 2.8 | 793.8% |
| Total Number of employed full-time Workers | — | 2,047 | 1,479 | 899 | 897 | 36,900 | 2.4 | (43.8% of 1938 figures) |

N

for roofing thatched cottages. Grass as a crop has become more important and the increasing use of silage has seen a decline in the acreage of swedes and turnips grown, but there are signs that this trend has been arrested. Early this century some flax was grown and processed into a coarse type of linen from which sheets were made. For a number of years small amounts of sugar beet were grown, the green tops of the beet providing a valuable early winter feed. Growing stopped when the Scottish beet factory was closed down. Potato growing is mainly in the hands of a few specialist growers whose product caters for a thriving trade to England in high quality seed. Yet, the potato acreage in recent years has shown a continuing decline, because many of the small scale producers have given up business.

*Stock*

Moray, particularly its uplands, has long been renowned for the fine stock produced and this is reflected in the sales at market centres such as Keith and Elgin. To many it is regrettable that there has been a marked decline in the number of herds of pedigree cattle of Aberdeen-Angus and Shorthorn breeds (Plate 24), largely because of the expense involved. The number of beef animals reared shows a steady increase; the stock is of a very high standard and many would argue that the best quality beef in Britain originated in the Laich o' Moray.

Around the bigger population centres of Buckie, Keith, Elgin and Forres there are several large dairy enterprises. Ayrshire and Friesian cattle supply the demand for milk which is both retailed directly and sent to creameries. The numbers of dairy cattle are still increasing although the number of producers is declining.

Specialists play their part in the breeding and rearing of pigs many of which are fattened under contract with factories. The increase in the number of pigs is now levelling off; pig populations are very volatile and go in cycles depending on economic circumstances. A number of poultry units, mostly batteries, have been built for egg and broiler production.

By the 1790's the small light sheep of the Moray District were being replaced by heavier breeds such as the Linton. Sheep breeding for cross-bred lambs is practised but is on an insufficient scale to supply the needs of farms on the low ground where half-bred and Cheviot ewes are the most popular. Lambs, to feed as hoggs and to bring out as ewe hoggs, are brought in at the autumn sales. Only on the hill areas is the Blackface variety found. The steady decrease in numbers of sheep reared over the past half century appears now to have been arrested. The upland moors can carry flocks of sheep but there is considerable competition for land from afforestation and sporting interests, so that very few areas actually have ewe flocks.

*Horticulture*

An important fillip to the fruit growing industry (particularly raspberries and strawberries) has been the commercial success of Baxters of Speyside. Table 8 shows that there has been a steady increase in the acreage under small fruits.

*Doo'cots and Farm Buildings in Moray*

Undoubtedly the oldest type of farm buildings extant in Moray is the freestanding doo'cot, examples of which can be found dating from the late 16th to the early 19th century, thus constituting the widest chronological range of any one type of secular building within the District, and incidentally comprising the most northerly group of "cotes" within the United Kingdom. Several forms are to be found, each with individual features. They vary in size and the number of birds they can accommodate, the smallest having 32 nesting boxes and the largest well over 800. A wall, lined from floor to apex with hand-dressed stone boxes, as at Burgie or Wester Elchies, is an impressive sight.

The beehive doo'cot is usually considered the oldest type. Two good examples remain at Gordonstoun and at New Elgin (Plate 25). Stone-built with gable ends, the rectangular cotes at Pittendreich and New Spynie are unique. The large stone roofing slabs from Dallas measure approximately 91 cm wide by 76 cm deep (3 ft x  2 ft 6 in). They are supported on the gables by two stone arches springing from the walls, constituting a kind of segmented "pack-saddle" roof.

Of the lectern variety of doo'cot, peculiar to Scotland and to the south of France, there are several examples: Burgie, Findrassie (dated 1631), Knockando, Leitcheston, Milton Duff, Edinglassie and Reccletich (these last two ruinious). Knockando and Leitcheston are very similar, but Leitcheston is sub-divided internally into four small chambers and has 660 nesting boxes as opposed to 400 in the former.

Cylindrical doo'cots at Greenbank, Pitgaveny and Orton

(this last with existing potence) date from the late 17th or early 18th century, as do the rectangular ones at Wester Elchies and Ballindalloch (dated 1696) and the square one at Rothiemay. Later cotes, like the hexagonal one at Grangehall and the tall, rectangular one at Mains of Seafield are, in effect, pigeon lofts with accommodation for the birds in the upper part of the building. Burnside of Duffus and Lesmurdie House both have small cotes built in the early 19th century. By this time the birds were being farmed as much for their valuable manure and for the sport of trap shooting as for their flesh.

In the garden of Urquhart Manse there is an unusual early 19th century doo'cot built of clay-dab, a composite of clay, straw and small pebbles much used in the Urquhart/Garmouth/ Spey Bay area, there being little stone close by.

The practice of building freestanding cotes died out by the end of the first quarter of the 19th century, but accommodation for some pigeons continued to be provided, and entrance holes are frequently to be seen in the gable ends of stables and farm buildings constructed throughout the rest of the century.

Most farm steadings in Moray reflect the culmination and success of the agricultural "improvements" initiated in 18th century Scotland which were established by the mid 19th century. Impressive sturdy ranges of stables, granaries, cowhouses, cart-sheds and "chaumers" (living accommodation for the unmarried male farm servant), stone built, roofed with pantiles, stone slabs, or, after the opening of the Caledonian Canal, with Ballachulish slates. Later in the century Welsh slates were used. The masonry is of excellent quality, with dressed stone lintels and arches to cart sheds, corners rounded where beasts might rub and then corbelled out on the square near the wallhead (Kaim and Drumbain). Sometimes the mortar courses are galleted (decorated with tiny fragments of slate or stone), as at Inverugie. In the Laich and the richer cornlands of the District the steadings are usually large and symmetrically planned in a square "U" shape, "E" shape or a hollow square. This square was frequently roofed over later for under-cover wintering of cattle. Sometimes the hollow square gives scope for grandoise entrances capped with tower and weather-vane e.g. Rothes Glen. In the uplands the buildings reflect the sparser land and poorer returns. As a result they are usually less spacious and claim no pretentions to architectural exuberance.

To motivate threshing machines water wheels are found on many farms situated on a slope and near water (Shougle), while farms without water power had horse mills. A feature of the larger farms in the Laich of Moray were the Horse Engine Houses, circular, hexagonal or octagonal buildings sheltering an overhead shaft and two or three pairs of horses. The internal diameter of these buildings is usually 9 m to 10.5 m (30 ft to 35 ft) and the walls are pierced with openings to allow air to circulate, thus keeping the building and the working horses cool. Circular horse engine houses remain at Woodlands, Channonry and Pitgaveny. Hexagonal ones with pantile roofs are found at Coltfield Mains and an octagonal building at Innes Home Farm has nicely proportioned arcades on its seven outside walls and the roof topped with lead finial. A good many more of these horse engine houses have been demolished.

Water and horse power were succeeded by steam evidenced by the tall farm chimneys at Earnhill and Cothall. Where chimneys have been taken down the large engine house remains with capped chimney which has been seen to serve as a useful bullpen!

At Rothiemay there is a unique 17th or early 18th century kilnbarn, while there is an unusual range of farm buildings in the Round Square at Gordonstoun (Plate 23) and the contemporary half round at Dallas Lodge, both built by Sir Robert Gordon of Gordonstoun at the end of the 17th century. The Round Square is a hollow, circular building with an internal diameter of 42.75 m (139 ft), arched entrances, a roof line varied with different heights, covered with stone slabs from Dallas and decorated with corbie steps. Seen in evening light, reflecting brown, grey and gold from its roof and rubble masonry, with its impressive proportions and simple lines, it is indeed outstanding.

Letterfourie has an elegant, Adamesque granary capped with a cupola, decorated with the Gordon Arms and dated 1776. Another good granary, later in date, is at Kinloss, a worthy successor to the farming tradition established there by the Cistercians in the 12th century. Blairs has a complete steading built in an Italianate style in the early 1900's — convincing on a hot summer's day but incongruous against a grey winter sky!

Drystone dykes and enclosing fields are of good workmanship

and serve well where maintained. Those in the Findhorn valley are built of stones smoothed by glacial action, giving the surface texture a "velvety" appearance. In the Fochabers area some dykes have turf copings, and in Garmouth clay dab walls are to be found.

What a contrast today's steadings provide with those of bygone days: concrete buildings roofed with asbestos, big enough to house the stock, their feed needs and the new large farm machines, presenting a very different picture to the old stone walled and slate roofed buildings with small and low doorways.

In conclusion to this chapter one must add that the National Farmers' Union, Farmers' Clubs and Young Farmers' Clubs have provided a splendid service and stimulation to the welfare of the District's agricultural interests. The advisers of the North of Scotland College of Agriculture have been of inestimable help to the farming community in connection with crop husbandry, the use of fertilisers, the testing of soil and the preparation of plans for new farm buildings. Throughout the history of farming in the area one must not overlook the significance of the role played by the farmworkers: their skill, their interest, their diligence and their loyalty.

*Doo'cots in Moray*

| | | | | |
|---|---|---|---|---|
| 1. | Burgie | (map ref. | | NJ033593) |
| 2. | Burnside of Duffus | ( " | " | NJ170697) |
| 3. | Ballindalloch | ( " | " | NJ178367) |
| 4. | Dalvey | ( " | " | NJ004586) |
| 5. | Edinglassie | ( " | " | NJ423387) |
| 6. | Findrassie | ( " | " | NJ194654) |
| 7. | Grangehall | ( " | " | NJ062608) |
| 8. | Gordonstoun — Beehive | ( " | " | NJ184690) |
| 9. | Gordonstoun — Windmill | ( " | " | NJ187693) |
| 10. | Greenbank of Letterfourie | ( " | " | NJ442613) |
| 11. | Kininvie | ( " | " | NJ399441) |
| 12. | Knockando | ( " | " | NJ204426) |
| 13. | Leitcheston | ( " | " | NJ399626) |
| 14. | Lesmurdie | ( " | " | NJ215636) |
| 15. | Milton Duff | ( " | " | NJ182602) |
| 16. | Mains of Seafield | ( " | " | NJ516668) |
| 17. | New Spynie | ( " | " | NJ183643) |
| 18. | New Elgin | ( " | " | NJ220618) |
| 19. | Orton | ( " | " | NJ314534) |
| 20. | Pittendreich | ( " | " | NJ195614) |
| 21. | Pitgaveny | ( " | " | NJ239652) |
| 22. | Recletich | ( " | " | NJ286348) |
| 23. | Rothiemay | ( " | " | NJ555484) |
| 24. | Urquhart Manse | ( " | " | NJ283627) |
| 25. | Wester Elchies | ( " | " | NJ256432) |

*Farms mentioned in the script (in order of writing)*

| | | | | |
|---|---|---|---|---|
| 1. | Kaim | ( " | " | NJ156679) |
| 2. | Drumbain | ( " | " | NJ270499) |
| 3. | Inverugie | ( " | " | NJ154684) |
| 4. | Rothes Glen | ( " | " | NJ254526) |
| 5. | Shougle | ( " | " | NJ211511) |
| 6. | Woodlands | ( " | " | NJ210640) |
| 7. | Channonry | ( " | " | NJ231630) |
| 8. | Pitgaveny | ( " | " | NJ240651) |
| 9. | Coltfield Mains | ( " | " | NJ118642) |
| 10. | Innes Home Farm | ( " | " | NJ280646) |
| 11. | Earnhill | ( " | " | NJ013608) |
| 12. | Cothall | ( " | " | NJ019549) |
| 13. | Rothiemay | ( " | " | NJ555484) |
| 14. | Gordonstoun | ( " | " | NJ184690) |
| 15. | Dallas Lodge | ( " | " | NJ109528) |
| 16. | Letterfourie | ( " | " | NJ446625) |
| 17. | Kinloss | ( " | " | NJ065615) |
| 18. | Blairs | ( " | " | NJ028551) |

# 12

# FORESTRY

## ALASTAIR SCOTT

Anyone who has looked at the peat workings beside the moorland road from Dallas to Knockando or at many other cutover or eroded hill peats must have wondered at the old whitening stumps in such a treeless landscape. They are the ghostly remains of the "Atlantic" forest which some seven thousand years ago covered all but the high tops of the region. In the hill peats the stumps are mainly Scots pine, or Scotch fir to give the tree its older name. Immediately identifiable remnants of birch, heather and other plants can also be found, although a comprehensive understanding of earlier vegetation is dependent on laboratory techniques like pollen analysis. On the foothills and the plains of Moray the trees were predominantly oak, with elm, hazel, gean, bird cherry and other broadleaf trees; the hungry sands and gravels of the plain probably grew Scots pine and birch, while the wettest areas then, as now, supported alder, willow and ash. The Statistical Accounts, Old and New, make numerous references to trees in peat cuttings. To quote a few parish entries at random — "some large trunks of oak and fir are dug out of the mosses, of these the inhabitants make very strong couples and lath for their houses", (Birnie); "Fossil oaks have been found and of great dimensions" (Drainie); "Oak and fir roots, and sometimes whole trees, have been found embedded in the mosses. Hazel nuts have been found at the depth of twelve feet" (Knockando).

What is known about the disappearance of the forest from a combination of natural causes — accumulation of peat, wildfires — and the actions of man and his stock — has been reviewed by a number of recent authors, for example Fraser Darling, Steven and Carlisle, Anderson, and McVean. It has proved difficult to disentangle the causes but everywhere the effect has been re-markable — to reduce the natural forest to a handful of relict

sites. Places like the oakwoods of Letterewe by Loch Maree,
the Assynt birch woods, Rassall Ashwood at the head of Loch
Kishorn, and the remnants of the Caledonian pinewood such as
at Abernethy, Glenmore, Rothiemurchus, Dulnain or Glen
Feshie are as important to the forest ecologist as say, Skara
Brae is to an archaeologist. There are, regrettably, no such
prizes in Moray, but wherever native tree species appear in
some quantity they may well have an interesting pedigree. These
are the native trees: -

Oak, *Quercus petraea* and *Quercus Robur;* Birch, *Betula
alba;* Alder, *Alnus glutinosa;* Hazel, *Corylus avellana;* Aspen,
*Populus tremula;* Ash, *Fraxinus excelsoir;* Elder, *Sambucus
nigra;* Holly, *Ilex aquifolium;* Blackthorn, *Prunus spinosa;* Gean,
*Prunus avium;* Bird Cherry, *Prunus padus;* Rowan, *Sorbus
aucuparia;* Whitebeam, *Sorbus spp;* Crab apple, *Malus sylvestris;*
Hawthorn, *Crataegus monogyna;* Wych elm, *Ulmus glabra;*
Willows, *Salix spp;* Scots pine, *Pinus sylvestris;* Juniper, *Juniperus
communis.*

Among sites of particular interest are these: The copse-
wood oak just west of Elgin (mentioned by James Donaldson
in 1794 as being in "a thriving state"), the oakbank
at Kellas (a remnant of an extensive oak wood over the Wangie
Hill), the banks of the Findhorn from Dulsie Bridge downstream,
the birch woods along Avonside, particularly the bird cherry, a
fine stand of juniper above Downan Wood, Drumin, and inaccessible crags like the Eas of Glenlatterach, where vegetation
has survived out of reach of fire, tooth, and saw.

Climate and weather are discussed in detail in Chapter Two.
It is sufficient to say here that, for tree growth, the most
important features are the length of the growing season and the
total warmth during that period, the balance between rainfall
and transpiration, the occurrence of late or early frosts, and
wind.

A glance at the fascinating maps prepared by Birse & Dry
show immediately that, in these terms, there are important
variations from the warm, relatively sheltered but overdry coast,
to the high hills where water is plentiful but summer warmth is
much less and wind a constant hazard. Even within these climatic
"zones", the elevation or the aspect of a particular site has an
important bearing on tree growth.

Geology and land use are discussed in Chapter One and it is again sufficient to say here that from the earliest times forestry has usually been confined to soils unsuitable for agriculture, because they were too shallow, wet, steep, stony or hungry. By and large this has meant that forests occupy four major land types: the flanks and gently rounded tops of the lower hills, the steep slopes of the river valleys, infertile fluvioglacial sands and gravels, and the acid coastal flats. It so happens that there is in Moray a substantial area of such land closely interspersed with excellent agricultural land. It may be that the property associated with the latter has been the main factor in the development of plantations from the 1680's onwards. Whatever the reason, travellers during the second half of the 18th century, like Donaldson, Pococke, and Newte had much to report. Here is James Donaldson in 1794: "From the diversity of ground . . . . . in the low parts of districts, perhaps no country of so wide an extent in Scotland, afforded so much the means of establishment by ornamental plantations. The Earl of Fife . . . . . displayed the superiority of his taste in selecting and planting such uncultivated rising grounds, as he judged would contribute most to this effect. The Earl of Findlater and other proprietors, soon followed his lordship's examples; and, to so great an extent is this mode of improvement now carried on, that, it is possible, the whole of the grounds inaccessible to the plough, in the low lands of Moray, will soon be covered with all the different species of forest trees, propagated in the Kingdom". Among the areas mentioned are Arndilly, Auchlunkart, Green Hill Deskford, Hill of Mulderie, Kenninvie, (sic) Innes House, Logie, Relugas, Cuthall (Altyre), and Lochnabeau. Scots pine was the chief species, though European larch was often mixed with it, and the more exacting oak or elm, or other broadleaf trees were sometimes introduced once the pine had become established. Around the houses and in the policy woods a wider range of trees was being tried. This bald list of trees on offer in 1763, from John Home's nursery at Banff should be read as a shorthand history of the era: English oak, American oak, Silver fir, balm of Gilead fir, larch, spruce, fir, pinaster, Weymouth pine, Cedar of Lebanon, Virginian red cedar, American white spruce, Tulip tree, American bird cherry, laurel and sweet bays, Horse chestnut, beech, Scotch fir, ash, elm, gean, hornbeam, American white ash, service tree.

The New Statistical Account of Scotland (1845) and numerous 19th century authors show the establishment of plantations continuing on large and small estates alike with an increasing range of planting stock available thanks to the intrepid expeditions of such as the Scotsman David Douglas. The fir which bears his name was introduced in 1827, the Deodar cedar in 1831, Monkey puzzle extensively in 1844, the first major consignment of Sitka spruce in 1852, and the Wellingtonia in 1852.

For many of the proprietors they were heady, affluent days — read for example the factor's account of the "improvement" of Aberlour, Edinvillie and Buchromb in the years 1887-89. It is to such activity that we owe many striking punctuation marks in the landscape of Moray. Think for example of the fine trees round Arndilly House, Gordon Castle, Ballindalloch, Drunnuir, Forglen, or Cullen House, of the superb beech shelter belts at Westertown, of the avenues at Brodie (sadly knocked about in the 1953 gale), of the Findhorn valley past Logie, Relugas, Dunphail and Altyre, especially the magnificent European Silver fir above Randolph's Leap, and the giant Douglas fir at Relugas —the tallest tree in Moray? — of the splendid European larch at Innes House, of the red-barked Scots pine surrounding the loch and providing the proper shelter for rhododendron at Blackhills, of the tall Sequoia at Carron, of the treescape of Forres, particularly the shapely Monkey puzzle at Park Hotel and the Spanish silver which stands beside it.

Most of these examples are policy woods or individual trees, but the broad areas of plantation were and are of equal importance in the landscape of Moray. It would be a very different countryside without, for example, the Altyre Woods, or the Pitgaveny plantations or, though they lie outwith Moray, the trees of Darnaway. The extensive planting or replanting of these years was some counterweight to the earlier massive felling of the old pine forests in Upper Speyside (mainly outside Moray) so vividly documented by Elizabeth Grant of Rothiemurchus.

There is not space here to tell the dramatic story of rafting timber down the turbulent Spey or the rise and fall of Kingston. It must suffice to quote an inscription:

In the Year 1783

WILLIAM OSBOURNE ESQUIRE

Merchant of Hull, purchased of the Duke of Gordon, the
forest of Glenmore the whole of which he cut down in the
space of twenty years and built during that time, at the mouth
of the River Spey, where never vessel was built before, forty
seven sail of ships, of upwards of 19,000 tons burthen. The
largest of them 1050 tons and three others little inferior in
size, are now in the service of His Majesty and the Honourable
East India Company. This undertaking was completed at the
expense (of labour alone) of above £70,000. To his Grace the
Duke of Gordon this plank is offered as a specimen of the
growth of one of the trees by his Grace's most obedient
servant.

Hull      September 26      1806                William Osbourne

The 19th century saw the upsurge of two populations that
no forester can look at ambiguously. In the words of C. F. Gordon
Cumming of Altyre, "although rabbits were tolerably numerous
along the sea coast, they were so scarce in the Woods that their
occasional appearance was noted with interest". This was before
1816. In 1840 a Norfolk rabbit catcher killed 7,000 rabbits in the
Altyre Woods. The red squirrel, near extinction in the late 18th
century, had returned in such numbers and was so destructive
that 14,123 were killed at Cawdor between 1862-78. Changed
days too when Sir Archibald Dunbar of Duffus could note the
arrival of a pair of woodpigeons as an interesting topic for the
naturalist in the 1870's.

The Moray forests have suffered a number of catastrophies.
Besides the notorious floods of 1829, there was severe wind
damage in 1879, large fires at Culbin in 1915 and 1938, and at
Teindland in 1942, and the Great Gale of 31st January, 1953 is
not likely to be forgotten, but the two worst "disasters" were
the fellings required in the national interest during the 1st and
2nd World Wars. During 1914 - 18 over 12,000 hectares (30,000
acres) were felled within the old counties of Moray, Nairn and
Banff. Since, on even the best soils available to forestry, current
rotations are not shorter than 45 years and many owners prefer
to leave their pine plantations for over a century before felling,
much of the contemporary treescape of Moray derives from the
replanting of these areas during the '20s and early '30s.

A roll call of the Estates represented at the first meeting of
the Moray and Nairn Foresters Society in 1927 shows a

remarkable continuity from the earliest plantations to the present
day: Altyre, Blackhills, Blervie, Burgie, Castle Grant, Dalvey,
Darnaway, Dunphail, Elgin, Forres, Glenferness, Gordon Castle,
Innes, Lethen, Logie, Orton, Pitgaveny, Pluscarden, Rothes (Seafield), Wester Elchies. Matthew Freaks of Darnaway was the
first Chairman. John McEwen of the recently formed Forestry
Commision was the first secretary, heralding a major change,
state involvement in forestry, and the beginning of the happy
partnership of the past 50 years. The first aquisitions of the
Forestry Commission, much of it felled woodland, were at
Monaughty, Culbin and Teindland between 1920 and 1924. Now
the holding is some 21,000 hectares (59,000 acres) in Moray
District. In the same area well managed privately owned
plantations cover about 15,000 hectares (40,000 acres). The
Commission areas are grouped into four forests called Laigh
of Moray, Speymouth, Craigellachie and Glenlivet, with centres
at Newton, Balnacoul, Archiestown, and Tomintoul respectively.

This period has seen the gradual change from a silviculture
based mainly on the Scots pine, European larch, and Norway
spruce — the dominant trees of the northern European forest —
to one based on those conifers from, mainly, Western North
America, mentioned earlier as being introduced experimentally
a hundred years ago or more but now proven as hardy and
productive in our conditions. The most important are Sitka
spruce, Douglas fir, Grand fir, Western Hemlock and, within
the last years, Lodgepole pine. The development of ploughs
tailor-made for forestry has had much to do with this change.
Now wet moors can be drained, and hard hills cultivated so that
trees have enough soil in which to grow. As a consequence the
planting limit has been pushed up to at least 400 metres (1,300 ft)
above sea level and as far as 530 metres (1740 ft) if the site is
sheltered by yet higher ground to the west. The highest
plantations are in the Glenlivet Forest just below the summit
of Carn Daimh at 570 metres (1866 ft). Typical new moorland
planting can be seen, for example, from the old Mannoch track
between Knockando and Shougle: The writer in the 1842
Statistical Account of the parish of Grange noted that "Even
the mossy and healthy hill of Aultmore is rapidly creeping
under the plough". He would be astonished to see the hill
today for he believed that "there is much soil which no tillage
will ever make good".

A spectacular demonstration of the change can be seen at Findlay's Seat, Teindland. Here research into the treatment of the north-eastern moorlands has been going on continuously since 1922. The experimental plantations are classics of their kind and a mecca for foresters far and wide. Cheek by jowl with one of the most dramatic is a patch of untreated moor deliberately left so that visitors may see 100 year old pine not much larger than tall bushes.

Research work showed early on the critical shortage of phosphate in many of the Moray moorlands, so that the application of phosphate has become nearly routine at planting time. Sometimes this is insufficient, especially when the young trees are in competition with luxuriant heather for available supplies, and aerial fertilising may be necessary. The sandy soils of the coastal forests are a special case. Absorbing detailed work by the Macaulay Institute at Culbin has shown both the characteristic shortage of nitrogen and the dramatic response of the pine to its application. Treatment of plantations on these sites is now routine.

The instinct of earlier foresters that they should use seed from particularly well formed or vigorous trees was sound, and this generation of foresters in Moray must thank their predecessors that so much of the Scots pine they planted came from the Altyre Woods or other local areas of similar quality. The science of forest genetics is however comparatively young, being pioneered in this country by John Matthews, now Professor of Forestry at the University of Aberdeen. Newton, near Elgin, is an important centre for the painstaking laborious work involved, made the more difficult because of the time lapse before results are apparent. Part of the work of the forest geneticist is to collect grafts from trees interesting for their size, form, or history, and to plant out the grafts in a "tree bank". Should anything happen to the parent tree, a replica is secure. The national Scots Pine Tree Bank is at Newton.

Trees are not of course the only occupants of the forest, and timber is not the only product. The name Deer Park is a reminder that the first "management" of the natural forest, by the Normans, was principally to benefit the chase. When the Gordon Castle Deer Park was established, probably in 1725, the fallow deer might have been equally for ornament and for sport, but trees were there mainly as browse. The park no longer exists as such, though a few descendants of the stock are occasionally to be seen.

Red deer live mainly on high hills to the south, but a few beasts occur in the lowlands, descendants of introductions at Pitgaveny this century. The delicate, shy, roe deer has benefited most from the extension of woodland. Too many mean damage to the plantations and legitimate complaints from neighbouring farmers and so their numbers are controlled.

Other indigenous creatures of the old Caledonian pinewood such as red squirrel, capercailzie, crested tit and the plants particularly associated with the pines such as twinflower, creeping ladies' tresses and the lesser twayblade have found a secure refuge in the new forests. There are persistent reports that even the pine marten may have reached Moray. Totally unwelcome would be the grey squirrel. This pest appeared on Deeside during 1973 in its remorseless northern spread.

As soon as people had leisure they have liked to use the forests — particularly the older woods and edges — for relaxation. The woods near Fochabers for example, are laced with pathways first laid out by the Dukes of Gordon and used extensively by the people of the village. The Oakwood, just west of Elgin, has fulfilled the same purpose for many years now, and belongs to the town, as do the developing woods at Millbuies.

Owners, where the sporting requirement is not too intense, have been generally tolerant of people in their woods, though they become understandably irritated when the privilege is abused and litter and vandalism leave their sorry marks behind. The Forestry Commission has recently developed forest walks and picnic areas at Torrieston (Monaughty Forest Walks), just east of Fochabers (The Winding Walks), and in Burghead Bay (Roseisle).

The climate and soils of lowland Moray are admirably suitable for growing young trees (Plate 4) and forest nurseries have been established here for many years. Reference has already been made to John Home's nursery in Banff in the mid 18th century. John Grigor, the author of an invaluable account of forestry in his era, founded the nursery at Forres in 1826. It has been in the Christie family since 1922. Another Christie in 1820 founded the Fochabers nurseries which still maintain a fine tradition. There is too a major and expanding nursery at Seafield Estate, Cullen, and many other smaller estate nurseries grow plants for their own use. The nursery at Newton, started in 1931, is one of the largest in the Forestry Commission. Each year some 25 million young trees leave the Moray nurseries, sufficient to stock about 11,000 hectares (27,000 acres).

A number of age old nursery practices have changed with the past decade. Irrigation is used more and more to minimise the effect of dry spells; cold storage of plants eases the rush at the end of April, and techniques borrowed from the farmer have helped to reduce weed problems. No doubt there are more changes on the way, but there is no substitute for the dedicated, green fingered nurseryman.

Major changes have taken place too in the harvesting of the wood and the destination of the products. The light axes and crosscut saws which the Canadians brought to fell the Orton woods in the last war, have given way to chainsaws, the garron to the universal tractor, the man to the mechanical loader, the horse-drawn bogey to the articulated lorry. New tools and techniques are waiting in the wings drawn from those countries, Scandinavia in particular, where the economy is heavily dependent on the forests and self interest demands research and development on a major scale. Some 81,000,000 kg (80,000 tons) of timber are removed from the Moray woodlands each year. Half of this goes to the pulp mill at Fort William, or to chipboard factories in the south. Much of the rest is sold to local mills, particularly Riddochs of Rothiemay at Mosstodloch and James Jones & Sons (of Larbert) at Forres, both firms with a long and fine tradition in the North-East, not only of sawmilling but of woodcutting.

Since the last war successive governments have agreed that forestry in private land must be supported. The reasons are not hard to find. Britain imports over 90% of its timber requirements. Imports are principally from countries which have "mined" their natural forests. Prices for home grown wood have thus reflected these costs of harvesting and shipping, not the cost of growing trees here or abroad. Even the world's natural forests, however, are not inexhaustable and the Food and Agricultural Organisation of the United Nations is forecasting a world shortage of timber by the year 2000.

No account of forestry in Moray would be complete without a particular mention of the work at Culbin. The story is well known of how, during the last half of the 17th century, the

Barony of Culbin was overwhelmed by sand and the unfortunate owner, Alexander Kinnaird, already embarrassed by debts was obliged to petition Parliament to reduce the cess, or land tax. The story has lost nothing in the telling about the fertility of the estate, the size of the mansion house, the character of Alexander Kinnaird or the supernatural circumstances surrounding the occasion.

For 250 years the north-east section of the contemporary Culbin Forest was a true desert — the sand dunes up to 30 metres (100 ft) in height — and a happy hunting ground for collectors of arrowheads and the like (see Chapter 6). From 1840 onwards proprietors neighbouring the sands, particularly Robert Grant of Kincorth, and Major Chadwick of Binsness established wide shelter belts of pine and larch. From 1922 onwards the area was acquired by the Forestry Commission and plantations were gradually established over the entire sand system. Work started to the west of the dunes so that each new planting contributed to the shield between dunes and prevailing south-west wind. Initially the sand was fixed by planting marram or bent, latterly by "thatching" with enormous quantities of branchwood. Major Chadwick had demonstrated the possibilities of Corsican pine in this situation, as well as the traditional Scots pine, and the confidence of early foresters in the tree has proved entirely justified. Conversely, they were right to abandon after trial the maritime or pinaster pine that had proved so successful in a similar role in the Landes area of south-west France.

The Moray forests and woodlands today are therefore as they have been for nearly 300 years, the raw material for a highly competent industry, but they are many other things besides. No likely future will reduce the demand for timber products, or the dependence of the British market on imports. Even Moray, the most heavily forested District in Scotland, with over one-fifth of the land surface under trees, and three times more than the Gt. Britain average, is well below the European mean. The technology and expertise exist to plant many thousands of hectares in open hill ground in Moray. To the foresters the "Atlantic" forest restored is an exciting and challenging vision.

O

# 13

# THE FISHING INDUSTRY

## MALCOLM GRAY

On a coast that fronts upon a sea so productive as the Moray Firth the catching of fish is an obvious, almost an inescapable, way of ensuring a food supply and it is likely that all through history some time has been given to the catching of fish, if only for the sake of subsistence. But when men first became fishermen, depending largely on the pursuit for their livelihood and how they were then organised, history does not show. There are signs that the first groups of fishermen must have appeared within agricultural communities. Later names were to be found in common between fishing villages and surrounding agricultural settlements; fisherman and farmer would have the same landlord; and in the late 18th century fishermen had at least vestigial fragments of land. All this suggests that the fishing communities were created by a probably slow process of specialisation within earlier agricultural communities. But we know nothing of the manner of life of the people while the parturition was occurring.

Even after fishing villages are first found in the historical records it is only by bare mention that we know of their existence. The plotting of their growth and of when particular communities appeared from the 16th to the 18th centuries depends upon the hazards of the historical record. There may have been some groups of fishermen, existent for centuries, who did not find a mention in the surviving record. It is then, only a minimum picture that we can draw of villages in existence at particular times; there may well have been more of which we have no record. But certainly there were true fishing villages, communities where the main occupation and source of livelihood was fishing, in being by the 16th century. Yet none of those traced in this period were to have great future importance. One, Covesea, disappeared and the others remained as minor fishing settlements. By the 16th century, however, there had appeared Cullen, Portknockie, Buckie and Lossiemouth, communities which were to stand out in the great era of fishing in the 19th century. With the 18th century the records broaden and we begin to find a genuine interest in, and description of, fishing villages as distinct forms of social organisation. It is now that we can begin to build up the picture of how the fishermen lived. We can also be fairly sure that we know of all the communities that then existed. It is not only a matter of plotting the names on a map; a social process can be discerned in which new villages were created by the migration from the older ones, which makes it clear that the fishers were a distinct stock of people whose aid was needed for the expansion of fishing enterprise. And the 18th century was undoubtedly a time of expansion. With the addition of Findochty, Portessie and Burghead to the list, there was now a line of eleven villages which made possibly the most active fishing area in the whole of Scotland. There were four more names to be added in the early 19th century but on the whole they were secondary offshoots of the main groups which were all active centres by 1800.

To all appearance, then, the fishing population continued to grow slowly through the three hundred years closing at the end of the 18th century, while the communities hardened into a a mould that left them sharply separate from the rest of the population. There was by then a clear type of fishing community to which all the eleven villages in essentials conformed. This typical community was in the first place small. The greatest, not only by the reputation of its fishermen but also by sheer size, was Buckie with fourteen boats of the largest type. More typical was a village such as Portessie which had five large boats, seven yawls and contained 178 inhabitants. The villages showed their social isolation in their physical characteristics with the cottages packed tightly together and quite obviously distinct from the wider-spread buildings of the agricultural population. It was usual for the buildings to be placed in an irregular huddle close to the water where the foreshore was reasonably flat. But towards the end of the 18th century an idea of planning was beginning to prevail, as in Burghead and Cullen. The people within such clusters were evidently solidly devoted to fishing and there was little mixing with people of other occupations.

The life of the fisherman of the time was indeed harsh. The coast, except at Lossiemouth and Cullen, was notably lacking in harbours and the boats, operated always directly from the home village, had to be hauled above high-water mark at every return to shore and to be shoved over the beach into the water at every launching; to be so handled they had to be small and entirely open. Yet at the appropriate season they might be taken 64 km (40 miles) offshore, being at sea for days at a time, exposed to treacherous weather, while the crews had to live upon cold tack. There was no season without its fishing and small boats would be launched for the inshore haddock fishing throughout the winter. For the women-folk life was equally hard. Their life is vividly described in the Old Statistical Account.

> The fisher wives lead a most laborious life. They assist in dragging the boats on the beach, and in launching them. They sometimes, in frosty weather, and at unseasonable hours, carry their husbands on board, to keep them dry. They receive the fish from the boats, carry them fresh or after salting, to their customers, and to market at the distance, sometimes, of many miles, through bad roads and in a stormy season . . . . It is the province of the women to bait the lines; collect furze, heath or the gleanings of the mosses, which, in surprising quantity, they carry home in their creels for fuel, to make the scanty stock of peats and turfs prepared in summer, last till the returning season.

Fishing itself had settled into unvarying annual sequence, broadly uniform for all the villages. There were two main types of fishing each with its particular apparatus and season. Most of the year was spent in fishing for haddock and other small fish with small-lines. Each of these formed the link for up to 3,000 hooks, which were baited usually with mussels, by the women folk on the shore. In the catching operation it was paid out from the boat to lie upon the sea bed. The winter and the autumn would be devoted to this type of fishing, which might well be in inshore waters with the small yawl type of boat. Some of the haddock, which comprised the greater part of the catch, would be sold locally as fresh fish, with the women acting as retailers, either around the individual houses of the locality or at a market such as Elgin. But a proportion, possibly half, was cured either by smoking or — as in the spelding form of cure — by salting and drying, and was exported from the region.

The second type of fishing was with the great-line, a form of apparatus similar in principle to the small-line, but shorter in length, greater in calibre and fitted with fewer and larger hooks. It was adapted to catching the 'great' fish such as cod, ling and halibut, but most of all cod. This fishing was taken up in the spring and early summer and the boats of the largest type — that is of about 7.5 m (25 ft) keel and open — would be taken to distant grounds, staying at sea for two or three days at a time. The Buckie men, for example, were wont to fish off the Caithness coast, still using Buckie as the base. This type of fishing used small fish such as herring or haddock as bait and was less dependent on the shore work of the women. The product too, was nearly always cured and exported. Curing was by drying. The fish having been cleaned and lightly salted were, in alternate phases, piled and laid out on the beach to dry in a sequence extending over some weeks. Some cod, too, were sold to curers to be cured by pickling. The product of the season's fishing would be loaded aboard the fishing vessels and transported to one of the markets in the south, such as Leith, to be sold; with the proceeds the fishermen would make purchases and arrive back with their boats as full as when they had left.

The fishermen were men of some substance. Landlords might put money into provision of boats but they took a fixed rent in exchange, leaving the fishermen to operate as they wished. In any case the crews put up all the money for their lines and most of the money for their boats and were in most important respects the owners of the boats they used. Within the crews they provided generally equal amounts and took equal profit. A rough equality prevailed throughout the fishing community. Each man would in due course become the holder of a full share in a boat and each family would stand in near equality with its neighbours. Nor were the fluctuations through time very severe. Thus by all accounts the fishermen of the Moray Firth were modestly prosperous.

Just after 1800 there came a sudden break in this long slow evolution of fishing life which had left the fishermen in a string of tightly-knit but small communities along what used to be termed the Banff and Moray coasts. The cause was the sudden raging growth of herring fishing. In the 19th century the Scottish herring fishing was to become the greatest in Europe, displacing the old leaders, Holland, and achieving a strong grip on a market which extended from the Rhine eastwards into Russia and from the Baltic southwards for some 1300 km (800 miles) into Austro-Hungary. In this growth the villages of the Buckie district played an outstanding part and in doing so underwent deep change.

The beginnings of continuously successful herring fishing were made in Caithness, in the last two decades of the 18th century. But crews from the south side of the Firth would move across for the herring season. Indeed they were the leaders, almost the instructors, among a population that had no great traditional commitment to fishing; but they also learned the techniques of what was for them a novel fishing and the great profits that were sometimes to be made out of it. In the second decade of the 19th century this experience was brought to fruit along the south shore itself, as herring stations were established wherever a harbour was available or could be speedily built. Cullen, Burghead and Lossiemouth were all lively centres, pulling in crews, curers and yard staff for the weeks of the fishing season. Thus herring fishing from being the activity of an adventurous minority on a strange shore became the seasonal standby of every man on the coast.

This herring fishing remained an affair of a fairly short season, from late July to mid-September, and for the rest of the year the fishermen would return to their traditional line-fishings for haddock and for cod. Almost all the catch was cured by pickling. Curing yards were often no more than flat open areas — 'stances' — on which would be gathered the salt, the barrels and the labourers, these being women who operated in teams, or crews, of three, with one woman packing and two gutting. Much of the initiative in the herring fishing came from curers. It was an attractive if speculative trade and men of varied origin flooded into it, particularly in the first boom days (when profits, in fact, were much helped by the government bounty on cured herring). The custom grew of curers engaging crews of fishermen, that is, they promised a set rate for the first 200 or 250 crans (1 cran = 3 cwt or 700-1,000 fish) to be landed by the crew; then there might be a re-negotiation but many of the crews would not reach this level. Contracts only ran for the one season and before the beginning of each fishing there would be a fresh bout of bargaining with re-adjustment of rates and some shift of the parties in agreement. Most of the cured herring from the Moray Firth area was sent to the growing continental market.

Even a seasonal switch to herring fishing was more than a mere change of routine, for it brought pervasive and deep social changes. It was accompanied — without necessarily being a cause — by a rapid increase in the fishing population. Three

new villages made their appearance in the 19th century but
much greater was the accretion of people within the existing
units. Between the 1790's and the 1840's increases of three or
fourfold are recorded for the villages between Buckie and Cullen
and there was to be a further growth at least up to 1871. Through
the last quarter of the century, however, the increase slowed
and possibly halted entirely. The increases that are recorded are
probably fairly typical of the general experience and the total
growth served to bring an existing array of villages to new
levels of size. Thus by 1870, the typical village of the coast would
have between 200 and 300 fishermen, representing total
populations of up to 1300, aggregations which had grown out
of the intimate groups of less than 200 that had been typical a
century before.

The fishing communities remained close-knit and exclusive
groups. Few of the indwelling families did not devote themselves
to fishing in its various aspects and even in the period of rapid
growth there was little immigration by people of other
occupations The young men, too, would all in due turn take up
fishing by the old process of acquiring a place in a crew as
a boy and going on to a share, adulthood and marriage. The
fishing which they had to learn and the tests and opportunities
of their life were much changed from those of their forefathers.
Herring fishing, for one thing, altered their prospect of income.
It was much more fluctuating than line-fishing, not only in the
catches that were made but also in the dependence on a volatile
market in which price might fluctuate for a host of reasons well
beyond the horizon of a small community in the north-east of
Scotland - the size of the Norwegian fishing, the potato and
grain crop on the continent, even the wine vintage might create
windfall, gain or sudden loss. These matters on the continent
concerned primarily the curers but their effect came back to the
fishermen usually in the high or low rate for the following
season. On the whole, with much fluctuation from season to
season the gains made from herring, as a weekly rate, were
markedly greater than those to be made from the older forms
of fishing, and in a long period of high prices from the early
fifties to the era of the early eighties these gains were tending
to increase. Then there came collapse of price and of income
and slow recovery from the mid-nineties.

In the value of their possessions, too, there came a remarkable change. One influence was the desirability of larger boats which were needed to carry as great a length of net as possible, for length of net determined the size of the catch. Thus while in 1800 the largest boats would be of 7.5 m (25 ft) keel and open, by the end of the century some were of 21 m (70 ft) and decked; in expense this meant an increase from £20 or £30 to £500. Similarly the 'drift' — the chain of nets that fastened to form a continuous wall to be hung vertically in the water during the fishing operation — was increased from twenty to eighty. By 1900 it cost over £1,000 to set a herring boat on the water, ready for fishing; this was well over ten times as much as it had done in 1800. Another influence was an increase in the number of boats greater than the increase in the number of fishermen. This was effective because groups of two, three or four local fishermen — owners of the boats — would take on hired men, incomers generally from the west of Scotland, to make up the crews in the summer herring season. These were tendencies to be seen all along the east coast of Scotland but the men of the Buckie district were foremost in the value of the equipment which they acquired and in the size of the income they earned with it.

The whole adaptation to the changing challenges and opportunities of the 19th century was determined not only by the uncertain movement of the herring shoals, which might cause the fishing to move from one part of the coast to the other, but also by the degree of success in a running effort to improve or provide harbours on a coast naturally devoid of protection. Cullen, Lossiemouth and Burghead had artificial harbours in use by the early days of the herring boom but they were all tidal and closed to traffic at certain states of the tide; and the majority of fishermen lived in villages which had no harbour at all. Then started a continuing push for improvement. Lossiemouth was extended and the Buckie fishermen improvised a small shelter for their boats but in the 1840's there still remained a mass of fishermen without a harbour to their village and the general provision of the locality was poor in quality and inadequate to support the fishing effort even of the local boats. In 1877 Buckie acquired a fishing harbour which gave entry at all states of the tide and good shelter and working accommodation to the largest fishing boats of the day and in the next two decades efforts were almost continually being made to provide for the large and flourishing villages, with hundreds of boats to their name, which had never had harbours. By the early nineties, then, there were eight harbours along the coast.

Thus the majority of the fishermen never found themselves with a close-by harbour which could be used with full convenience by the boats which they were currently using and the convenience of the new harbours of Fraserburgh and Peterhead, together with the rise of Aberdeen as a herring fishing centre, decisively drew the bulk of the herring fleet to the east Aberdeenshire coast. The men of the Banff and Moray coasts, then had to adapt to hold their long-standing leadership in skills, income, and value of their equipment. Many of them had been forced from the earliest days of herring fishing to move some few miles to find curers to engage them for the season; in the mid 19th century they were increasingly forced to move longer distances and in greater numbers for the summer herring season. Other distant herring fishings would be exploited. In the 1840's an early summer fishing, from late May to July was established as an annual activity on the west coast and it drew extensively on the Moray Firth communities. In the early eighties, a similarly early fishing was established in Shetland, with great takes being made for a number of years and this visit to Shetland might well be continued through the whole summer. Finally, towards the end of the century an increasing number of boats were making an autumn trip to East Anglia, a move which had been pioneered by Fife men in the sixties and which slowly took hold further north. In 1900, however, about half the Buckie crews are found on the way to East Anglia. In the intervals of this wandering, the men would return to fish on their own coast. The small-line fishing for hadocks remained on important activity. It was pursued with small boats, it might be from open beaches or from the poorest of local harbours, and for it the village, almost dead when many of the men and many of the women removed themselves to the distant fishings, came alive again with all the shore activities of baiting of lines, of preparing and launching boats, and of curing in which whole families would participate in the traditional fashion. Great-line fishing, in which large boats were an advantage, tended to be carried on locally but in the better harbours, as did the winter herring fishing which arose in the sixties. The activity of the fisherman, then, was a changing blend of effort with small boats from the home village, of possibly more distant use of larger boats with the great-line and of herring fishing in remote regions.

The fact that so much of the fishing was now conducted in boats that could not be locally operated did not bring any strong move to the centres with good deep-water harbours. But the restless movement of the fishermen crews took the heart out of some of the community functions, for much of the year the village had become a mere residential shell, often indeed drained of much of its population, and only sporadically did a full activity encompassing whole fishing families return. Yet, there were no signs of decline in the population of fishing towns and villages.

The enormous growth of fishing and particularly herring fishing since 1800 had been supported by the use of wooden sailing vessels of increasing size and ever more complex furnishing. Yet an increase which almost trebled the keel length of the boat never obliterated the distinctiveness of the Moray Firth design of boat. The Buckie boat of the 18th century was "of a peculiar construction and formed like a Wedge very sharp at the Bow and broad beaft, and much resembling the shape of a Coble only rounded at the stern with a deep sharp keel". This design was developed into the 'skaffie' still with the angled bow and stern and the fishermen of the east coast continued to be divided between those who favoured the Moray Firth type of boat on this basic design and those who went for the type originating farther south. Buckie, as the original seat of this design and the surrounding districts, stuck to the skaffie while Caithness to the north and the coast from Fraserburgh southwards generally used the Fife type. The final flowering of this evolution of the sailing vessel was the Zulu, still with some of the lines of the original Buckie boat but now turned into a powerful instrument of fishing of over 18 m (60 ft) keel, decked and often equipped with a steam capstan which could be used to haul in its eighty nets. Along with its companion, the Fifie which had been developed out of the more southerly designs of boat, it represented an unequalled concentration of fishing power on which there was needed a crew only one man in excess of the six who had manned the small rowing boats of early in the century. Yet, introduced in the eighties, its reign was not to be long for it was overtaken by a type of vessel which suddenly doubled the power of catching — the steam drifter. And the steam drifter  started changes within the fishing community just as deep as those which grew out of the switch to herring fishing just one century before. The serious arrival of steam power for herring fishing almost exactly coincided with the arrival of the 20th century but purchases of the new type went slowly and steadily till 1905. Then good fishings, high prices and bumper profits brought a sudden rush to invest in steam vessels, so that by 1908 the whole composition of the fishing fleet was completely changed; by that year the greater part of a herring catch which itself was much higher than ever before was being made by steam vessels. From 1908 till 1914, the steam fleet continued to increase with a moderate annual addition. In this whole dramatic shift the men of the Buckie district were the leaders and by 1913 they had owned nearly one third of all the steam drifters in Scotland, while more than half the local fishermen worked on steam rather than sailing vessels.

The changes that came to the fishing community with the steam drifter stemmed largely from its high initial expense. To cover its costs it had to be used intensively through a large part of the year. This meant that owners were thirled to the type of fishing for which it was suited much more completely than they ever had  been even with the relatively expensive types of sailing vessel. It might indeed be used for great-line fishing but it was pursued solely by herring fishing through the greater part of the year and to the exclusion of all other types of fishing. This concentration on herring fishing was seen most in the Buckie district, where the ownership of steam drifters was particularly high, as opposed to Lossiemouth in which both the type of boat and the forms of activity were more varied. Dependence on catching herring in its turn meant dependence on the vagaries of the market for herring. By far the greater part of the catch went to the continent as pickled herring. Thus the fishermen, particularly of the Buckie district, by their heavy investment in steam drifters, were forcing themselves into dependence on the herring fishing; they contributed considerably to a sharply rising output and the resulting product could only be sold on the continent. The whole livelihood of the men of the district had come to depend on selling at the high levels of the immediate pre-war period.

In fact, while the steam drifter had an undoubted wide superiority in catching power, its earning power was more qualified. The mere operation of the craft involved an expense, unrelated to catch, which had to be covered before any surplus arose to be shared among the crew; the typical expenses of the standard annual routine of summer fishing on the east coast of Scotland or in the Shetlands followed by the voyage to East Anglia were indeed greater than the normal total earnings of a sailing boat. But the apparently great catches of the steamers did not mean high earnings for the crew. This tended to be more sharply divided into grades than had been the old partners in the sailing vessels. Engineer and fireman were paid a fixed rate of wages and tended to be men from outside the community. This left six or seven 'fishermen'. These were now mainly men of the local community although a few west coast men were still hired. The fishermen fell into distinct groups. In the Buckie district in 1911 nearly all boats were at least in part owned by one or more members of the working crew and in all, rather less than half the fishermen had shares of this type. The owners would also provide nets but there were also some members of the crew who provided nets alone; 95% of fishermen had shares in boats or nets — or both. The remaining 5% was without property in the means of fishing, although the remuneration of such men was on a share rather than a fixed wage basis. In Buckie and the surrounding villages, with the changeover to the steam drifter, the general run of the fishermen had succeeded in maintaining some share in boat or nets better than in most other districts. But the new forms of fishing did create a major division between those who had shares in the boat and those who had only nets. This meant a difference on property owned, since the man with shares in a boat generally also provided a proportion of the nets. It also meant a considerable difference in earnings, since the owners took a share for each, together with a basic share as a crew member.

The era of the steam drifter coincided with, if it did not cause, the appearance of a minority within the fishing community who were of considerably greater wealth than their fellows although the extreme differences between the man of all forms of fishing property and the man of none were not so evident in Buckie. But the fishing community on the whole enjoyed good earnings in the ten years up to the First World War. In a good year — such as those between 1905 and 1908 — an ordinary crew member would make about £2 per week, while owners would have additional spending money after making due allowance for spending and upkeep. A man with shares in a boat and nets might well be making £4 per week in these years, and the earnings on a top boat might be twice as great. For the years from 1908 to 1914 the basic earnings might fall to 15 s (75 p) per week and on the average boat owners could not do more than cover the charges that fell upon them.

Between 1920 and 1939 herring fishing, which had become the universal and often the sole dependence of the fishermen of our coast was afflicted by a progressive blight, alleviated slightly in the late twenties. With the contraction of the continental and particularly the Russian market on which all depended, output had to be cut down. Price collapse was averted but a work force and a fleet only slowly diminishing from pre-war levels were forced into dependence on selling a moderate amount of herrings at moderate prices. Drifters were unable to meet their full costs; earnings were often desperately low; and with boats long past their normal life and nets neglected and in disrepair an ultimate cruel contraction was forced by the loss of the means of fishing.

Buckie and its nearby fishing community were peculiarly hard-hit. The men of the area had a heavy and very widespread investment in steam drifters and their gear and they were thus committed to make whatever use they could of these diminishing assets. The wage-hand could drift to other work — and it was paradoxical that even in a time of unemployment it became difficult to make up the crews with the required complement of hired hands — but the men with an investment in boat or gear had a deeper compulsion to struggle to the end. Any attempt to use the steam drifters brought with it the old limitations; Buckie was very lacking in alternative forms of fishing. Thus the fishing families found themselves struggling to live on the small and occasional surpluses that accrued above the running costs of the vessels. On the whole, matters only became worse as the vessels aged: by the mid-thirties the great bulk of them was thirty years old and the nets stiffened by too long use. Even in the period between 1925 and 1929 when something like equilibrum was reached between catching capacity and market and when for a few years nets began to be replaced and upkeep could be properly looked to, there came the coal strike of 1926 which caused great difficulties. Hopes that the herring industry could regain its old health were dashed by the onset of depression in 1930. For three years the boats, sole source of livelihood for their crews, failed to produce a living wage. In 1931, 1932 and 1933 average annual earnings of the deckhands on the Buckie drifters were respectively £16, £22 and £12, although it should be remembered that food during the season was additional. 1934 and 1935 brought some improvement but by then it was too late for a fleet now far gone in age and neglected through lack of funds. Year by year the number of boats made ready for the fishing diminished, not in a deliberate honing of the industry to the size of the market but by the sheer failure of strength. Herring fishing had to diminish but those who were dropping out were drained of all capital and any means of adopting new means of fishing.

It was in the eastern part of the district that the depression cut deepest. Farther west in Lossiemouth, from 1921, a new form of fishing which gave a more secure livelihood was being pioneered. This was the use of the Danish seine-net, a form of bag net which is pulled through the water by manipulation of ropes. This was used in smaller motor-powered boats which did not have the heavy working expenses of the steam drifter. It also resulted in the catching of white fish for which the market, being a domestic one, was expanding during the inter-war years. The profits of seine-netting were moderate and even the Lossiemouth men did not swing over to the new form of fishing with sufficient speed to avoid being partially caught in the trials of herring fishing.

The Second World War brought to an end the death-agony of the herring fishing in its old form, pursued from steam drifters, normally to the virtual exclusion of any other form of fishing. Twenty years before at the end of another war, a fleet still relatively new had been returned to its pre-war owners and activity, but in 1945 there was no such fleet to be returned. Perhaps it was fortunate that a new fleet had to be built for it could be done with boats that were adapted to the new conditions, both of technique and of market. The labour force had been diminishing for years but in 1945 there were still enough fishermen, born and bred, and willing to pursue their hereditary craft to make it a major industry if the right means could be found. They were. Salvation was found in the diesel engine and the seine-net, although there were still intermittent good earnings by drift-netting for herring. A new fleet was accumulated with the help of government grants, consisting of wooden vessels of up to 21 km (70 ft) length; the fishermen had gone back to a type of boat similar in its hull structure to a time before the steam drifter. It was efficiently powered by diesel engines and could be turned to either white or herring fishing. The steady basis of livelihood lies in white, mainly haddock, fishing on grounds which may be up to 65 km (40 miles) off shore and which may be to the east or the west of the country.

The villages from Portnockie to Portgordon and farther west, Hopeman, Burghead and Lossiemouth have notably held their character as fishing communities, even when they are not all seats of active fishing. The number of fishermen has, it is true, been continuously declining as some of the young men from the fishing families have made for other occupations; inevitably they are all less completely of the one occupation but here have reverted to the status of the dormitory or holiday shell. The fishermen who remain are still mainly of families that have produced generations of men for the boats and old customs of ownership by small partnerships of working fishermen are still maintained. But they have entered a new technological age. The boat and its gear, much of it now scientific, represent major investments and the incomes earned are commensurate. Some of the fishing is conducted from the ports at, or nearby, the home; landings of white fish at Buckie (Plate 26) itself have risen steeply. But when they turn to herring they have to go elsewhere and some of the crews fish the year round for white fish at west coast stations. Another gadget of the age — the motor car — has given them the freedom to fish the productive waters of the west and return to their homes every weekend. It is a last turn in the long process by which fishing communities and families stable in geographical position and in devolution to the one occupation have adjusted to changing opportunities and crisis by wandering and return.

# 14

# DISTILLERY COUNTRY

## KENNETH WOOD

Moray, that ancient province which was the prize of many an acquisitive campaign in the chequered history of early Scotland because of its fertility and natural resources, still stands high in any estimate of desirability to-day. There are, of course, a number of important industries in the province as befits a fairly rich and stable area, such as agriculture and building, distributive trades and fishing, woollen manufacture, forestry, engineering and a large number of professional and administrative services, ship building and repair, food canning. All these businesses and occupations maintain a fairly continuous level of prosperity, and the population of the "Laich" is, unlike other mainly rural areas, on the increase. Apart from the equable and attractive climate and variety of countryside and coast which it possesses, the District is the seat of one of the most important industries — as also one of the ancient activities of people in the land — the art and craft of distilling whisky.

The important constituent of "Scotch" is malt whisky, a single distillation which imparts flavour, character, and personality to whisky everywhere. Most whiskies are blends of "malt" with "grain" whisky, and the particular flavour of any blended whisky depends upon the proportion and individual flavour of the "malt" ingredient which a blend contains. Whilst one may distil whisky from rye or other grain, the product is quite a different creature from the whisky produced from malted barley together with the peat-filtered water of the Moray hills. The "single malt" is the true original drink which the world knows as whisky.

Distilling spirits from this or that grain is one of the early arts of mankind. Its origins are lost in the ocean of time. No date can be assessed for the beginning of distilling, or indeed brewing, but it is certain that the process goes far back in human history even to the legendary world of Homer and his heroic contemporaries. It is doubtful whether they would have recognised "whisky" in its present form, although they would undoubtedly have enjoyed it!

It is quite clear however that increasingly during the 18th century people were turning to the distillation of whisky as a means of supplementing their meagre incomes. Soon the sideline had developed into a substantial cottage industry. It has been suggested that to minimise the amount of malt tax payable, a high proportion of raw grain was used with just enough malted barley to ensure saccharification of the grain by diastase of the malt. As a consequence genuine highland malt whisky is likely to have been of a better quality than the legally distilled product and would therefore be in great demand. There were 200 small stills in Glenlivet in the 1820's and income from the developing whisky trade was so good that people gave up the land to make the "barley bree". Whether the trade was lucrative or not, several writers claim that the making of whisky was the only means by which many tenants could pay their rent. This extract from the Old Statistical Account suggests a happy, if potentially dissolute, view of Tomintoul: "Tammtoul . . . is inhabited by 37 families, without a single manufacture . . . . All of them sell whisky and all of them drink it. When disengaged from this business, the women spin yarn, kiss their innamoratos, or dance to the discordant strains of an old fiddle".

A considerable trade in illicit Highland whisky developed in the lowlands of Scotland and England. Legal distillers of spirits put pressure on the Government to deal with this competition of illegal stills and several Acts of Parliament resulted. The first in 1814, prohibited all stills with a capacity of less than 2285 litres (500 gallons), within the "Highland line". The earliest of the Moray distilleries is Glenburgie-Glenlivet (1812), followed by Linkwood and Miltonduff (1821). Macallan, Cardow and Balmenach were all founded in 1824 following the Distillery Act of 1823. Thereafter there is a list of illustrious names, twenty-five bearing the distinguished "Glenlivet" appendage, through the late 19th century, until one reaches the last to be built "from scratch", the Tormore Distillery at Advie (Plate 28). All premises have, of course, been modernised and output as far as possible has been expanded to meet ever increasing world demand.

The water of the Spey and its tributary rivers and burns is the source, and its banks the home, of the finest whiskies on earth. The Lossie Valley and that of the Findhorn and Nairn have

P

their distilleries, at Birnie, Forres and Cawdor. Nonetheless it is the Spey basin with its waters from the distant Monadhliath Mountains, and other waters from the outlying Cairngorms (for water is the essential ingredient of scotch whisky) and the surrounding peat-mosses which provide the heart land of Highland Malt Whisky distilling (Fig. 11). Those rivers like the Avon, the Livet and the Rothes Water whose names are poetic to the

Fig. 11 The Distilleries of Moray.

connoisseur and layman alike, provide the reality and romance of "the malt".

The industry has of course, like many others, been rationalised and combined by large firms. Almost gone are the days of the "individual still". The size of the industry is truly revealed in its outstanding record of earnings from exports to almost every country in the world, except of course, those countries which are officially "dry". Many attempts have been made to emulate Scotch Whisky in other lands and climes, but none has been even slightly successful, since the particular local conditions of whisky making cannot be matched elsewhere. Indeed it is true to say that the intimate secrets of whisky are not completely understood or assessed even within the scientific laboratories of the distillers themselves, despite the research and analysis which continue year by year.

It is of interest to note that the individual whisky produced

## DISTILLERIES OF MORAY

| No. | | No. | |
|---|---|---|---|
| 1 | Benromach-Glenlivet | 23 | Glenfarclas-Glenlivet |
| 2 | Dallas Dhu | 24 | Dialuaine |
| 3 | Glenburgie-Glenlivet | 25 | Benrinnes |
| 4 | Miltonduff-Glenlivet | 26 | Aberlour-Glenlivet |
| 5 | Glenmoray-Glenlivet | 27 | Craigellachie |
| 6 | Linkwood-Glenlivet | 28 | Convalmore |
| 7 | Glen Elgin-Glenlivet | 29 | Balvenie |
| 8 | Longmorn-Glenlivet | 30 | Glenfiddich |
| 9 | Glenlossie-Glenlivet | 31 | Parkmore |
| 10 | Coleburn-Glenlivet | 32 | Glendullan |
| 11 | Speyburn-Glenlivet | 33 | Mortlach |
| 12 | Glen Grant-Glenlivet | 34 | Pittyvaich |
| 13 | Glen Spey | 35 | Towiemore |
| 14 | Glen Rothes-Glenlivet | 36 | Glentauchers |
| 15 | Macallan-Glenlivet | 37 | Auchcroisk |
| 16 | Imperial-Glenlivet | 38 | Aultmore |
| 17 | Knockando | 39 | Strathmill |
| 18 | Tamdhu | 40 | Strathisla-Glenlivet |
| 19 | Cardow | 41 | Glenkeith-Glenlivet |
| 20 | Tormore | 42 | Inchgower |
| 21 | Glenlivet | 43 | Knockdhu |
| 22 | Cragganmore | | |

by each distillery is unique. There are instances in Moray where two or three neighbouring stills, using the same sources of water, the same barley and closely similar methods in what are intended to be identical stills, owned by the same company, produce entirely different whiskies, with different characters, which have recognisable individualistic identities. The distillers are obviously most concerned to keep these characteristics and take the utmost care that this quality should persist.

In recent years, while the process of manufacture has seen little change, there has been an enormous increase in the capacity of the industry, which is one of the principal focal points for the acquisition through excise duty of public revenue. The export of whisky continues to rise, and the duty upon spirits raises an enormous amount of public money. At the same time, the industry has steadily increased its exports, something which becomes more important with every year that passes. Therefore, it can be rightly said that the distilleries are providing large amounts of internal revenue through duty and external revenue through selling abroad on a scale incomparable with the contribution of any other industry in the country. This is achieved by remarkably few people, by comparison with those very large but labour-intensive manufacturing industries or extractive industries, elsewhere in the entire country. One only has to observe the vast expansion of bonded warehouses adjacent to most distilleries to appreciate both the scale of investment and the enormous gallonage of whisky which is being aged and matured for the correct length of time throughout the area. Even now, the storage of whisky requires further expansion of warehouses.

Distilleries lie in the heart of the countryside, often in situations of great natural beauty. They frequently form the nuclei of small village communities, where the workers and craftsmen are housed. They are the mainstay of villages such as Archiestown, Rothes, Dufftown and Tomintoul. The "Peatreek" from the distillery is one of the fine familiar sights among the glens in which they lie.

One important feature of distillery country is the existence of other crafts alongside that of the whisky-maker. There are for example the coopers, practitioners of an ancient and honourable trade, who are responsible for making and repairing the casks which are designed to store the whisky in its bonded warehouses.

Sherry casks, of course, have to be imported, but with increasing production new casks have to be made especially for the distillers. There are the maltsters and the engineers and coppersmiths and plumbers. The distillers also operate farms of their own, and premises and plant for manufacturing animal feeding-stuffs from the draff and fertiliser from the pot-ale, two of the residues of the distillery process.

The movement of barley, the by-products of distilling, the bulk whisky and the bottled spirit, the malted barley, all contribute to the earnings of road and rail services — a feature which has helped to keep these economic through difficult times.

Centralisation of malting has been accomplished by Scottish Malt Distillers by the use of the large malting unit at Burghead. Besides all this, there are numerous jobs for other contractors in the area — in building and repairing, steel-erecting, welding and the manufacture of specialist items. Whisky-making also benefits the advertising and catering sectors, and has a direct influence on the tourist industry — being of itself a "tourist attraction" with a great deal to show to an interested public.

All in all, the business of making Scotch is highly suited to the small population of a rural countryside, and goes a long way to illustrate a fact which is frequently forgotten in these days of growth of urban industries which dominate huge populations — that quite small units may be immensely profitable and productive and infinitely more attractive. The strength of the whisky industry lies in its administrative structure — which is large, co-ordinating a number of relatively small production units. The presence of a distillery gives a large measure of permanence to small rural communities which would rarely exist in any other form of industrial activity. Whilst technological change, economic misfortune, obsolescence and other variable factors tend to strike at most activities, there seems little likelihood of any decline or diminution in the demand for whisky. The reverse is the case.

# 15
# OTHER INDUSTRIES

## JOHN PHILP

At first glance it might seem that a chapter on the industries of the Moray District from which agriculture, forestry, fishing and distilling have been excluded would be rather threadbare. A casual trip round the District from the fishing ports on the coast through the farmland and forests to the valleys with their seemingly innumerable distilleries would seem to suggest that a large proportion of the population must be employed in these industries. Statistics, however, tell us otherwise. 79% of the working population of the Moray District is employed in "Other Industries". As with all statistics this is far from the whole truth. Service industries necessarily tend to play a more important part in a rural economy and about 50% of all jobs do fall into this category which covers a wide range of employment in transport, distributive trades, the professions, local government and so on.

Again, many are employed in industries ancillary to the primary industries. The Moray coast has a long tradition of boatbuilding and marine engineering while agricultural and distillery engineers are found in most of the towns. Food processing, too, is important although not nowadays so directly related to local produce. There are also industries of importance not related to the primary ones and these range from textiles to the manufacture of electric lamps.

If one turns first to marine engineering and boatbuilding, Buckie must be the first port of call. Here grouped round the harbour are three boatyards with long traditions in the building of sturdy wooden fishing vessels. Herd and Mackenzie are the largest of the three Buckie yards. The yard builds steel as well as wooden vessels and in fact their range of 17 m (56 ft) stern-working steel fishing boats has been particularly successful. Close to Herd and Mackenzie lies Jones's Buckie Shipyard which dates from the beginning of the century and has built over the years many boats between 18 and 24 m (60 and 80 ft) for the Scottish inshore fleet. At the west end of the harbour is the yard of G. Thomson and Son which was founded in 1880. All boats built here are of timber and vary from 20 to 27 m (65 to 90 ft) in length. Indeed such has been the traditional quality of finish that these yards have found little difficulty in adapting to the needs of the leisure market. Many solidly built and beautifully finished yachts and cabin cruisers have come off the Buckie slips. One of the most spectacular triumphs of recent years was the launching of the sail training vessel *Captain Scott*. Traditional skills and modern techniques met to create a truly beautiful vessel which is now operating for the Dulverton Trust off the west coast of Scotland. She still returns to Buckie from time to time for refits and is a delightful reminder that in these days of mass production superb "one offs" can still be created.

Other marine engineering firms operate in Lossiemouth where firms such as Henry Fleetwood & Sons (Marine) and D. F. Sutherland have established their reputations over the years. These reputations for skill and reliability allow these family firms to operate not only throughout North East Scotland but far beyond. Fleetwood propeller shafts will be found in vessels over a wide area while Sutherland winches have, for long, been exported even to the eastern seaboard of Canada.

It is at Lossiemouth that one of the Buckie based boatyards has been experimenting with what is a novel departure for this part of Scotland, a concrete vessel. Contrary to local expectation, it floated and more may yet be heard of this type of construction.

Agricultural engineering is less easy to pin down and describe as a distinct industry. Over the years agricultural machinery has become more and more sophisticated and relatively little machinery is now manufactured in the area. Repair facilities do of course exist, ranging from factory trained staff operating from local agents to the smaller firms who can still in the tradition of the old fashioned village blacksmith "fix most things". Many firms in Moray who have started out as agricultural engineers have now diversified into other things and are described later.

The textile industry is one which bears little direct relation to the primary industries nowadays but was originally based on local supplies of wool and water power. In the Moray District the textile industry is confined mainly to the towns of Keith and Elgin. There are two mills in each centre and together they employ nearly 900 people. All of them have their roots in the last century or even earlier and have expanded by adapting readily to changing conditions.

Three of the mills operate fully vertical manufacturing, carrying out all the processes involved in converting raw wool to finished cloth. Wool used in the mills comes not only from local sources but from many other parts of the world and especially New Zealand. The care and attention shown throughout all the processes, the rigorous inspection and meticulous hand finishing, ensure that the cloths produced from all the mills maintain the high quality on which the textile industry in this area has built its reputation.

In Keith, the town's twin industries (whisky and textiles) are long established and were attracted originally by the same resource — water. G. and G. Kynoch (Plate 29) was founded in 1788 and the Isla Bank Mills, built in 1805, were originally driven by water power. This is still an independent public company and the management of the mill remains in the hands of the Kynoch family.

Compared with Kynoch's, the firm of Robert Laidlaw and Sons is a relative newcomer to Keith. The Seafield Mills were first opened in 1901. The company produces quality fashion fabrics sold to garment houses for ladies' clothes. Equally important is the production of Shetland type knitting yarns for knitwear factories. More recently Laidlaws have started producing men's fabrics. In 1961 the firm was taken over by Grampian Holdings who have carried through a modernisation and expansion programme.

In Elgin the larger of the two mills is that of James Johnston & Co. which was established at the end of the 18th century, using water power, to process local wool into cloth for local use. By the middle of the 19th century the company was already experimenting with working rarer wools, such as cashmere and vicuna, for which the firm is now internationally famous. Being one of the first, Johnstons of Elgin remains one of the country's major producers of cashmere with a specialist knowledge of the cleaning and dehairing process required in its preparation. Supplies have come from China, Manchuria and Persia.

Reid and Welsh is the smallest of the four mills. It is associated with J. & G. Crombie of Aberdeen, makers of the famous Crombie tweed overcoatings. Reid and Welsh buy in the yarn and weave twist worsted suitings and sports jackets materials.

Although these four mills provide the bulk of employment in textiles in Moray there are a number of other points of textile interest in the area. Handwoven cloth for example is still being manufactured by Speyside Weavers of Archiestown while throughout the District can be seen evidence of a number of old mills. One of these at Knockando has only recently ceased production and all the machinery is still in position. It could yet be brought back into use reviving a traditional craft on its original scale.

While not strictly textiles, it is interesting to note that protective clothing for the oil platform construction yards is now manufactured at Forres.

The food and drink industry in Moray is dominated by whisky distilling (see Chapter 14) and that apart is fragmented into small units with a number of notable exceptions. Baxters of Speyside is not only a household name, it is also still very much a family concern. In the late 1860's George Baxter was one of fifty gardeners for the Duke of Gordon and Richmond at Fochabers. His wife Margaret was well known for the quality of her home-made jams and demand for them grew to such an extent that George was able to leave the Duke's employment to open a shop. Their son, William, added to the enterprise by taking the train to Wick or Fort William and then cycling home picking up orders on the way. He purchased the factory site in 1914. Production was confined at first to jams and then during the 1920's the first of the famous soups was introduced. At W. A. Baxter & Sons the emphasis is still on old fashioned quality; to this is added the advantage of up-to-date production techniques and skills. Family concern though it may be Baxters' products are sold in over 80 countries.

Another family concern whose quality products are found throughout the country are Speyside bakers, Joseph Walker of Aberlour. Their success has been built particularly on the sales growth of their high-quality all-butter shortbread which now accounts for three-quarters of their total turnover and makes the company the country's third largest shortbread manufacturer. No mean achievement for a family firm based in a tiny town in the heart of Speyside. Joseph Walker founded his bakery business in Torphins, Aberdeenshire in 1898. In the 1920's he bought over Catto's of Aberlour and expanded operations. The business is now run by his three grandchildren who employ 140 people. One measure of their quality and success is that if you buy your shortbread in the 'top people's' shop with its own Harrods' label on it then that shortbread was made by Walkers in Moray.

Fish processing is obviously a significant part of the food industry in Moray and a wide range of firms is involved from the large concerns such as Seagull Seafoods in Lossiemouth and the Buckie Fish Processing Co. and Moray Fish Supply, the two major firms in Buckie, to the small businesses run by one man perhaps employing half a dozen women on a part time basis.

There are differences even between the larger firms. Seagull Seafoods, for example, concentrates almost entirely on scampi processing while Moray Fish Supply processes a wide range of fish and shellfish. There can indeed be few more outward-looking firms than this and refrigerated vehicles regularly leave Buckie for all corners of Europe and beyond.

Specialist items are often left to the smaller firm and many traditional skills are married to modern techniques, for example, in the smoking of salmon. Local Spey salmon smoked in a kiln fired with oak woodchips from the Speyside cooperages is to many a delicacy well worth seeking out around the old harbours at Portsoy or Portnockie.

One would think that it is a long step from fish processing to electrical engineering but in Buckie the two are found side by side. The unexpected can always be encountered in North East Scotland and here on the Moray coast in a relatively remote fishing port we find a substantial factory manufacturing light bulbs. The lamp factory in Buckie which is now operated by Thorn Lighting was built in 1956 for AEI. The first extension was erected after only five years and a third bay was added in 1968. Yet another extension has recently been completed.

Although the Buckie factory is fairly remote from its main markets and other company factories, the plant has still been relatively profitable. The factors which first brought the company to the area still play a large part in the continuing profitability.

Rents and rates are lower than in the south although recent developments have eroded this differential. The more important factor, however, is the availability of a labour force which the management believes maintains its high level of output both through skill and more especially through dependability.

The greater proportion of the workforce of over 300 people are women and the management has been greatly impressed by the quality of work. This is not really surprising along a coast where for generations the women have worked at the fish. Cleaning out fish in cold running water requires a degree of manual dexterity even to keep one's fingers intact and the transfer to a warm factory and the fitting of lamp filaments has come as an agreeable change. Output continues to increase and now three large articulated lorries leave every week for the south with the factory's products.

The factory manufactures a wide range of lamps as well as specialist equipment for bodies such as the Post Office and British Rail. Indeed lamps from Buckie have been exported to Japan and success in that market reflects credit on the Buckie factory. One would certainly not expect that this typical North East fishing port could produce electrical equipment to be sold in what must be one of the most difficult markets in the world particularly for products of that type.

Throughout the rest of the Moray District are a number of other engineering firms of a more traditional nature who have nevertheless adapted traditional skill to meet demands not only from agriculture and the distilling industry but also from the oil exploration and production industry. No major oil related development has yet to come to Moray but such is the speed of change in the industry that this situation could alter very rapidly. At present, however, the Moray area is well situated to take advantage, on a less dramatic scale perhaps, of developments at the service bases at Aberdeen and Peterhead and the spectacular platform construction yards at Ardersier to the west of Nairn and at Nigg Bay on the Cromarty Firth. Already a number of new companies have set up at Elgin and Keith to take advantage of this central position; nor have a number of local firms been slow to see the opportunities.

One such company is Newmill Ironworks (of Elgin), a long established company whose principal products are process plant for the distilling and brewing industries in which they are recognised specialists. Indeed the name "Newmill" is synonymous with the 'mashing' process and conveying plant in these distilleries and breweries. Engineering and marine castings in grey iron and brass are produced in the foundry while the machine shop manufactures plant and machinery to the company's own design. More recently it has also done work for oil related industries. The fabrication workshops turn out stainless steel vessels and structures.

Elgin Central Engineers is another company which has expanded from traditional agricultural engineering into further fully-equipped workshops. The firm now offers a range of specialist engineering and fabrication services to the offshore oil industry. Another interesting development at Elgin Central is the operation of a friction welding machine for British Aluminium. The machine, which when installed was the largest of its type in Western Europe, is used for making anode rods and is capable of welding 8 inch steel round rods to aluminium bars.

Inevitably in a short survey of many industries such as this it is not possible to mention every development of interest and this is particularly the case in the engineering field where there tends to be a considerable number of smaller companies each, nevertheless, making a significant contribution to the local economy.

It is worth noting, however, firms such as Hendry Hydraulics in Elgin manufacturing a wide range of hydraulic equipment for agriculture, fishing and general industry, William Reid (Forres), an agricultural and general engineering company and Hamilton Brothers of Buckie, structural engineers with a very sophisticated workshop capable of turning out prefabricated sections for industrial buildings of all types.

Two incomers worthy of mention are Speyside Engineering which provides a design and construction service in its fabrication and engineering shops, and Anderson Engineering, Keith, which also designs and manufactures stainless steel, mild steel and aluminium fabrications.

While not precisely an industry itself, although quite a substantial employer, Elgin Technical College plays a vital part in the industrial and commercial life in Moray. Before the College opened in 1971 firms who required training services had to send their employees to Inverness or Aberdeen and were often understandibly reluctant to do so. Now they have the services of a fully equipped modern Technical College.

As growth has taken place in the whisky industry, fishing, food processing and the new oil related industries, the College's strength in engineering trades is proving of great value to firms in Moray. The College's workshops are equipped with machines and training is adapted to meet the needs of particular firms as well as off the job full-time technical training. While the technical department is the largest, the College offers a wide variety of courses in its other departments.

Although related to forestry, passing mention must be made of the three major sawmilling firms in Moray. Elgin City Sawmills perhaps has the most impressive local presence with their concentration of workshops at the Wards, Elgin, where a massive new joinery workshop has been recently completed. This is still a locally owned family firm producing from both home and imported timber a wide range of supplies for the building trade. Riddoch of Rothiemay have recently moved their headquarters into Elgin. 1974 was a particularly exciting year for this well known timber firm as not only did their new Kilmallie sawmill at Fort William come on stream but they also opened one of the most up-to-date treatment plants at Mosstodloch. John Fleming & Co. (Elgin), the third of the trio, are also timber importers, sawmillers and manufacturers of wood products although they do also act as agents for other timber products.

In trying to draw together all these aspects of "other industries" there must inevitably have been omissions. One wonders, for example, how many of Elgin's own citizens realise that within a very short distance of each other they have small factories manufacturing cod liver oil and plastic minnows! Much could be made of the rural craft industries but, fascinating though they are, they do not yet provide the daily bread of a significant number of people. Perhaps this will change. There is no doubt that demand is growing for items like the beautiful, wooden, cane-backed chairs hand-made in the wilds of Glen Rinnes.

There is, however, one thing which sets many of these other industries apart from fishing, agriculture, forestry and distilling, and that is change. There will certainly be changes within these industries but as industries they will continue. The people of Moray have already seen many changes and have adapted their ways and their skills. The signs are there that they will continue to do so and that Moray and its industries, whatever that "other" may encompass, will continue to prosper.

# 16
# SETTLEMENT PATTERNS
# AND COMMUNICATIONS

## JAMES GUTHRIE

*Introduction*

As we enter the last quarter of the 20th century it is
tempting to think that patterns of settlement depend upon the
business and decisions of men: upon organisation, government,
commerce, communications and economics — even upon ex-
traneous factors like world commodity markets. Certainly all
these things have an influence, as do other facets of human
activity including medical science, the control of disease, religion,
education, and the provision of amenities and services. By far
the most influential and traditionally most important of human
activities of the North East are those which date back to the
earliest settlement, namely farming and fishing.

We are still very much dependent upon our basic needs:
food, water, fuel and shelter materials. Where these are available
people will settle. Having become accustomed over centuries
to sharing their basic requirements, people have also been
conditioned to living in groups and now feel deprived if they
cannot enjoy the social amenities which only group-living can
provide. Thus there has always been a tendency to "nucleated"
as opposed to "dispersed" settlement and this process seems to
be accelerating as the benefits of technology are expensive and
can only be justified in economic terms by sharing among large
groups of people. Indeed the basis of the planners' philosophy
seems to be that populations should be concentrated.

Settlement in Moray is determined to a considerable degree
by the physical landscape which in the District can be divided
into a highland/upland area and a lowland one (see Chapter 1).
The latter rises to the 120 m (400 ft) contour, the former into
the Cairngorms, over 1200 m (4000 ft) in height. Within the
lowland lies the Laich of Moray, the most fertile part of the

District where the greatest density of population is found in an area renowned for its genial climate.

*River Mouth Settlements*

The major rivers flowing through Moray, the Findhorn and Spey, are too swift of flow and particularly at their estuaries, too erratic in their behaviour to encourage large settlements. Tidal streams and long-shore drift have, over the centuries, moved large quantities of sand and gravel westwards along the Moray shore causing shoals in the river estuaries and creating sand bars. These not only make the river mouths too shallow for shipping but also cause diversion of the river outlets.

The estuary of the Findhorn was formerly 3.2 km (2 miles) west of Findhorn Bay. The village at the mouth of the river was lost when the drifting Culbin Sands caused the course of the river to change. A second Findhorn site was inundated by the sea in 1701 causing the villagers to settle where Findhorn stands today. Formerly the most important port for the Laich of Moray, Findhorn decayed rapidly from 1860 because of the growth of large shingle spits across the mouth of the bay.

Kingston was created as a port at the mouth of the river Spey in 1784 by two Englishmen from Kingston-upon-Hull (hence the name) to exploit the woodland resources in the Spey forests, floating timber downstream to build ships in the pre-steam era, but the lack of draft for bigger ships and the shifting of the river mouth prevented real development. Kingston is now a dormitory village, a quiet place for holiday makers, still threatened as the Spey estuary moves westward. Following a season of heavy rain the broad Spey estuary is an awe-inspiring sight, particularly at high tide. One has the feeling that here is a turbulent and mighty river which has fought its way down from the mountains and now is struggling violently before succumbing to lose its identity in the waves.

The nature of the rivers Findhorn and Spey has discouraged large settlement but their influence, together with that of the river Lossie, has been crucial in determining the pattern of settlement. Until bridge building techniques were developed to overcome these difficulties both rivers created real barriers to the natural line of communication between Aberdeen and Inverness. The Findhorn in particular, with alternate stretches of gravel-floored shallows which make difficulties for ferries, and rocky gorges which are unsafe, has no good crossing point. It is noticeable that the people of Forres have a dialect more akin to that of Invernessians, quite different from that of Elgin, which seems to be more influenced by the east. It seems likely that many were attracted to settle in Forres when awaiting a suitable opportunity to make the westward crossing at Waterford. James Donaldson writing on the agriculture of the county of Moray in 1794 noted: "when swelled by floods, the progress of the traveller is often interrupted for days and on some occasions lives are lost. The year 1782 is remembered with grief, when thirteen persons in passing the Findhorn were drowned."

The more languid river Lossie must have played a part in the siting of Elgin providing water power for mills as well as water for brewing, domestic purposes, and fishing. Between 1189 - 1195 William the Lion granted Richard, Bishop of Moray, leave to build a mill above the cruives, (salmon traps), on the river Lossie below the castle. It is also probable that small boats would reach Elgin from the sea prior to the establishment of Lossiemouth harbour. But the principal reason for the establishment of Elgin seems to have been its defensive strength. Indeed the Old Statistical Account contains a reference suggesting that the derivation of the name of Elgin is from Elgyn — meaning a peninsula. It is clear from a Charter of Malcolm IV that a castle existed there in 1160, and it is likely that this site was occupied much earlier. The security of the site (Plate 19) combined with its position near the fertile lowland area enhanced its settlement potential. This was recognised and assisted by the establishment of the Cathedral just to the east of the town in 1224 and guaranteed Elgin's permanence and development.

*Rural Settlements*

The earliest true "settlements" are thought to be those of the neolithic period. An important site (Plate 9), possibly of the first farming peoples, was found in Forestry Commission land near Fochabers in 1971. This discovery was remarkable for the large number of pieces of pottery, together with human bones and skeletons discovered in the burial mound. The time of the arrival of these settlers is not known but it seems that they cleared a small area of the woodland for cultivation and radio carbon-dating of oak wood found in the area suggests that the site was first colonised in 3,500 B.C.

Q

Archaeological evidence from Bronze Age times is associated mainly with burials rather than domestic dwellings and it is not until the Pictish period that a clearer pattern of settlement distribution emerges, as outlined in Chapter 7.

The maps of Timothy Pont show that most of the habitable areas of Moray were settled by the 16th century. However, inadequate diet, poor housing and clothing, lack of sanitation and hygiene, poverty, epidemics and famine tended to restrict natural increases in population and life was often "nasty, brutish and short". What would now be described as subsistence living was nevertheless possible throughout the rural areas.

It is difficult for us, as we drive past well ordered fields, combine harvesters, and fat cattle renowned for their quality, to imagine that as recently as some 250 years ago only the drier patches of land could be cultivated; weeds grew in profusion; the value of crop rotation and manuring was not understood; wooden carts were scarce and primitive with fixed axles and irregularly shaped wheels; primitive wooden ploughs were drawn by half-starved cattle in greater numbers than the land as then used could sustain; lime could not be brought for lack of roads and wheeled vehicles, and crops were in the main restricted to oats and barley; the potato had not been introduced. Up to the middle or late 18th century, people were dependent almost entirely on the local production of food. There were no nucleated settlements in the form of villages, only irregular collections of dwellings in "ferm-touns, kirk-touns and mill-touns." It is estimated that 75% of the people relied on primitive agriculture. Lack of drainage limited the available farmland and primitive soil — exhausting methods restricted the distribution of farm-touns to the fertile areas in the river valleys and drier areas of the lowlands.

Given these circumstances the rural areas were over-populated in relation to the natural resources of the soil. Consequently famine, not unknown in earlier years, and particularly in the North East in the period 1693-98, recurred throughout the 18th century. With a diet restricted to cereals (mainly oats), cabbage and kale, failure of the harvest resulting from wet summers, protracted winters and early frosts, particularly in the upland areas, caused disastrous famines.

In desperation people came down from the upland areas hoping to obtain food in the lowland towns. This was, no doubt, the primary reason for the large numbers of beggars and vagrants in the towns giving rise to the Scottish Poor Law which struggled to provide a primitive form of social welfare. Although it is likely that Moray with its more favourable climate than more easterly areas of the North East suffered fewer deaths, the seriousness of the situation is reflected in the following quotation from Elgin Town Council Minutes for April 6th, 1741: "The Council considering that by reason of the scarcity of victuall has occasioned tumults and mobbs wherby the inhabitants are in danger everie night therfor the Councill appoint the Magistrats the Baillies . . . to take ane quarter of the town and appoint twenty men to guard everie night . . . and . . . also to search everie familie they suspect that lodge vaggrants . . . ." The people living in the coastal areas seem also to have suffered: "At Cullen 10th July 1699, given to the bedall for burying several poor who dyed through famine and were brought dead into the churchyard, 15s" (Cramond).

From 1779-1781 the crops again suffered from frost, snow, rain and cold winds, resulting in failures of the harvest and in famine. In the Cabrach (Upland Banffshire) the population of 960, (Webster 1755), was reduced by 200 and meal multures to "a ninth part only of what they were in ordinary years". Even in the parish of Keith "the produce could not supply the farmer's family above six weeks or three months" (Old Statistical Account). Although there were other contributory factors, these famines gave the impetus for improvements in farming methods less vulnerable to climatic conditions.

The present pattern of settlement in rural areas (Fig. 12) emerged from the "Age of Improvement", between 1750 and 1850 (for detail see Chapter 10). The changes of that period were so profound that few signs of previous settlements and land use systems are visible today. Domestic buildings in the early 18th century were built of such poor materials that few, if any, would have remained; roads were almost non-existent.

The open-field, run-rig system and common grazings gave way to enclosure of larger fields for cultivation, stones cleared from the fields often being used to form the enclosing "dry-stone dykes".

Along with the change from the open field system which discouraged long-term husbandry of the soil, progressive landlords granted longer leases giving tenants the incentive to nurture resources. Farms were consolidated and usually enlarged, one farmer taking the place of several. The numbers of tenants, or peasant-farmers, were reduced, some being turned off the land completely, others finding employment as farm-servants. In the parish of Drainie, by 1809, 68 farms had been reduced to 38 in less than 20 years. Although the effects of these changes were harsh for individuals and their families, the famines had

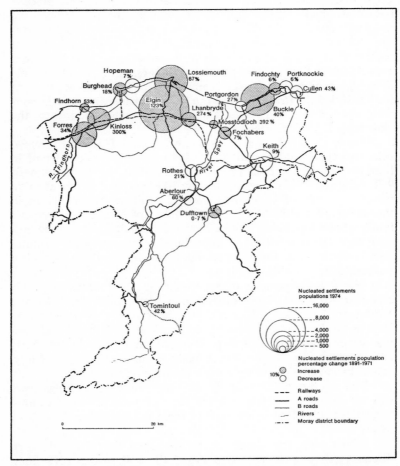

Fig. 12 Moray: Settlements, Communications and Population Changes

shown that over-population* was a greater evil. In many cases the settlements increased in area, displaced peasants breaking in new ground at the edges of the moorland to form crofts. But much of this marginal land settlement was short-lived; most of the land was of poor quality, difficult to manage because of its exposure and inferior soil. Many of these crofts were ultimately absorbed into the farms, others were later abandoned when crofters could exchange a precarious and poor existence for more secure employment and better living conditions in the towns.

## Planned Villages

A great many settlements, between 120 and 150, were created in Scotland between 1745 and 1845 (Smout). These were the "planned villages", most of which are still easily recognisable from the symmetry of their streets. Nine were founded in Moray: Archiestown (1760), Rothes (1766), Fochabers (1776; Plate 4), Tomintoul (1779), Cummingstown (1805), Dallas (1800), Aberlour (1812), Cullen (1822), Dufftown (1817), and Newmill (1759), near Keith.

The motives of the founders, the lairds of the estates on which they were built, were no doubt mixed. Some had real concern for the suffering of people forced to move from enclosed farms; some no doubt felt there was a need to absorb the surplus rural population to avoid increasing emigration. Some had perhaps a real desire to raise the standard of living of their tenants and improve life generally in Scotland. Others realised that the setting up of these villages might be in their own interests. By attracting new tenants as well as giving more secure employment to their own, the amount and number of rentals could be increased. In the village of Cuminestown, Aberdeenshire, annual rents increased from £11 per annum derived from "a moorish part of the farm" to £120-£150 a year from the new village" (Smout). By the introduction of "manufactures" — which, in this period, in rural areas, still meant cottage industries, trade could perhaps be fostered where poor conditions made it necessary to supplement agriculture. "Industries" were mainly textiles — the spinning of flax and

* During a period of unprecedented population increase from 1811 - 1831, the population of the upland parishes of Cabrach, Dallas, Inveravon, Kirkmichael and Mortlach increased by an average of 35%.

wool. Linen, with government stimulus, was Scotland's main industry of the 18th century but landlords encouraged those with other skills, glove makers, bakers . . . . . to take feus. At this stage these settlers were still partly dependent on home-produced food supplies and crofts were attached to most of the houses. The villages also domiciled estate and farm labourers.

The village planners' motives were well expressed in a letter written in January 1769 by Alexander Shaw, a leading figure in the linen industry to Jas. Grant of Castle Grant who founded Grantown-on-Spey in 1767:

> It is in the interest of every gentleman possessed of ane Estate in the Highlands to collect a number of Mechanicks, and other industrious people, into some centricall spot. For over all that Country, there is double the number of people necessary to cultivate the ground, so that it's impossible for them to live, and pay ane adequate rent to the Master; and they are so strong attached to the place of their nativity, that they rather starve than remove from it. This contributes to their poverty . . . and from their mean, scanty subsistence proceeds that sloth and idleness, so remarkable in the Country . . . . This Village would be productive of any good effects. For the people Observing the different Mechanicks live more plentifully and better clothed, without being exposed to the hardships and fatigue in the farming way would readily fall in love with business and send their Children to be instructed by them which would rid the country of a Burthen, and raise a sett of useful people, for the different purposes in life. It would also create a Mercate, for the different productions of the Country, near at hand; and consequently induce the Farmers to be at more pains to inprove their Farms & raise many articles of subsistence more advantageous; which on Account of their great distance from Towns, the heavie Toll exacted, and other expense they are exposed to, presently discourage them from attempting. The Linen manufacture, being now considered the staple of our Country, I presume it will be the principall object of your village . . . . .

Some of the landowners had less altruistic motives. Doubtless arising from contact with their more affluent brethren south of the border since the Union of Parliaments in 1707, many of the Lairds sought to improve their own residences creating the gardens and parklands which enhance many Scottish castles today. In many cases the "castletouns", sited nearby to allow the villagers to have protection from the castle walls in time of war, were growing and detracted from the view of the laird's seat. This was the situation at Fochabers where Alexander, 4th Duke of Gordon, forced the inhabitants of the old castletoun of Fochabers to move to the site of the present village.

"Sir
The Duke is anxious to have the present town of Fochabers removed — And, with that in view, has marked out a situation for a new Town — I have bargained with a few of the present Tenementers — and some houses are going on in the New Town — The fact however is, that many of the present possessors are unwilling to part with their old Habitations, but as the Duke is determined and intent upon it, Every method must be taken to force their removal . . . ."

(Letter to Mr Charles Gordon, Edinburgh, 20.11.1776).
(Gordon Castle Letter Books).

The old town of Cullen was likewise demolished to make way for improvements to nearby Cullen House. The new town, built in 1822, on higher ground rising above the ancient Fisher town of Seatown has fine wide streets and a large square, which like those of Fochabers, Grantown and Keith are typical of the new towns.

Some of the "new" villages were really extensions of existing ones. These included New Keith and Fife Keith (1817), New Elgin and Bishopmill which have in more recent times been absorbed into Keith and Elgin. The new town of Burghead replaced the existing village at the beginning of the 19th century. Branderburgh established as a new village in 1830 became part of the Burgh of Lossiemouth in 1890.

After a slow start, most of the new villages prospered but few attained industrial status as we now understand it because, by the early 19th century, the weaving industry was languishing. The points made by Mr Shaw in his letter concerning access to markets (for agriculture) and lack of roads prevented the growth of "exports" of manufactured goods from these towns in competition with Aberdeen and the towns in the south. The development of machines and factories in large towns put an end to cottage industries. Nevertheless population increased in the 19th century in many of the new villages which now became agricultural and service centres and tourist resorts. As the centralisation of services continues, many of these small towns and villages survive only as dormitory towns and holiday resorts. In the Spey Valley area, the towns of Aberlour, Dufftown and Rothes are too small to justify the provision of separate services such as sports facilities, community centres, secondary schools, and libraries. They can thus be seen as rivals, fragmenting the population which might otherwise form a unit and justify the provision of these services, although it has recently been agreed that a new secondary school should be built in Aberlour.

## The Growth of Population

During the period from 1755-1820 the population of the land increased by roughly two-thirds and as late as 1820 seven out of ten Scots still lived in rural areas. There is no clear explanation for this growth in population but it is likely that the main reason was the reduction in the death rate in infants which had formerly been very high ("it is not uncommon, I have frequently been told, in the Highlands of Scotland for a mother who has born twenty children not to have two alive" (Adam Smith).

The reduction in the death rate can be attributed to improvements in nutrition deriving from agricultural improvements producing more varied crops including carrots, turnips and particularly potatoes. The availability of potatoes might well have prevented repetition of the serious famines when grain harvests failed. Other contributory factors could have been the introduction to the Highlands of inoculation against smallpox — the worst epidemic killer at that time — and perhaps improvements in child care inspired by Dr. Wm. Buchan's "Domestic Medicine" which was published in twenty-two editions from 1769-1826.

In Moray between 1811 and 1831 there were unprecedented population increases ranging from 22% in the parish of Botriphnie to 75% in the parish of Duffus. By the 1830's however the parishes of Inveravon, Kirkmichael and Cabrach had reached their maximum populations and thereafter rural depopulation has continued right up to the present time.

The collapse of the rural linen industry due to competition from the south affected many parts of Moray, but the greatest exodus from the upland areas occurred in the period of economic depression in agriculture from 1880-1910. This was mainly attributable to the import of vast quantities of low-priced wheat and barley from North America. Between 1871 and 1911 the number of farm-holdings in Banffshire decreased from 4,550 to 3,418, because they were unprofitable. The depressed agricultural labourer suffered poor living standards, poor pay, long hours, poor housing, no amenities — and left. Although total natural increases in population continued, parish populations decreased as the rate of emigration increased. It is estimated that between 1880 and the early 1900's some 750-1,000 people left Moray to go to the USA, Canada and the colonies as well as other parts of Britain. Reductions in parish populations in this period ranged from 11.5% in Kirkmichael to 28.3% in Dallas. Emigration was highest from the upland areas (J. R. Gordon).

Many of the people leaving the upland areas settled in Elgin, Forres and Keith where there were more job opportunities, a range of occupations and better pay. Small industries in Elgin in 1915 included woollens, tweeds, leather, breweries, sawmills, cornmills, nurseries and iron founding. The population of Elgin increased from 6,286 in 1881 to 8,250 in 1911 (+31%) while Forres increased by 29.6% and Keith by 9.5%. Rothes by contrast lost 17% and Dufftown 11% (J. R. Gordon). In 1913, 1500 people left Moray for the USA, Canada, South Africa and New Zealand.

Rural depopulation continued after the 1st World War (Fig. 13) which had widened the horizons of men and women from the upland areas where life was often dull and monotonous. As farming suffered in the post-war depression many of the more remote crofts were abandoned. Primitive conditions, the bothy system, and long hours of work compared unfavourably with the shorter working day, housing, shopping and entertainments available in the towns. In the 1920's Banffshire lost 568 farmers and crofters; in the same period 121 crofters and 339 agricultural servants left farm-work in Moray (J. R. Gordon).

During the national economic depression, thousands left this whole area, but Elgin, which had lost 880 peoples by 1921, increased its population again by 1,034 in 1931 mainly as a consequence of the drift from the countryside. People were employed in light industries, service and administrative occupations in Elgin which then, as now, was the natural centre of the area.

As a consequence of rural depopulation, it was realised in the 1950's that the cost of various services could no longer be justified in relation to the numbers of people remaining. 37 pupils attended Achnarrow school in Glenlivet in 1900 but there were only 5 children on the roll in 1958 when the school was closed. Kirdels with a roll of 49 in 1885 closed when fewer than 10 attended in 1953. As the numbers attending rural schools decreased, it became more difficult to justify the improvement of old school buildings to bring them up to modern educational standards. In the 1950's Moray and Nairn Education Authority decided to close all one-roomed schools and establish area schools where necessary. Whereas, since the establishment of schools in 1872, there were about 60 primary and 10 secondary schools, there are now (1974), only 22 primary and 5 secondary schools in the County of Moray.

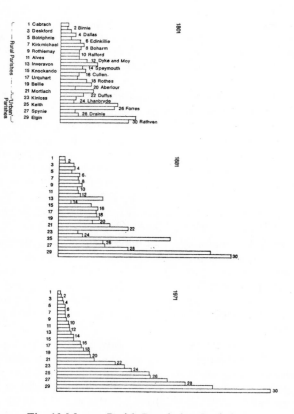

Fig. 13 Moray: Parish Population Statistics

*Whisky*

Whereas marginal farming in the upland areas was even more precarious in the 18th century than it is now, the heavy rainfall, the mountain streams and abundance of peat encouraged the making of whisky. There were 200 small stills in Glenlivet in 1822 and the income from the whisky trade was so good that people had given up crofting entirely. Whisky making guaranteed a living — until the exisemen came. The act of 1814 prohibited all stills with a capacity of less than 2285 litres (500 gallons) within the "Highland Line" but this only led to increased smuggling. As roads improved and supervision became more effective, particularly after the 1823 Act (which required the licensing of distilleries) people were obliged to leave the Cabrach and Glenlivet areas. George Smith of Glenlivet however, shrewd enough to see which way the wind was blowing, decided to establish a legal distillery, the first of the many legitimate highland distilleries. There are now about 45 distilleries in the Moray District — more than in any other part of the world and new distilleries are still being established. They give employment in many of the upland areas particularly in the Spey Valley and are the mainstay of most of the villages including Archiestown, Rothes, Dufftown and Tomintoul.

In the early days of the Glenlivet distillery the whisky had to be taken in carts drawn by Clydesdales over 56 km (35 miles) of mostly difficult country to the ports of Garmouth and Burghead for export to southern Scotland and England. Even as late as 1924 horses were used when steam traction engines could not be used in difficult winter road conditions to carry whisky from the distillery to the railway at Ballindalloch. As has already been mentioned the development of farming and the textile industries were similarly hampered by inadequate transport facilities.

*Transport Developments*

Up to the early 19th century it was almost impossible for people or goods to move over any appreciable distances. Only those whose work necessitated travel moved around the country on horseback: young university students walked from Moray to Aberdeen at the beginning of term. A start was made in improving communications following the 1715 rebellion when military roads were made to control the highland areas, but it was not until the 19th century, following the appointment of Thomas Telford to survey new roads and improve existing highways, that the foundations of the modern road system were laid. In less than two decades 148 km (920 miles) of roads were constructed and 1200 bridges were built. These made it possible to distribute goods more quickly. A toll bridge replacing the dangerous ferry over the Spey at Fochabers was opened in 1804. The post road from the Spey to Nairn was made a turnpike road under the provisions of an Act of Parliament passed in 1805. The prospects of revenue from tolls encouraged landed proprietors to raise more than £4,000 for construction of a road from the Findhorn bridge to Elgin. These roads enabled the introduction of stage coaches, the earliest form of public road transport. From 1811, a Mail coach operated daily between Aberdeen and Inverness. Commencing in 1825, the Star coach, which ran from Aberdeen, left Burnett's Inn, North Street, Elgin, "every lawful day" at 8 a.m.

Until the passing of the 1831 General Turnpike Act, road conditions were often poor particularly when heavy rain eroded primitive surfaces as this advertisement following the great floods of 1829 indicates:

> "In consequence of the great difficulty and obstruction occasioned in crossing the river Findhorn, and the general bad state of the roads at this season, the proprietors of the Elgin and Inverness STAR COACH, . . . have re-arranged arrival and departure times. By the arrangement the Coach will be enabled to complete her several journeys with day-light, which is so essential to the comfort and safety of the Passengers during the continuance of the present obstructions from the want of a Bridge over the Findhorn." — Elgin Courier, Friday, November 20th, 1829.

Before the roads, everything apart from local produce carried in primitive carts, or panniers, was transported by coastal sailing vessels. Although coasters became quicker and more reliable with the development of steam ships, (which gave a great impetus to the cattle trade in the south), for a long time most of the coastal trade was borne by sailing vessels which were, of course, vulnerable to bad weather and adverse winds which could delay cargoes for days and sometimes weeks.

The development of road and rail communications as well as the increasing trade by sea has had a decisive impact upon the settlement pattern (Fig. 12). The great improvements in roads opened up extensive areas formerly isolated and inaccessible for commercial farming, e.g. lime could now be brought from Keith and Dufftown for use in eastern Moray.

Road construction brought about a considerable advance in communications but in the 19th century before the development of the internal combustion engine horsedrawn vehicles were unable to exploit the area's commercial potential. And so it was the steam engine and the railway which opened up Moray, as elsewhere. "Railway mania" reached here in the 1840's, when many companies were set up and Acts of Parliament obtained to develop railways throughout Northern Scotland. The small scale and ease of the building operation over an easy level route enabled the Morayshire railway to be first on the track with the Elgin-Lossiemouth railway opened in August 1852. The building of the Great North of Scotland Railway Company Line which eventually ran from Aberdeen-Inverness with branches to Banff and Garmouth started in 1852. The rival Inverness and Aberdeen Junction Railway, which became the Highland railway in 1863, was extended from Elgin to Keith in 1858 but for some time passengers had to detrain and cross the Spey by road bridge until the railway bridge at Orton was completed.

The line to Orton, Rothes and Craigellachie also opened in 1858. Strathspey was opened up but while conditions must have improved, the overall effect was to cause more movement of population out of the area as country dwellers found new opportunities to move around and become aware of better conditions to be enjoyed in the towns. The coming of the railway assisted the commercial development of the fishing industry. No longer was it necessary for boats to sail the whole length of the Firth to land their catches. This of course caused the concentration of the industry in the larger ports. The Banff, Portsoy and Strathisla railway serving the coastal towns started in 1859 connecting to Elgin in 1863 (becoming part of the GNSR in 1867). One of the last lines to be constructed was the Elgin-Garmouth line in 1884.

The development of communications led to the growth of Elgin and assured its prosperity as the natural centre of communications in Moray. Roads and railways converged upon it from Strathspey, the coastal towns and from the main axis of east and west travel. By 1881 the population of Elgin had risen to 6,286 from its 1841 level of 4,493. It had been a little higher twenty years earlier in 1861 — possibly the result of the influx of railway construction workers. Similarly Keith became the most important inland settlement in Banffshire, with roads converging from the Banffshire highlands, from Moray and from the fishing towns and for a time it served as a rail junction. In 1964 villages in the Spey Valley lost their rail services, a direct result of the policy enunciated in the report on "The Reshaping of British Railways", (the "Beeching report"). The stations at Dava, Dunphail, Alves and Kinloss were also closed. All passenger branch railway lines throughout the Moray District are now closed; even the Aberdeen-Inverness line has not escaped the threat of closure. Although many feared the effects of the rail closures it is interesting to note that in 1963 a Ministry of Transport survey of transport use in rural areas discovered that only 10% of all journeys were made by public services. The Tomintoul area was one of a few Scottish rural areas chosen as typical for this survey which also indicated that more than 40% of households owned private cars — significantly above the national average.

With a fully developed road system, bus services and private cars have had sometimes contrary effects on settlement. Before the widespread ownership of personal transport the ubiquity of the omnibus again helped the development of Elgin as a market service centre since the principal bus station was situated there and all roads led to Elgin. Places such as Lhanbryde developed, while nearby Urquhart, not on the main bus route, did not have this advantage.

*Fishing Settlements*

The earliest recorded fishing settlements were those at Cullen, Garmouth, Lossiemouth, Covesea, Burghead and Findhorn. Findhorn and Garmouth were both ultimately abandoned as fishing ports as a consequence of the movements of the river mouths and sand bars.

The Seatown of Cullen had existed for well over 500 years. Like the neighbouring coastal ports it grew in the 19th century; by the late 1920's there were 273 fishermen living there owning 42 boats including 25 steam drifters (Anson). That is not to say that all these vessels used Cullen harbour, or certainly not at the same time. The harbour was small and subject to silting. Like most of the former coastal ports, with the exception of Buckie, Lossiemouth and Burghead, commercial fishing from Cullen harbour ceased some years ago.

Although the three villages of Covesea, Lossiemouth and Stotfield had been in existence for many years before this, it was not until 1698 that Elgin Town Council acquired land at the mouth of the river Lossie for its first harbour which was built in the early 18th century establishing a port for fishing and trade with the continent. In 1830 the proprietor of the land west of the river mouth founded Branderburgh which, together with Stotfield, formed the Burgh of Lossiemouth in 1890. The harbour was improved in 1837 and 1860; in 1881 there were 149 sailing boats and 395 fishermen; by 1929 there were 44 steam drifters and line fishing boats, 27 motor boats and 474 fishermen (Anson).

Burghead is unquestionably one of the most ancient settlements in Moray (see pages 115 - 118). According to the Old Statistical Account, the old fishing village of Burghead, (demolished to give way to the new town), had 400 inhabitants in 1793. In the early century a company was formed to develop a port. The harbour was built about 1807, part of the old port being demolished to provide foundations for the large warehouses which still stand along the quayside. By 1828, 93 fishing boats sailed from Burghead. Improvements to the harbour were made in 1858 and the branch line to the Elgin-Forres Railway was opened in 1861. (Grain, potatoes, timber, free stone, herring and oatmeal were exported; imports included coal, slates, ore and guano).

In 1929 there were 23 steam and 13 motor boats owned by 268 fishermen. Burghead became an important trading and fishing port, steamers from Inverness calling regularly before proceeding to Leith and London. Trade was also carried on with Russia and the Baltic ports and this traditional trading goes on up to the present day: vessels of about 800 tonnes call regularly importing timber from Finland, Sweden, Poland and Russia carried in Dutch and German chartered freighters. In 1974, 40 vessels brought in about 35,000 tonnes* of timber valued at about £3,200,000. The annual value of the fishing industry at Burghead is about £500,000 currently derived from winter sprat fishing and summer prawn fishing carried on by about 25 boats.

Burghead is the location of the largest maltings in Scotland providing a supplement to the malt production in the many distilleries throughout the Moray District. The maltings were established in 1966 and were extended to double the production capacity in 1971. About 15,000 tonnes of distillers' dry grains from the maltings are exported annually, from Burghead harbour, for cattle feed to Germany and Holland.

According to the Old Statistical Account, Portessie became a fishing station in 1727, the original fishermen coming from Findhorn, but Anson suggests that a reference to the "Boat Hythe called Rottinslough" in the records of Cullen indicates that "The Sloch" was settled in 1594. The modern village of Findochty first settled in 1716 by men from Fraserburgh was laid out in 1833. Its harbour was enlarged in 1883. The first house in Portknockie is said to have been built by a man from Cullen in 1677; his colleagues followed, attracted by the natural harbour there. The present harbour was built by the Seafield Estate in 1880. In 1855 there were 595 fishermen at Portknockie and even in 1929 there were 555 men owning 58 steam drifters engaged in a flourishing herring trade. Portgordon was founded in 1797 by the fourth Duke of Gordon.

The first house in Hopeman was built in 1805 and although there were 445 people living in the village by 1831, the harbour was little better than a natural creek until 1865 when the present harbour was built. In 1881 there were 250 men and boys engaged in fishing, sailing 119 boats from Hopeman, where the population had increased to 1323. Like so many of the harbours of the small fishing ports of the Moray Firth, Hopeman harbour has become silted up in recent years. The fishing fleet must use other ports, principally on the west coast and the harbour is now mainly a haven for pleasure sailing craft. The village however continues to grow as a dormitory town for Elgin and Royal Air Force personnel.

Cummingston, (Port Cumming), is an example of a "planned

*1 tonne = 1000 kg. = 2205 lb.

village" conceived with rather more enthusiasm than the situation warranted. The "pleasant, convenient and desirable situation" to quote from the poster printed for the proprietor, Sir William Cumming Gordon (Gordon Cumming) in 1808, suffered from two clear disadvantages. Almost equidistant from the ancient settlement of Burghead which was growing, and the newly settled village of Hopeman, both conveniently situated at the shore, Cummingston is about 15 m (50 ft) above, and a few hundred yards from, the creek, known as "The collach", which was advertised as "a safe and convenient landing place for boats". As any sailing man knows, it requires a fair degree of skill to negotiate the rocks on entering the Collach with an onshore breeze; it is not surprising therefore that by 1814, of the 18 houses built in the village, only 6 were occupied by fishermen. While the populations of Burghead and Hopeman had grown to more than 1,000 in 1851, that of Cummingston was only 155, about 50 fewer than the present day population.

The lack of transport, roads and railways which hindered development of farming, industry, trade and service centres paradoxically caused the fishing villages to develop during the 19th century. Poor land transport facilities existing when the harbours were built required these villages to be as self-sufficient as possible and helped to create local commercial monopolies.

Without the safety which harbours afford in bad weather many lives were lost at sea in the 18th century: a writer in the Old Statistical Account maintains that deaths at sea at that time exceeded those from natural causes.

As the harbours were built, boats became larger and eventually became steam powered, the older settlements in creeks where harbours were not built fell into disuse and disappeared. The industry became concentrated on the larger ports which could offer marketing and maintenance facilities for ships designed to work the more distant fishing grounds. Larger boats brought about commercial development of the fishing industry and it became more economical and convenient to move fish by rail to southern markets from a limited number of ports.

The development of the coastal ports is closely connected with the development of the herring fishery industry which began about 1815 (see pages 199 - 202). By 1840, a flourishing export trade in herring with the Baltic countries, Germany, Russia and Ireland brought prosperity to the fishing towns. This

R

resulted in immigration to the coastal villages. Many came from
the rural areas, farm labourers attracted by the higher wages
paid for curing and barreling. Hopeman had a population of
630 by 1841; Lossiemouth increased in population from 300 in
1791 to 1061 in 1841. At Burghead the population rose to 829
in 1841 and 1662 in 1891.

This prosperity resulted in the development of the towns,
especially Buckie and Lossiemouth. It was during this period
that most of the solid, well-built homes of the boat owners in
the new town of Buckie were built above the "yardie", where the
irregular pattern of small houses and sheds of the old fisher-
town still form a striking contrast with the symmetry of the new
town. Buckie grew out of several separate villages. "Buckie-west
the-burn", near Buckpool harbour, dating from 1645 was "by
tradition, the oldest village in the parish" according to the
Old Statistical Account. The other villages formed what must
be one of the longest towns of its size in the country: stretching
5 km (3 miles) along the coast are Gordonsburgh, Ianstown,
Portessie and Easter Buckie.

The first harbour of Buckie, at the Hythie, was not built
until 1843. A wooden structure, it cannot have been very
substantial, for within six years it had been washed away.
Buckpool (Nether Buckie) harbour, completed in 1857, played a
significant part in the development of Buckie as a fishing port
but it too proved inadequate and was replaced in 1878 by the
Cluny deep water harbour in Easter Buckie.

The population of Buckie rose slowly until 1851; by 1861 it
had 2165 inhabitants, but then it grew at a remarkable rate
its 5231 inhabitants in 1881 increasing to 5849 in 1891, to
7461 in 1901 and in 1911 to 8897, making it the biggest centre
of population in the Moray/Banff area at that time. In 1891
there were more than 3,500 fishermen living there and about 250
boats used Buckie harbour. They were supported by a large
number of curers, coopers, boatbuilders, sailmakers and workers
in other ancillary industries. Between 1900 and 1920 there
were more fishermen from Buckie engaged in the herring industry
than from any other British port.

By 1921 it was clear that the fishing industry must find
new methods and new sources of income. Fortunately an
alternative was available, the seine net or "snurrevod" developed
and perfected in Denmark. Once again the Moray ports were to

the fore in exploiting new methods and Lossiemouth fishery district, which included Hopeman and Burghead with Lossiemouth as its chief port, became the leading seine net centre in Scotland. Lossiemouth maintained this position, reaching a pre-war peak in 1937 when landings of 7,500 tonnes (147,765 cwt) equalled 45% of the Scottish catch. Meanwhile Buckie although used as a base for the first seine netters in the Moray Firth, carried on traditional herring fishing, seine-net fishing being regarded as an ancillary between the herring seasons.

The 2nd World War once again affected the Moray Firth ports, 50% of Scottish fishermen being called to service and almost as many boats were requisitioned. Although landings became concentrated in a limited number of ports, the demand for fish to augment the nation's food supplies, price controls, and the adoption of seining by older men resulted in the Scottish fishing industry emerging from the war with greater productivity than in 1938; the 1945 total landings were more than double those of the pre-war years. In fact the war years can be seen as a period of take off leading to greatly increased catches attained in the last three decades.

The visitor to the Moray ports other than Buckie, seeing them as they are today, may be excused if he is puzzled. Here is a series of bright, clean, attractive little towns, each providing homes for about 1200 people with no apparent means of economic support. Yet they show no sign of neglect or deterioration. On the contrary many of the old houses are carefully preserved and have a real charm (Plate 27). The answer to the puzzle is threefold: firstly, these are dormitory towns for fishermen, their families and others who find employment in the service industries in the larger centres, Banff, Buckie, Keith and Elgin. Secondly, many Banff and Moray people return here and others come from industrial areas in their retirement, and thirdly all these towns have a developing tourist potential. The Moray Firth climate, the clean beaches, unspoiled by the commercialism of southern "seaside holiday resorts", the character of the old towns and their harbours make this whole area particularly attractive for young families. Almost all the towns and villages of the new Moray District have a thriving tourist industry. Supporting statistics are not readily available but people familiar with recent developments cannot have failed to notice the growth in numbers of hotels, restaurants, caravan and camping sites in the area. In addition there has been a significant increase in bed and breakfast accommodation.

*Conclusion*

This chapter began with the assertion that settlement is determined by physical characteristics. This is still true of Moray but much depends upon man's reaction to these characteristics. Settlement in Moray has been greatly influenced during the last thirty years by the decisions of politicians and Service chiefs in establishing and maintaining large air-stations at Lossiemouth and Kinloss. Kinloss, established during the war, has become a base for maritime reconnaissance and anti-submarine training aircraft operating in the North Sea and the North Atlantic. The station at Lossiemouth, established in the late 1930's by the RAF as a flying training school, was the main base for the Fleet Air Arm's strike aircraft. "HMS Fulmar" provided training facilities and served as a shore base for Buccaneer squadrons when not at sea on aircraft carriers. The station was taken over by the RAF in September 1972 when aircraft carriers were phased out.

The importance of these service stations to the economy of Moray is crucial. In an area heavily dependent upon the primary industries, farming, forestry and fishing with little manufacturing industry, the Ministry of Defence is one of the largest employers in Moray. It is estimated that, including service personnel, about 6,500 people are employed, directly or indirectly. About half the income (c. £13 million) of the area is derived from the Service stations. Service and civilian employees spend an estimated £1.5 million on goods and services in the Elgin, Lossiemouth and Forres areas.

This brief review of settlement in Moray seems to indicate that the planners are simply following a trend rather than setting one. Assisted by improvements in communications and the attending benefit of greater freedom of movement for the individual, throughout the last 200 years there has been a clear trend towards concentration of people in towns. Whereas in 1801 the landward areas contained about 77% of the total population and only 23% were resident in the burghs, more than two thirds now live in the towns and burghs in the Moray District. Whether one should welcome this trend is an open question. When one considers the advantages and disadvantages of city living there may be some who would agree with sentiments recently expressed by Thor Heyerdahl, which seem to be particularly appropriate to Moray! "Progress can today also be defined as man's ability to complicate simplicity . . . . Without the farmer and the fisherman modern society would collapse, with all its shops and all its pipes and wires. The farmers and the fishermen represent the nobility of modern society, who share their crumbs with the rest of us who run about with papers and screwdrivers, attempting to build a better world without a blueprint."

# 17

# PLACE NAMES

## DONALD MACAULAY

Various sources for the names have been consulted. The primary source, and the one from which forms of the names have been adopted, is the Ordnance Survey 1 inch: 1 mile map (OS) and the OS Books of Reference to the plans of the parishes. The pronunciation of the names, as far as this was possible, was checked with local informants. This showed up some errors in the OS forms (Auchinlech for Auchinclech [Rothiemay], is a typical example). Place-names are referred to the parish in which they occur eg. *Auchinclech* (Rothiemay).

Some of the names occur in early documents. The most notable of these is the Registrum Episcopatum Moraviense (RM), the Episcopal Register of Moray, published for the Spalding Club in 1837. It contains material dating to the beginning of the 13th century.

Early maps are also important for the historical perspective they give us of the names. The earliest geographer to take an interest in Scotland and whose work remains is, of course, Ptolemy. Unfortunately there is little correspondence between the names that he gives us for our area and any names to be found in later documents or maps. It is difficult even to correlate places named on the Ptolemy map with actual localities. The name given to what appears to be the river Spey is *Tuesis* and the name given to the river Findhorn is *Loxa* (which looks as if it ought to refer to the Lossie but is, perhaps, too far displaced for that to be likely). The tribe who, we are told, occupy the area, the *Vacomagi,* leave no trace of their name, either; and the same is true of the 'towns' ascribed to them.

Later cartographers, however, such as Blaeu, Sir Robert Gordon of Straloch and Timothy Pont give us valuable evidence.

Such evidence, it should be said, must be used with caution. The RM contains a map of the area based on Gordon.

A comprehensive study of the names of the Moray District would run to a large volume. Here we can only try to give a general picture of the nomenclature and its implications.

Part of the problem of dealing with the names is that the history of the area, especially its linguistic history, has been complex. The earliest identifiable, historical inhabitants were the Picts. The best information we have about them suggests that at least two languages were spoken in their domain. One of these languages is not intelligible. Name elements from such a language would, of course, not be intelligible to us, and probably some at least of the obscure names are of this origin. The other appears to be a language akin to the ancestor of Welsh (W) and to Gaulish. That is to say, it is a Celtic language; but it belongs to a different group of Celtic languages from Gaelic — although certain elements of the one are so similar to the other that confusion can arise.

We would expect certain elements from this Celtic language, which we may call British, to appear in the names of the Moray area, and indeed we find that they do. We will look first of all at elements which are accepted as being British and not Gaelic (G). The most important of these is the element *pit, pet*: a piece of land. The distribution of this element has been shown to coincide with the known territory of the historical Picts. It occurs eight times in our area. On each of those occasions it is combined with a Gaelic second element.

*Pitchaish* (Inveravon) *pit chais*: steep 'pit'
*Pitchroy* (Knockando) *pit chruaidh*: hard 'pit'
*Pitcraigie* (Rothes) the locative case of *pit creageach*: rocky 'pit'
*Pittendreich* (Elgin) *pit an dreich*: 'pit' of the face
*Pittensier* (St Andrews) *pit nan saor*: 'pit' of the artificers
*Pitgaveny* (St Andrews) *pit gamhna*: 'pit' of heifer
*Pitglassie* (Mortlach) *pit glasaich*: 'pit' of grassland
*Pittyvaich* (Mortlach) *pit a' bhathaich*: 'pit' of byre

Another element in this class is *cardden*: copse. Examples of this are: *Urquhart ar*: 'on' and *cardden, '*the place on the copse'.
*Cardenhill* (Alves) which shows the combination of *Carden* as a place name with English 'hill'.

*Cardnach* (Knockando) This is *cardden* with the Gaelic termination -*ach* which means 'having the property of' or 'full of'. *Allacardoch* (Keith) This is the previous name preceded by G. *al*: rock, cliff.

*Nether Carnach* (Dyke & Moy) is probably the same name with the -d- lost between r and n.

A related element *pert*: 'bush' occurs in *Bolnapiart* (Inveravon). It is *buaile na peart*, 'the fold of the bush'. Another word for bush *pres* is not found in Irish but is common in Scottish Gaelic as *preas*. There are two occurrences in our area: *Prescaulton* (Knockando) is Gaelic *preas calltuinn*: 'hazel bush'; *Presley* (Dyke & Moy) is probably an old British name *presle*: 'bush place'.

The element *aber*: confluence (in early documents *abir*, *obir*) is British. Its Gaelic equivalent is *inbhir* (inver). Aber- is widely distributed in Scotland. In our area it occurs in *Aberlour* (see page 259). There appear to be no *aber*- names in the area immediately west of the Spey.

There is then considerable evidence of speakers of a British language in the area. We notice that in most cases the British elements are compounded with Gaelic ones which shows us that the names belong to the era of the Gaelic takeover of the territory, probably from the late 8th century onwards.

One of the other linguistic groups to leave their mark conspicuously on the nomenclature of Scotland is the Norsemen. However, in Moray they have left no direct impression. There are no Norse names to be found.

Most of the names are either Gaelic or English in origin. They give us a picture of a Gaelic settlement (superimposed, as we have seen above, on a previous language group) with, superimposed upon it, a settlement by English speakers. The exact dating of the beginning of this English settlement and the speed of its development are not entirely clear. Unfortunately, the names do not help us much in determining them. The forms in RM do not, for the most part, suggest an acquaintance on the part of the clerks with Gaelic literacy. This suggests that the Church was an Anglicising agency, as well as a 'civilizing agency' for the central authority in the area, and that in this it supported the cultural displacement being affected by the feudal barons, at least as early as the end of the 12th century. This is no more than we would expect. The actual patterns of settlement do not seem, as far as we can see from the nomenclature, to have undergone radical changes. There are no signs that the process of English settlement entailed large population replacements. On the contrary there is clear evidence of bilingualism. This is especially evident in the adoption of the English -s plural ending for plural name forms in Gaelic e.g. Ordens, G. *ordan*: protruberances; Knockans, G. *cnocain*: hillocks.

The proportion of English to Gaelic names is now, of course, strongly weighted towards the former. However, if we look at the origin of name elements we find that the balance is fairly even. We also find a strong correlation in elements across the two languages, which reflect a socio-economic continuity over a very long period.

As to the distribution of English and Gaelic elements, again the picture is what we would expect from our knowledge of the history of the area. There are Gaelic elements to be found over the entire District but they are fewer on the coastal plain than in the inland areas. On the coastal plain, also, Gaelic names are much more obscured in form by long adaptation in the mouths of English and Scots speakers. By contrast, in areas such as parts of Kirkmichael, Gaelic names are preserved in their original form. Inveravon is clearly an intermediate area. This gives us a general picture of a pattern of early displacement of Gaelic by English in the fertile lowland areas and a much more gradual displacement in the inland parts.

Since we are unable to deal with all the names it seems a reasonable compromise to look at the most common name elements. Since the English names and the elements of which they are composed are almost all transparent, I have concentrated on Gaelic elements, which present considerable problems of interpretation. Reference is made in passing to corresponding elements of English origin.

*baile: settlement*

The commonest Gaelic element denoting a settlement is the element *baile* which corresponds closely with *-town, -ton* from Early English *tun*.
Examples are:
*Ballachurn* (Inveravon) *baile a' chuirn*: settlement of the cairn.
*Baile a' Mhuileann* (Kirkmichael): settlement of the mill (cf. English Milltown).

*Bailebeg* (Kirkmichael) *baile beag*: little settlement.

*Ballindallochkan*: (Inveravon) *baile a' chnocan*: settlement of the hillock.

*Ballanlish* (Kirkmichael) *baile an leis*: settlement of the enclosure.

*Ballanloan* (Kirkmichael) *baile an loin*: settlement of the meadow.

*Ballantruan* (Kirkmichael) *baile an t-sruthan*: settlement of the stream.

*Bailebain* (Kirkmichael) *baile bàn*: white settlement, or settlement no longer cultivated.

*Ballcorach* (Kirkmichael) *baile corrach*: tapering settlement.

*Ballenreich* (Boharm) *baile an fhraoich*: settlement of the heather.

*Ballenteem* (Aberlour) *baile an tuim*: settlement of the hillock.

*Balgreen* (Boharm) *baile na gréine*: settlement of the sun (sunny place).

*Ballimeanach* (Knockando) *baile meadhonach*: mid town. This name is of a type found more commonly in the English toponymy of the area eg. *Midtown*, going with *Eastertown* and *Westertown* and the distinguishing elements of *Upper* and Lower.

*Balliemullich* (Aberlour) *baile mullaich*: top (highest) settlement.

*Balnabreich* (Boharm) *baile na braich*: settlement of the malt, ie. where malt was made.

*Balnacoul* (Aberlour) *baile nan coll*: settlement of the hazels.

*Balnacree* (Boharm) *baile na craoibh*: settlement of the tree.

*Balnaferry* (Forres) *baile na feuraich*: settlement of the grasslands.

*Balnakyle* (Aberlour) *baile na coille*: settlement of the wood.

*Balnageith* (Forres) *baile na gaoithe*: windy settlement, or settlement of the marsh.

*Balnaglach* (Knockando) *baile nan clach*: settlement of the stones.

*Balnagone* (Knockando) *baile nan gobhan*: settlement of the smiths.

*Balvenie* (Mortlach) *baile a' bheannaich*: settlement of the blessing (shrine).

*Shanwell* (Dyke & Moy) *sean bhaile*: old town. This is a common type among English names especially in the form *Newtown*. There are no 'Newtowns' among the Gaelic names unless

*Belno* (Inveravon) is *baile nuadh*. The element *bel-* I take, in most cases, to denote *buaile*: a fold; (see below).

It will be seen that for the most part the defining element that goes with *baile* is topographic: it names some distinctive feature of the landscape associated with the settlement. Some, such as *grassland* and *meadow*, refer to land use. Only two refer to the profession of the settler. Two refer to function; one has religious connotations. Most of these defining elements appear also in the English farm names of the area. Some English elements such as *Tennanttown, Cottertown, Mains, Home Farm* and *Pauper's cottage* have no Gaelic equivalent. This reflects the changing social structure of the community in the later period.

### Land division and field names

We may next look at elements that denote land divisions, and land use.

*Davoch* (Grange) G. *dabhach*: vat, tub. The most convincing explanation of this is that it was a land measure denoting the amount of land that could be sown with a vatful of grain. Certainly it is the commonest land measure in documents relating to early Gaelic Scotland.

*Daugh of Corinacy* (Kirkmichael) *dabhach* appears in several forms in early documents and on maps e.g. *daugh, dauch, doch*. Incidentally, *Corinacy* is likely to be *coire an fhasaidh*: corrie of the settlement; *fasadh* is related to the element *fas*, also meaning a settlement or station (See *Dallas* p. 260).

*Drumdauch* (Knockando) *druim nan davoch*: ridge of the davochs.

*Halfdavoch* (Dyke & Moy). This illustrates the adoption of the term into English and also central place of the notion as a land measure.

*Lettoch* (Inveravon) *leth dabhach*: half davoch is the Gaelic form of the previous name. *Craiglethie* (Grange) is probably *creag lethdabhaich*: rock of half davoch.

*Reddavie* (Elgin) is probably *reidh an dabhaich*: plain of the Davoch.

*Squaredoch* (Dyke & Moy) shows the combination of English *square* with *davoch*.

There are other elements denoting land divisions. For

example, many names throughout the area begin in *Auch-* which is Gaelic *achadh* the most common element denoting field.

*Clune of Elchies* (Knockando) Clune is from G. *cluain* a piece of pastureland.

*Croitanloin* (Knockando) *croit an loin* the croft of the meadow. There are numerous English names containing the element *croft*.

*Gortons* (Knockando) *gortan*: arable fields, plots. The ending -an is the Gaelic plural ending. The English plural -s is added to this.

*Inchkeil* (Duffus) *innis na coille*: pastureland of the wood. All *Inch-* names contain this element.

*Lesmurdie* (Cabrach) contains G. *leas, lios*: an enclosure: In modern Gaelic it means 'garden' (cf. Gardenhead (Grange)). (The element *-murdie* is obscure to me).

Many names beginning with *Dal-, Del-* are probably field names but as *dail* usually means 'hollow' in Gaelic this is difficult to determine (cf. *Dellachaple, Delnabo, Delchirach* below).

*Pennycairn* (Inveravon) *peighin a' chàrn*: pennyland of the cairn.

*The Ochts* (Dallas) probably derives from *na h-ochdamhan*: the eights (from *ochdamh*: an eighth, which was a common land measure (cf. Midthird (Botriphnie)).

There are some interesting English names such as *Newtack* (Grange); *Southfen* (Elgin); *Teindland* (Elgin) (land of the tithes); *Acres* of Balintomb; *Plewlands* (Drainie), which have no Gaelic equivalents.

## Crop names

Surprisingly few names refer to crops.

*Dalachale* (Kirkmichael) *dail a' chàil*: hollow of the cabbage.

*Lynachork* (Kirkmichael) is *linne a' choirce*: pool of the oats or of the oatfield. (cf. *Tom chork* (Dallas) *tom a' choirce*: hillock of the oats (probably put there to dry)).

*Inaltrie* (Dyke & Moy) *ionaltraich*: pasture.

*Shougle* (Birnie) is probably *seagal, siogal*: rye (cf. Ryeyards Elgin)).

## Domestic animal names

There are several names referring to domestic animals.

*Auchnarrow* (Inveravon) *achadh nan tarbh*: field of the bulls
(cf. *Tarulian* (Kirkmichael) *tarbh liana*: bull meadow).
*Clachnagour* (Inveravon) *clach nan gabhar*: stone of the goats
(cf. *Lochan nan Gobhar* (Kirkmichael): little loch of the
goats; *Knocknagore* (Knockando) *cnoc nan gabhar*: hill of
the goats; and *Gawrie* (Rothes) *gabhraich*: place of the
goats).
*Dalchirach* (Inveravon) *dail chaorach*: sheep hollow (or field).
*Delmickmore* (Inveravon) *dail muic mór*: big pig hollow (or
field) (cf. *Glackmuck* (Botriphnie) *glac nam muc*: gap of
the pigs).
*Delnabo* (Kirkmichael) *dail nam bó*: hollow of the cows. (cf.
*Lochnabo* (Urquhart & St Andrews) *loch nam bó*: loch of
the cows).
*Rynamarst* (Kirkmichael) *raon nam mart*: plain of the cattle.
With this group also go:
*Auchavaich* and *Lagavaich* (Inveravon) *achadh, lag a' bhàthaich*:
the field, hollow of the byre (cf. *Byres* (Bellie).
*Badivochel* (Inveravon) *bad a' bhuachail*: the herdsman's clump.
*Bolnapiart* (Inveravon) *buaile na pert*: fold of the bush and
other names in *Bol-*, *Bel-*.
There are a few *shiel-* names e.g. *Shielpark* (Rothiemay) but
there seems to be no name extant clearly containing the element
*àirigh*: shieling.
There are similar English names e.g. *Goatlees* (Mortlach);
*Oxwell* (Keith); *Ramsburn* (Rothiemay); *Stotfield* (Dallas);
*Wedders Hill* (Duffus) and so on.

*'Activity' names*
Some names denote activities performed in the locality.
*Allt a' bhainne* (Kirkmichael): burn of the milk (cf. Milkburn
(Grange)).
*Auchenhalrig* (Bellie) *achadh na h-eilrig*: field of the deer trap.
(Deer were driven into a valley with a narrow opening and
slaughtered as they tried to escape through this opening).
*Beinn a' chruinnich* (Kirkmichael): peak of the gathering.
*Cnoc na Croiche* (Boharm): hill of the gallows. (cf. *Gallowshill*
(Inveravon, Mortlach and elsewhere)).
*Knockshalg* (Inveravon) *cnoc nan sealg*: hill of the hunts.
*Maggieknockater* (Boharm) *magh an fhucadair*: plain of the
fuller or waulker (cf. *Bleachfield* (Dyke & Moy)).

*Balnabreich* (Boharm): *baile na braich*: farm of the malt (cf. *Maltkiln* (Mortlach)).

*Tomnamoin* (Dallas) *tom na mónadh*: peat hillock (cf. *Peathillock* (Dyke & Moy)).

*Tomnavoulin* (Inveravon) *toman a' mhuileann*: hillock of the mill. There are many English hill-names throughout the area.

*Church names*

There are several names with church connotations.

*Ardemanoch* (Keith) *àrd nam manach*: height of the monks. (cf. *Dalmany* (Alves)); *dail manaich*: monk's field; *Mannochhill* (Rothiemay); *Monkland* (Forres).

*Balvenie* (Mortlach) *baile a' bheannaich*: settlement of the blessing (shrine).

*Bomakellock* (Botrphnie) *both Mo-Cheallag*: hut of Mo-cheallag. This saint's name occurs also in Islay.

*Incharnock* (Elgin) *innis Earnag*: field of Earnag. The usual form of the saint's name is *Mo-Earnag* which gives English Marnock (cf. *Kilmarnock*).

*Rechlerich* (Inveravon) *rèidh a' chléirich*: plain of the cleric (cf. *Clerkseat* (Grange)).

*Stràthandean* (Kinloss) *srath an deadhain*: dean's strath (cf. *Deanshillock* (Speymouth)).

There are few *Kil-* names, from *cill(e)* - church. Only four occur in our area. There are only four names beginning with *Kirk-*, also, which is somewhat surprising. There are many English ecclesiastical names; e.g. *Chapelhill* (Dyke & Moy); *St. Peter's Well* (Speymouth); *Priest's Well* (Cabrach); *Abbeylands* (Kinloss); *Blackfriarhaugh* (Elgin) and so on.

*Topographic elements*

We may now look briefly at the topographic elements.

(a) *Water names*

*Aldavallie* (Dyke & Moy) *allt a' bhealaidh*: burn of the broom.

*Auchness* (Dallas) *achadh an easa*: field of the waterfall.

*Buineach* (Dallas) *buineach*: place of the springs.

*Bogentenie* (Elgin) *bog an teine*: bog of the fire (phosphorescence).

*Corskie* (Urquhart) *crasgaich*: place of the crossing (G. *crasg*: crossing).

*Eskmore* (Inveravon) *uisge mór*: large water (i.e. stream).
*Enoch* (Mortlach) *aonach*: upland plain.
*Fuaran dearg* (Inveravon): red spring.
*Findouran* (Cabrach) *fionn dobhran*: little white water.
*Keichan* (Keith) *caothan*: torrent (cf. *Lochliesk* (Boharm) *loch leisg*: lazy (still) loch).
*Lynavoir* (Kirkmichael) *linne mhór*: large pool.
*Pollflasgan* (Knockando) *poll nam fleasgan*: pool of the branches.
The commonest English elements are *burn* and *strype* e.g.
*Burniestripe* (Urquhart); *Strypeside* (Keith; Dyke & Moy) and so on.

(b) *Names of raised ground*
*Alnaceo* (Mortlach) *al na ceó*: cliff of the mist.
*Ardoch* (Dallas, Dyke & Moy) *àrdach*: high place (àrd: high, height).
*Barmuckity* (St. Andrews & Lhanbryde) *bàrr mucadaidh*: *top* of the place of the pigs.
*Cairnliath* (Kirkmichael) *carn liath*: grey cairn (or hill).
*Craigellachie* (Knockando) *creag eallachaidh*: cliff, rock of 'eallachie' (the meaning of the element is obscure).
*Drummin* (Inveravon) *druimean*: little ridge (cf. *The Drum* (Dallas) *(an) druim*: (the) ridge).
*Edingight* (Grange) *aodan gaoithe*: face of the marsh (or of the wind).
*Knapernaich* (Grange) *Cnaparnaich*: humpy ground from *cnap*: hump, lump.
*Knockbog* (Grange) *cnoc bog*: soft hillock; (cf. *Cnocnavae* (Kirkmichael) *cnoc na fèith*; hill of the bog; *Knockan* (Boharm) *cnocan*: hillock).
*Latternach* (Grange) *Leitirneach*: the place of the steep slope(s) (from *leitir*: steep slope).
*Tomintoul* (Kirkmichael) *tom an t-sabhail*: hillock of the barn.
*Tor* (Rafford) *torr*: protuberance; appears also as Tar(r).
*Tulloch* (Rafford) *tulach*: hillock. This element appears most usually as Tilly-, sometimes in Aberdeenshire, e.g. as Tough.

(c) *names of low ground*
*Clashdhu* (Rafford) *clais dhubh*: black depression, ditch.
*Mayen* (Rothiemay) *maighean*: little plain from *magh*: plain (cf. *Rothiemay* (below) etc).

*Retanach* (Rothiemay) *rèidh tamhnach*: fertile (smooth) plain. There are twelve names with this element *Re-*, *Rae-*, in Moray.

*Slacks* (Dallas) *slag*: hollow, with English plural -s; so the original name was probably plural *slagan*.

(d)   *'valley' names*

*Ballochford* (Cabrach) *bealach*: pass, valley, with English -ford added.

*Belneddan* (Kirkmichael) *buaile an fheadan*: fold of the narrow valley from *feadan*: pass, narrow valley.

*Glack* (Aberlour) *glac*: defile, pass.

*Glenlatterach* (Birnie) *gleann leitireach*: glen of the steep slopes.

*Urlarmore* (Kirkmichael) *urlar mór*: large floor, bottom of valley).

*Mostly defining elements*

(i)   *non-domestic animals and bird names*

*Blairshinnoch* (Rothes) *blàr nan sionnach*: field of the foxes.

*Brocloch* (Rafford) *broclach*: badger's den.

*Rinafiach* (Knockando) *rinn nam fitheach*: point of the ravens.

*Tomneen* (Knockando) *tom nan eun*: hillock of the birds.

(ii)   *vegetation names*

*Ardcanny* (Rothes) *àrd canaich*: height of bogcotton.

*Ballenreich* (Dyke & Moy) *baile an fhraoich*: farm of the heather.

*Collie* (Rothes) *coille*: wood. There are many names containing this element.

*Colltom* (Dallas) *coll tom*: hazel hillock. (cf. *Coldhome* (Dallas, etc) which is the same name. *coll*: Hazel *(col-, cal-, cow-)* is the commonest element of this class by far).

*Darnet* (Rothes) *darnait*: little oak (wood), from *dar*: oak.

*Drummuir* (Cabrach, Botriphnie) *druim an iubhir*: ridge of the yew.

*Fernyfield* (Speymouth) *feàrnaich*: place of the alders, with English 'field' added.

*Rinaitin* (Aberlour) *rèidh an aitinn*: plain of the juniper.

*Shalloch* (Boharm) *seileach*: willow.

*Tom na brilach* (Inveravon) *tom na braoilich*: hillock of the whortleberries.

These elements are almost all reflected in English names.

(iii)  *shape and size names*

*Achfad* (Inveravon) *achadh fada*: long field.
*Bailebeg* (Knockando) *baile beag*: little settlement.
*Crumalt* (Cabrach) *crom allt*: crooked stream.
*Invercarach* (Cabrach) *inbhir carach*: twisting confluence.
*Knockmore* (Birnie) *cnoc mór*: large hill.

(iv)  *colour names*

*Aultderg* (Bellie) *allt dearg*: red stream.
*Bogbain* (Keith) *bog bàn*: white bog; cf. *Whitecross* (Dallas).
*Breacach* (Dyke & Moy) *breacach*: speckled place, from *breac*:
    speckled.
*Clashdon* (Dallas) *clais donn*: brown depression or ditch.
*Corr Riabhach* (Kirkmichael): brindled corrie.
*Craigroy* (Knockando and several others) *creag ruadh*: red rock;
    cf. *Redstone* (Dyke & Moy).
*Dounduv* (Dyke & Moy) *dùn dubh*: black fort.
*Feabuy* (Dyke & Moy) *fèith buidhe*: yellow bog; cf. *Yellowbog*
    (Dallas).
*Glaschyle* (Dyke & Moy) *glas choill*: green wood.
*Knockyfinn* (Dyke & Moy) *cnocan fionn*: white hillock.
*Tom Lea* (Knockando) *tom liath*: grey hillock.

Finally we may examine the name *Moray,* the names of the
parishes, and the names of towns within the area.

*Moray* The modern Gaelic form is Moireabh. The Annals of
Ulster have 11th and 12th century forms Muireb, Moreb;
the usual Norse form is Morhaefi. These forms point to a
first element mori-, the compositional form of the Gaelic
word for 'sea'. The second element is probably Celtic -treb,
G. -treabh, W. -tref, in the meaning 'settlement'. The
meaning of the name would then be 'sea settlement'.

*Names of parishes*

*Aberlour* (RM Aberlower). The first element is clearly *aber,* the
    British correlate of Gaelic *inbhir* (inver), both meaning
    *confluence.* The second element is a common one in Celtic
    river names and probably (cf. Watson p. 432-3) means
    'loud': G. *labhar* W. *llafar.* *Labhar* would be the name of
    the tributary of the Spey which joins it in that neighbour-

S

hood, probably the burn of Aberlour, or, less likely, a description of the confluence.

*Alves* (Alveys, Alnays RM). Possibly *al mhagh fhas* i.e. rock plain place, rock plain settlement, but on the evidence it is difficult to determine.

*Bellie* (Belethyn RM) The name is obscure to me.

*Birnie* (Brenath 1237, Brenach c. 1300 RM). Probably from G. *braonach*: a moist place. Locative case would be *braonaigh* which would give Birnie by the metathesis so common with 'r' plus vowel syllables in early Scots.

*Boharm* (& Bucharin RM) The first element is probably *both*: a hut. The second is obscure.

*Botriphnie* (Battruthin 1226 Butruthie 1275 RM) The first element is again *both*: a hut. We should probably relate the second element to the name *Ruthven* which is common in the east of Scotland and probably goes back to British *ruddfaen*: red stone.

*Cabrach* The meaning of the name is obscure to me.

*Cullen* (Inverculan RM) The RM form would lead us to look first of all for a stream name. However the most probable derivation is G. *cuileann*: holly. The older name would then signify the confluence where the holly grows.

*Dallas* (Dollays Mychel RM 1232). This belongs to a set of names in the area ending in -as. The most likely source for this ending is the British term cognate with W. *gwas*, G. *fos, fas*: steading. The first element is probably W. *dol*: a meadow, low-lying land. In modern Gaelic it is *dail*. The meaning of the name is probably 'steading of the meadow'.

*Deskford* The second element -ford is clear. The first is probably a stream name containing the an element Early G. *esc*: water; the d- may stand for *dubh*: black, a common appelative in river names (cf. *Deveron*). The name then would mean 'black water ford'.

*Drainie* (Drany; Dranye, RM) This derives from G. *draighneach*; thorny place.

*Duffus* (1290 Dufhous, 1512 Duffous). The first element is almost certainly *dubh*: black. The second may be the same as that in Dallas - *fas*: settlement. The name would then mean 'black settlement'.

*Dyke & Moy. Dyke* appears to mean simply 'dike'. *Moy* is from G. *magh*: plain.

*Edinkillie* (Edinkelye RM) This derives from the two elements G. *aodann*: face, of which there are several examples in the area, and *collie*: wood. The name means 'wood face'.

*Elgin* (Elgyn RM). There is considerable disagreement about the origin of this name. In Gaelic it is *Eilginn*. A possible explanation is that, like Banff *Banbha* and Earn from an oblique case of *Eire*, it is simply one of a set of names applied to districts in Ireland and Scotland. Elg, Eire and Banbha are all names applied, probably metonymously, to Ireland. This might suggest that these names were brought to Scotland by the Gaelic settlers but this is an open question as is the suggestion that these are in origin names of earth goddesses.

*Forres* (Fores, Forais RM - C1200) which latter corresponds to the Gaelic form of the name. Probably from *fo ros*: little wood.

*Grange* the meaning is transparent.

*Inveravon* The first element is G. *inbhir*: confluence -avon is a river name cognate with G. *abhainn*: river.

*Keith* (Keyth RM) The origin is obscure. It has been compared with *Cé* the Pictish territory of N.E. Scotland but there is no evidence beyond the similarity of the names.

*Kinloss* (Kynlos, 1229 RM) Kin- denotes 'end' from G. *ceann*: head, end. Watson says that the element -los is a form of G. *lus*: plant, herb. He derives the name of the river *Lossie* from the same source. The name would then mean 'river of the herbs'. There is no corroborative evidence for this.

*Kirkmichael* The church of St. Michael.

*Knockando* (Knockando RM) The first element is G. *cnoc*: a hill. The usual explanation is G. *cnocan dubh*: black hillock. But both the RM form and the stress on the second syllable make this impossible. The second element is obscure to me.

*Mortlach* (Murthilloch; Morthilache) Probably G. *mór tulach*: large knoll.

*Rafford* Probably from G. *rath*: fort, rampart, compounded with English 'ford'.

*Rathven* Possibly G. *rath* with G. *beinn*: peak of the fort; but cf. *Ruthven* above.

These names present great difficulty as the possible interpretations are many and decisive evidence does not exist.

*Rothes* (Rothes; Rothays RM) The Gaelic form is Rathais. The second element is probably *fos, fas* (as in Dallas). The first is probably *rath*: fort, rampart, again.

*Rothiemay* (Rothiemay RM) Almost certainly from G. *rath* and G. *magh*: 'fort of the plain'.

*Speymouth* The meaning is obvious.

*Spynie* (Spyny RM) The name is obscure to me; but cf. *Spey* which W. J. Watson (chap. XIV) says comes from British *spiath*: hawthorn. Perhaps the name correlates with e.g. Caisteal *Spiathanaigh* which possibly means 'castle of the hawthorn place'. *Spynie* would then mean the 'hawthorn place'.

*St. Andrews and Lhanbryde* The first part, St. Andrews, is transparent. *Lhanbryde* (Lamanbride; Lamnabride RM) presents problems. Clearly the last element is the female saint's name: Bride, G. *Brighid*. The first element looks as if it might be G. *lann*: an enclosure, cognate with W. *llan*: church. The *m* and the extra syllable in the RM forms are problematic. If it were -m- by itself then we could look at this as an assimilative form of -n- before -b-, ie. nb to mb, but this would positively require no intervening vowel. Possibly what we have is the hypochoristic form *mo*: my, which is very common with Gaelic saints names, giving *Mo-Brighid* in this case. The name would then be *Lann-mo-Bhrighde* the laman-, lanma- forms would be due to metathesis of m and n.

*Urquhart*: (Urchard RM) The Gaelic form is Urchardan. The earliest form of this name is in the *Life of St. Columba* by Adomnan which dates from the end of the 7th century. The form there is *Airchartdan*. The first element is *ar*: on; the second the British *cardden*: copse. The meaning would be 'the place on the copse'.

*Names of towns* (the names written in large bold capitals on OS are discussed).

*ABERLOUR* (see p. 259).

*BUCKIE* Watson derives the name from a stream name containing the element *boc*: buck; but the question is open.

*BURGHEAD* This is a late name referring to the ancient ruined fort on the headland. This may be the place referred to by

Ptolemy as *Pterodon Stratopedon*, which means 'winged fort' and seems to be a translation of Latin *Alata Castra*, with the same meaning. However, the assumption that the site was occupied by the Romans does not seem well-founded. The name gives us no information on the question at any rate.

*CRAIGELLACHIE* (cf. Elchyn, Elechyn RM) Craig- represents G. *creag*: rock, cliff. The second element is obscure.

*CULLEN* (see above).

*DUFFTOWN* Founded in 1817 by James Duff, 4th Earl of Fife - hence the name.

*ELGIN* (see p. 261).

*FINDHORN* (Findaryn RM) The first element is EG. *find*: white; the second is *Eirinn*, for which see under *ELGIN* above.

*FINDOCHTY* The first element is the same as in the previous name; the second is *ochtamh*: eighth, a land measure name.

*FOCHABERS* (Fochobyr RM) The second element looks as if it is *obir*: confluence, but the name is obscure. The final -s appears as early as the beginning of 16th century.

*GARMOUTH* The forms in the mid-16th century Garmoch, Germoch. This suggests a stream name G. *gairmeach*: the calling one (Watson, chap. XIV).

*HOPEMAN* Founded 1805. The origin of the name is unknown to me.

*LOSSIEMOUTH* Situated at the mouth of the river Lossie.

*KEITH* (see p. 261).

*PORTGORDON* Founded in 1797 by the 4th Duke of Gordon - hence the name.

*PORTKNOCKIE* This is the locative case of G. *port cnocach*: hillocky port.

*ROTHES* (see p. 262).

*TOMINTOUL* This is in Gaelic *Tom an t-Sabhail*: hillock of the barn.

# 18

# FAMOUS LOCAL PEOPLE

## IAN KEILLAR

In writing of the famous local people of Moray, the difficulty is not in finding sufficient worthy of the title but in cutting down the list of candidates to a chosen few.

What makes a person famous? There is only a thin line, blurred in places, between the infamous and the famous and the line is arbitrarily drawn by the selector. The names of the people selected for this chapter may not all be that well known in Moray; but they should be.

There are references given at the end of this chapter for those who wish to know more about the Moray personalities than is given here in these sketches. Most of the reference books are obtainable at local libraries. An invaluable book which gives biographies of 42 famous Moray men is Robert Douglas's "Sons of Moray", published in 1930, but as there were only 29 copies printed, it is not only invaluable but practically unobtainable.

### Macbeth

We all know about Macbeth, the hen-pecked murderer who took the life of an old man who was his greatest friend. Shakespeare tells us this, but when Shakespeare wrote his play he had at least one sycophantic eye on James VI, newly come down from Scotland. James Stuart had not a very strong claim to the Scottish throne and a weaker one to the English throne, so he must have been pleased by Will Shakespeare's play which inferred that he was descended through Fleance from the ancient line of Scottish kings.

Macbeth was the son of Findlaech, the Mormaer or Earl of Moray and he was also the grandson of Kenneth II (971 - 995) and the nephew of Malcolm II (1005 - 1034). Macbeth married Gruoch who was a grand-daughter of Kenneth III (997 - 1005). In those days, when primogeniture was unheard of, Macbeth had as good a claim, if not a better one, to the Scottish throne, as his second cousin Duncan (1034 - 1040) who was but a grandson of Malcolm II.

Duncan, who was younger than Macbeth, was not a particularly successful king. He impoverished the kingdom by attempting to fight on two fronts: against the English in the south and the Norse in the north and it was after a disastrous expedition against Duncan's Norse kinsman, Thorfinn, that Macbeth killed Duncan, allegedly at Bothgowan, believed to be near Pitgaveny.

Macbeth made peace with his cousin Thorfinn and ruled Scotland for some seventeen years. He made a pilgrimage to Rome and he and Queen Gruoch were generous to the church. But Malcolm, the son of Duncan, with English help, defeated Macbeth at Lumphanan and took the throne as Malcolm III.

*Freskyn*

The sons of Malcolm III and his English Queen, Margaret, were sorely tried by the men of Moray who attempted several times to restore the old Celtic succession. The sons of bigheaded Malcolm introduced Norman, Flemish and English knights to Scotland, giving them large tracts of land in return for feudal duties, which included keeping down the native Scots.

One such knight was Freskyn. Probably a Fleming, he was born in the late 11th century and assisted the Scottish crown to crush the Moray rebellions in the 1120's. As a reward he received the rich lands of the Laigh of Moray and built his Motte and Bailey castle on the shores of Loch Spynie at Duffus. His timber castle no longer survives but the Motte and Bailey, built under his instruction, still stands.

In 1150 he was entertaining King David I while that "sair sanct for the croon" was superintending the building of Kinloss Abbey. Freskyn died, an old man, about 1170 and was succeeded by his son William. One of Freskyn's great grandsons, Andrew became Bishop of Moray and was present at the foundation of Elgin Cathedral in 1224.

*Bishop David Murray*

In the wars of independence against the rapacious insolent and cruel Plantagent, Edward I, the Scottish Church was wholeheartedly on the side of the freedom fighters. Nobles, like Reginald de Cheyne of Duffus, who had married into the Freskyn family, might bend their knees to the usurper, while the Town Council of Elgin turned out the Town Band to greet Edward, but the clergy were made of sterner stuff. Bishop Sinclair of Dunkeld yielded a sword as he swept the English from Fife while David Murray preached that it was better to fight the English than the Turks or Saracens.

David Murray, a descendant of Freskyn, canon of the Cathedral Church of Moray, was elected and consecrated Bishop of Moray in 1299. A staunch supporter of Bruce, he was one of only three bishops present at the king's coronation. Because of Bishop Murray's steadfast support for Bruce, Edward I persuaded Cardinal St. Sabinus, the Papal Legate in England, to excommunicate the Bishop.

In 1313 Murray founded the Scots College in Paris. According to Macintosh ,the records of the Scots College of Paris, amounting to seven cartloads were deposited in Blairs College, Aberdeen. It is surely time that these invaluable records were edited and published. When David Murray died in 1325 he was buried in the choir of Elgin Cathedral.

*Florence Wilson*

Florence Wilson, or as he signed himself in Latin, Florentius Voluzene or Volusenus was born somewhere near Elgin about 1500. He probably attended the grammar school and graduated from Aberdeen but no record of this exists. He then studied in France and was on familiar terms with Cardinal Wolsey and Thomas Cromwell. In France he taught at the public school at Carpentras, near Avignon and there he wrote and published in Lyon the now lost work entitled "Commentatio quaedam Theologia quae eadem precatio est in Aphorismos dissecta".

In 1543 he published his great work "De Tranquillitate Animi" which is a discussion on the best means by which a man may obtain tranquillity or peace of mind. In it Wilson refers to the beauties of Moray, the running streams and the singing of birds.

In 1546 he set out to return to Moray and it is tragic that this talented Scot died at Vienne, just south of Lyon, not long after he had begun his journey home. Wilson was not antagonistic to the teachings of Luther and, had he lived, his experience and learning may well have mitigated the excesses of the Reformation in Scotland.

## James Ferguson

James Ferguson was born in 1710 at Core of Mayen, near Rothiemay, but not long after his birth his family moved to Cantlie some 5 km (3 miles) north-east of Keith where his father was a cottar. At the age of ten he tended sheep for a neighbour and by day amused himself by making model mills and spinning wheels, while by night he studied the stars and at an early age made simple astronomical instruments. In his studies he was greatly inspired by John Glichrist the minister at Keith, while Mrs. Duff of Dipple encouraged him to paint.

Moving to Edinburgh Ferguson supported himself by portrait painting but he longed for Strathisla and was soon back unsuccessfully trying to sell patent medicines. When he was aged about 30 he met Colin Maclaurin, Professor of Mathematics at Marischal College and armed with letters of introduction from the Professor he and his wife Isabella sailed for London in 1743.

In London he painted portraits and gave lectures in astronomy. In 1758 he was introduced to the Prince of Wales and when the Prince became King George III in 1760 he gave Ferguson an annual pension of £50 from the Privy Purse. In 1763 Ferguson was elected a Fellow of the Royal Society and shortly afterwards was defeated for the post of Clerk to the Society. The man who got the post promptly defrauded the Society of £1,000.

Ferguson's most successful publication was "Astronomy explained upon Sir Isaac Newton's Principles". He died on 16th November 1776 and with his wife lies buried in Old St. Marylebone, London.

## William Marshall

Interest in William Marshall (born in Fochabers in December 1748) and his music is becoming deservedly popular to-day. At that time the present Fochabers did not exist, the village being then sited nearer to Bellie. Ill educated, or more accurately, poorly schooled, Marshall, at the age of twelve, went to work at Gordon Castle. In 1773 he married Jane Giles and of their five sons, three died in army service while the fourth lost his right arm at Waterloo.

In 1790 Marshall took up farming at Keithmore, Mortlach and there he continued the composition of fiddle music which he had started at Fochabers. A handsome man, he was a keen sportsman. He fished and shot, danced and composed. He is reputed to have composed well over two hundred tunes, some of which were plagiarised by that other famous fiddler, Neil Gow.

Besides his musical abilities, he was an accomplished craftsman and he built a most wonderful clock, now in Edinburgh. This clock shows the time in minutes, hours, days, months and years. It illustrates the moon's revolution round the earth and points out the appropriate phase. The clock indicates the time of high water and the time of sunrise, with the length of day and night indicated and much more besides.

But it is as a musician that William Marshall is best remembered. When he left Keithmore for retiral at Newfield, Dandaleith, he composed "Farewell to Keithmore", a tune still played and popular to this day. Another of his famous tunes is "O' a' the airts the wind can blaw". He died in 1833 listening to his own melodies being played by Charles Grant, the dominie at Elchies.

Buried on the banks of the Spey at Bellie, his memorial looks across to the river where, three years before he was born, the army of Cumberland forded the waters on their way to Culloden.

### George Gordon

George Gordon was a giant among men: parish minister, scholar, botanist, geologist, historian, archaeologist and ornithologist — a polymath, the like of which Moray has not seen since. He was a true Moray loon, born at the old manse of Urquhart on 23rd July 1801, graduate of Marischal College and minister of Birnie from 1832 to 1889.

In the 1830's Gordon published his "Flora of Moray", a valuable source book to this day. As an archaeologist he visited every site in the District and made a fine collection of stone age tools, besides writing a paper on the "Archaeology of Moray".

He was a noted geologist and as early as 1832 he had written a paper to the Geological Society, followed by another in 1859 examining the geology of the whole of the coastal plain of Moray. One of the founders of the Elgin and Morayshire Association (now the Elgin Society) he contributed exhibits to the Museum and spent much time classifying and arranging the displays. He was without doubt the greatest of all the Chairmen of the Association.

Gordon protected birds and encouraged them to nest in his garden at Birnie. He published papers on the fauna of Moray. An active man all his life he published in 1892 a paper on the "Reptiliferous Sandstones of Elgin" and late the next year he closed his eyes for the last time after a hard but happy life.

## Hugh Falconer

Hugh Falconer, born on the 29th of February 1808, was one of the most gifted sons of Forres. He was educated at the Grammar School before taking his MA at Aberdeen at the age of 18. Before he was 22 he had gained his MD from Edinburgh and at the age of 23 he was appointed chief of the Botanical Gardens near Simla in the Siwalik hills.

Dr. Falconer believed that the Siwalik hills were of Tertiary age and he reasoned that they should contain fossil remains of extinct mammals. On 20th November 1834, in the space of six hours, he uncovered 300 fossil bones. Before he was 30 he had, very deservedly, been awarded the Woolaston medal for his geological work.

A few years later, on his recommendation, the growing of tea in India was started. By 1844 the tea industry was well established, solely due to the industry and enthusiasm of Hugh Falconer. While travelling through India looking for plantation sites he was continually making notes on the geological formations and corresponding about them with his contemporary polymath, George Gordon of Birnie.

He travelled in Afghanistan, Baluchistan and Kashmir, collecting plants, fossils and seeds as he went along. On being forced through ill health to return to Britain in 1842 he brought back with him 5080kg (5 tons) of fossil bones and geological specimens. For the next few years he was arranging his own and his colleague's (Captain Cantley's) collection, in the British Museum.

Recalled to India in 1847 he investigated the growing of the cinchona (quinine) tree, while he also examined the teak forests and wrote on the best woods to use for railway sleepers and for fuel.

Returning to Europe in 1855 he travelled extensively on the continent, examining fossils in many countries. At the time of his death in 1865 he was engaged in a work which would have established the antiquity of mankind, many years before such ideas were acceptable.

## George Stephen

George Stephen was born at Dufftown in 1829. The son of a carpenter, his father made fiddles and the works of composer William Marshall must have been heard by George at an early age.

After working in Aberdeen and London, George Stephen emigrated to Canada in 1850. In Montreal in 1866 he met his cousin, Donald Smith. Donald, born in Forres in 1820 was then a factor with the Hudson's Bay Company. The two cousins were destined to be largely instrumental in developing the railway system in Canada. Both were honoured for their work. George Stephen became Lord Mount Stephen while his cousin became Lord Strathcona.

Their first joint enterprise was to buy up and complete a railway between St. Paul and Manitoba. From then on Stephen was involved in Canadian railways and eventually he was asked to build the Canadian Pacific. This monumental task he completed in 1885 after five years of work. As the railway forged ahead, so did the settlers follow on, aided by schemes and bounties.

Stephen later retired to Britain, where he was friendly with Sir Garnet Wolseley (the "all cigaré" of First World War slang). The two friends fished from Faskally House, Pitlochry and it was there that George Stephen learned that he had been raised to the peerage. "All cigaré" wrote to his wife: - "I wish every peer was half as good . . . I never knew people so unchanged by richness . . . "

Stephen provided for hospitals at Dufftown, Aberdeen and London. A hard man, yet sympathetic to a genuine cause, he lived to see the country he had served grow into a great nation, held together from the Atlantic to the Pacific by the iron road that his strength and determination had forced through the hills of the east, the central plains and the mountains of the west.

## Constance Frederica Gordon Cumming

Constance Frederica, or Eka as she was known to her friends, was the daughter of Eliza Maria Campbell of Islay and Sir William Gordon Cumming of Altyre. Her mother, a noted beauty, had more than a pretty face, she entertained and went on excursions with Sir Roderick Murchison, Hugh Miller and the brilliant but unbalanced Swiss, Agassiz. Although Constance Frederica was only five years old when her mother died she remembered her mother coming home from fossil hunting expeditions and cracking open the nodules while other members of the family sketched and painted.

Born into an already large family in 1837 (one of her brothers was Roualeyn, the mighty lion hunter of South Africa) she saw most of them carried off to early graves. Perhaps this gave her a philosophical acceptance of hardship and danger, for when she was thirty she left Britain on a series of travels which must have appeared daunting, if not downright foolhardy to her contemporaries.

First, she went to join her half sister in India and there she wandered from Calcutta to the Himalays and then to Bombay. Returning to Britain she observed: - "After a spell in the tropics in sunshine and colour, avoid returning to our British Isles in February, or any other bleak wintry month! . . . it is very difficult to keep up the illusion that one is really glad to be back." Soon she was on her travels again: Ceylon, Singapore, Sydney, Fiji, New Zealand, California and then, in September 1878 she arrived in Japan.

She stayed and travelled in Japan for one year, meeting Henry Dyer, the Scottish creator of the Imperial College of Engineering. She climbed Fujiyama and sketched it as delicately as any Japanese. Returning to San Francisco she then sailed for China and wrote a book on the inventor of the numeral type for printing Chinese. She sailed the Pacific in a French Man of War and yet found time to sketch, paint and write travel books, including; "Wandering in China" and "At Home in Fiji". She wrote many magazine articles, some of which were strangely prophetic in title and content. Among these were; "Destruction of the American Bison" and "The World's Oil Supply", both of which appeared in 1884. She could have been talking about some parts of Scotland when she wrote: - "So they sold their land at an emormous increase, and now the once sleepy village . . . has upwards of five thousand money-craving inhabitants . . . More attractive to gambling speculators than any mining business was this new industry (oil), which, to the workers, offered a chance of more rapid fortune than any other known enterprise."

## William Cramond

At Fettercairn on 10th July 1844 was born William Cramond who was destined to become one of the greatest local historians of the North-East. At the age of 13 he became a pupil teacher at Montrose and in 1861 he gained a bursary to King's College, Aberdeen. He graduated MA with first class houours in classics in 1866. Later the same year Cramond began teaching English at the Misses Pringles' Boarding School for Young Ladies in Banff. In 1868 he was appointed to the Kirk Session school at Lumphanan and in 1871 he became headmaster of the school at Cullen-ad vitam aut culpam.

The school, now a private house called Aldersyde, was in the square at Cullen. Extracts from the school log book show that with respect to corporal punishment, Cramond was way ahead of his time: - "January 29. 1886. Two Seatown boys got 3 strokes and 6 strokes for rioting and disobedience — first use of the strap for nearly two years." "March 22. 1886. Two new teachers. I told them that punishment will be administered in my room and in my presence."

In other scholastic matters too, Cramond was a pioneer. In 1881 he led his 6th form to the top of the Bin to look round the country with a telescope. Five years later, within 8 days of the opening of the railway, he took the whole school to Elgin. He did all this while constantly harassed by lack of staff and enormous classes. At one time there were 180 infants in a room designed for 91. His helpers included pupil teachers, some as young as 13 years. After school was finished he would then have to teach his "teachers".

In addition to his duties during the day —and in those days a headmaster was expected to take at least one class — he taught navigation to the fishermen at night. Despite this heavy load he found time to research, write up and publish works of scholarship relating to local history. His monumental two volumes of "The Annals of Banff" are invaluable, all the more so now, for during the 1st World War, the ancient records of Banff were sent to be pulped.

According to Cramond's biographer, Dr. A. A. Cormack, he (Cramond) published some 59 articles, books and pamphlets. To obtain the material for his books, Cramond travelled the country by bicycle. Worn out by work and alcohol, Dr. Cramond, founder of the Banffshire Field Club, Freeman of Banff and Honorary Doctor of Law at Aberdeen died in 1907 aged 62 years.

### James Ramsay MacDonald

In 1866 Anne Ramsay was working as a housekeeper at a farm near Alves and on the same farm was a handsome ploughman, John MacDonald. Later that year Anne returned to her mother's but and ben at Lossiemouth and there, James Ramsay MacDonald was born.

He went first to Robbie Codlin's school at Lossiemouth and then to Drainie where, in his teens, he became a pupil teacher. He found time to engage in political activities on behalf of the Liberals and in 1883 he founded the Lossiemouth Field Club, established a small museum and issued a Lossiemouth Field Club Magazine. In 1885 MacDonald left Lossiemouth railway station en route for Bristol, with a single ticket and £1-7/- (£1.35) in coin of the realm in his pocket.

In Bristol he ran a Boy's and Young Men's Guild and he also joined the Social Democrats, a then small almost secret society. He became a socialist activist and was present in Trafalgar Square on "Bloody Sunday", November 13th 1887 when mounted police charged the crowd of peaceful demonstrators. In 1896 he married Margaret Gladstone, daughter of a wealthy Fellow of the Royal Society. It was a love match and when Margaret died on September 8th 1911 the light of James Ramsay MacDonald's life went out for ever.

MacDonald (Plate 30) was first elected to Parliament as member for Leicester in 1906 and he became leader of the Labour Party Parliamentary group in 1911. In 1918 the "khaki" election swept him away from his seat but he returned as representative for Aberavon in 1922 and in 1924 he became Prime Minister in a minority Labour government. He was Prime Minister again in 1929. In August 1931 he broke with the Labour Party and formed a National Government, a decision which still casts shadows to this day. Expelled from the Labour Party he went to the country and was returned by a massive majority. He retired from the premiership in 1935. Worn out with work and worn out by the vituperation of his former colleagues he died at sea in 1937 and his ashes lie at Spynie, looking across to the place of his birth.

MacDonald's actions of 1931 appear inexplicable to many,

yet his election adress of 1895, when he unsuccessfully contested Southampton as an I.L.P. candidate, contains the clue to why he acted as he did when the great slump hit Britain: - "No cry (is) more fatal to the well being of general progress and good government than that which you hear in Southampton: "Party! Party!" The fact is, both parties have broken down. Against that cry of my opponents I am to raise the answer: "Principle! Principle!" James Ramsay MacDonald paid a bitter price for adhering to principle rather than to party.

# 19

# THE SPEECH OF MORAY

## DAVID MURISON

Fortunately perhaps for the inhabitants who tend to be conservative in their outlook and habits, the Grampian region created under the new local government reorganisation does not differ materially from the old counties of Moray, Banff, Aberdeen and Kincardine, which in themselves correspond more or less to geographical actualities like mountains and rivers — and these are noted among linguists and speech-geographers as being barriers also as between one dialect and another. Of course much depends on how easily these can be penetrated by contact routes, roadways, bridges and ferries; a river valley may unite rather than separate a community and a hill ridge is no obstacle if it can be got round at either end; again, and this is important in the area under our present consideration, communication may be easier by sea than land and a coastal fringe may speak in a way distinct from its hinterland, a most marked feature in places like Newfoundland and Labrador.

The area now called Moray (roughly the old Moray and Western Banffshire) comprises, linguistically speaking, the western part of the total area of the North-East of Scotland which has enough features in common and different from those of the regions surrounding it to justify being called a separate and distinct dialect and this area is bounded by the Moray Firth, the North Sea and a line running in a curve from about Nairn across the hills to Tomintoul, over to Braemar and then over the Mounth to the sea a few miles south of Stonehaven. Within that area again there are sub-dialects with variations among themselves and two of these are represented in the Moray District, all of which will be more fully explained later. It is however most helpful at this point to give a short historical sketch of the speech of the area, so that its features and present state may best be understood as a development of its past.

What its very first language may have been we really do not

T

know as we have no records of it. Its first historical language we know to be Pictish, though that does not take us very far, as the remains of the speech are hard to interpret and there is much dispute among scholars on the subject. It does however seem to have been a Celtic language most akin to Welsh and to have left traces in quite a number of place-names, which must have existed before the language died out sometime in the 9th or 10th centuries, conspicuously in those prefixed with *Pit-* as in *Pitairlie, Pitcraigie, Pitcroy, Pittendreich,* and in *Aber-* as in *Aberlour, Abernethy, Aberchirder; Urquhart,* too, and *Keith* are very old names. The names of some rivers, too, generally the oldest element in any toponymy, may well go back to the Pictish period, as Nairn, Spey, Deveron (see also Chapter 17).

We are on much firmer ground with the next language that came to Moray, for it is well attested in the place-names in the area and in historical documents as well. The Scots came from Ireland to Argyll about 500 A.D., bringing the Gaelic language with them, and spread their rule east and north, till by conquest and intermarriage they united with the Picts to form the Kingdom of Alba. The Gaelic language triumphed over Pictish and it is from it that the majority of today's Moray place-names take their origin, as *Altyre,* 'river-land', *Alves,* 'rocky place', *Auchluncart,* 'campfield', *Balmeanach,* 'middle-town', *Bodnafiach,* 'raven wood', *Craigellachie,* (possibly) 'the rocky hill', *Cullen\*,* 'the nook or recess', *Dava,* 'the measure of land', *Edinkillie,* 'the wooded slope', *Lochnabo,* 'the loch of the cow', *Inveravon,* 'the confluence of the river', *Mulben,* 'the bare hill', *Rothes\*,* 'at the ring fort', *Tomintoul,* 'barn-hill', and of course all the Bens and Cairns of the Moray uplands. Moray itself is "the land by the sea" and it formed an important province in the coastal defence of Scotland against the Norsemen under a Mormaer or 'sea-steward', of whom the most famous was Macbeth in the first half of the 11th century. Macbeth in fact headed the Celtic resistance to the encroachment of a new regime and the new language which came in its train. The Feudal system which William the Conqueror brought from Normandy to England in 1066 found its way into Scotland through the English-born queen of the Celtic King Malcolm Canmore and the many English-speaking officials and clergy who came to administer the new system both

\*See Chapter 17 for alternative suggestions of derivation.

in its political and ecclesiastical aspects. It is true that the chief magnates, the barons, were themselves French-speaking but their stewards, estate agents, bailiffs, and the like were in the main from the North of England where these barons also had lands, and it was their speech, the Northern dialect of the speech that had once been Anglo-Saxon, but in the course of the centuries acquired a great many Scandinavian words from the Danes who had established a powerful kingdom at York, and finally had been radically transformed by the extensive influx of French words and sounds and spellings that came in with the Normans. In Scotland this speech got the name of 'Inglis' in testimony to its origin.

By the end of the 12th century documents drawn up in Elgin are being attested by Roman bishops and Norman French earls instead of Celtic abbots and mormaers. About the same time the clergy in Elgin are a mixture, with Gaelic, Anglo-Saxon and French names, and already the priories at Urquhart and Kinloss had been founded by David I, the son of Malcolm Canmore, with clergy from the south or Inglis-speaking part of Scotland. Soon after, in Strathisla for instance, we find place-names in the new tongue, Strype, Staneycroft, Muirford, Corncairn, Stobstane.

By the end of the 14th century the earliest literature in this 'Inglis' had been written in Aberdeen in John Barbour's *Brus*. In 1450 we have *The Buke of the Howlat*, the fable of the owl borrowing feathers from the rest of the birds, turned into a eulogy of the Douglas family, then Earls of Moray, written at Darnaway by a priest of Elgin, Sir Richard Holland. A few lines will illustrate the language of the period:

> I sawe ane Howlat, in haist, undir ane holyne,
> Lukand the laike throwe,
> And saw his awne schadowe,
> At the quhilk he couth growe,
> And maid gowlyne.

> He grat grysly grym, and gaif a gret yowle,
> Cheuerand and chydand with churliche cheir.
> 'Quhy is my far,' quoth the fyle, "fassonit so foule,
> My forme and my fetherem unfrely, but feir?
> My neb is netherit as a nok, I am bot ane Owle;
> Aganis natur in the nicht I walk in to weir;
> I dare do nocht on the day, but droupe as a doule."

More than a century later the Session Clerk of Elgin writes up his minutes for 25 September 1594 about a case of suspected witchcraft:

> "The said Cuming cam thryis to James Andersonis hous broght with her water in ane pig and weische the barne therwith, scho confessis and declaris that the said Janet Cuming bad her go to the place of the Kirk wher Grissall Urnellis first barne was bureit and thair unspoken tak up ane handfull of meildis and bring the same to the said Janet Cuming that scho micht put the same among the watter that suld wesche the seik barne with, scho declarit that scho yeid to the grave and did as scho bad hir also confessis that scho careit the watter that weische the barne at the command of the said Cuming to the rynnand wattir of Lossie and keist in the same thair that nane suld hurt thairby."

When we discount the obsolete spellings, there is nothing which would puzzle a modern native of the District and we can see the regular North-East forms of the past tense in *weische* (washed), *keist* (cast) and in *meildis* for moulds or soil, especially of a grave. It is interesting incidentally to note the first recorded instance of the word *Hogmanay* on 3 January 1604 from the same Session minutes.

In the 18th century the Jacobite risings brought the North of Scotland into the ken of Government and in the long series of investigations that followed, military, political, social and economic, the concept of the Highland Line, due in the first place to General Wade, was formulated and developed. This was the geographical boundary between Highlands and Lowlands, which divided Celtic culture and tradition from the Anglo-French, the clan system from the feudal, and linguistically, Gaelic from Lowland Scots as "Inglis" had been called from the beginning of the 16th century. As far as we are concerned the line ran as we have seen from near Nairn to the Aberdeen-Banff border at the top of Glen Livet leaving the parishes of Cromdale and Kirkmichael within the Gaelic-speaking area. But with the breakdown of the clan system, the making of roads and the expansion of an improved agriculture, the Lowland speech gradually prevailed in Kirkmichael and to a large extent also in Cromdale. As Cromdale has in any case been cut out of the old Morayshire, its speech, which is a mixture of Scots and Highland English, does not concern us here and as the number of people in Kirkmichael who understand Gaelic, let alone speak it, must be minimal we can for practical purposes leave Gaelic and the Highland English (not Scots) which succeeded it altogether out of consideration. The essential speech of our area is Scottish School English and the native vernacular Scots of the North-East.

In 1793 the writer of the 1st Statistical Account of the parish of Duffus for Sir John Sinclair's famous survey, gives considerable space to the features of its speech which in its particulars resembles that of the rest of Morayshire. These will be discussed in a few moments. This speech has not materially altered to this day in its pronunciation and grammar and indeed in the slow and even tenor of rural life up to the beginning of the 1st World War, it retained a great deal of the typical vocabulary of the North-East. Here is a description of a farm house in Dallas, written about 1885:

> "The horse an' nowte and fowk, an' a' kin' o' beasts, a' gied in at the same door, an' that's as sure as I'm sittin' here. At ae en' o' the kitchie there was a door leadin' into the stable, and there was seiven beasts steed there. The nowte, aifter gaen through the kitchie, hed to gae past the horses' tails. Farrer ben than the hoose, there war ten or twal' workin' owsen; Syne there were seiven or aucht kye, an' syne a curn hungry stirks, an' a puckle caur. The hooses were bigget wi' stanes an' fell like a dyke, an' plaistered weel up wi' clay, and thackit wi' divots."

And another specimen from Fochabers in 1914:

> "A hae a kin o' notion fat fowk mean fan A hear them spykin' aboot things 'at's gyaun on in the worl'. Gin that birkie cud live on fowerpence a day in the ceety, fat's tae hin'er me fae livin' on jeist hauf that in the country? A bawbee i' the day for milk, twa for mael, an' the lave in traicle — that mak's it oot richt eneuch. There maun be a fond set aside for extras aenoo, for A canna dae wintin' ma snuff an' ma paper, but fan A get ees's tae't A'll meebe can save't aff the traicle. Fat mair need ony daicent 'oman be seekin'? Ye'se mak' yer ain maet an' A'se mak' mine, for A'm gyaun tae live on tippence a day, an' nae mair aboot it."

Both of these passages would still be perfectly intelligible to the Moray native, but it is doubtful whether his own usage would be so correct or consistent. The effect of the "telly" has been too insidious.

The distinguishing characteristics of the North-East dialect, apart from its having retained a large vocabulary of Scots words which have become obsolete elsewhere, as *loun* and *quine* for boy and girl, are chiefly in certain vowel and consonant sounds. With regard to the vowels, what appears in English as a long o, almost o-w sound, and in Southern Scotland as -*eh*-, before an n, becomes *ie* in the north-East, as bone, *bane, been,* stone, *stane, steen,* one, *ane, een;* and this *ee* sound has also developed from what is usually written *ui* in the rest of Scotland and sounds like a French *oe, u* or German *ö* or *ü,* and in English is pronounced *oo,* as *beet* for *buit,* boot, *gweed* for *guid,* good, *speen* for *spune,* spoon, *peer* for *puir,* poor, *feel* for *fuil,* fool, and so on. The marked distinction in consonants is in the pronunciation *f-* at the beginning of words, where Scotland elsewhere has *wh-* and English *w-,* as in the relative words, *fa, fat, fan, far,* and in *fite,* white, *furl,* whirl, *fup,* whip, *fuskie,* whisky. The Session Records of Elgin for instance have *phippit* for whipped, in 1592.

When we come to examine the speech of the area more closely and study its vowel and consonant systems, we see that within the general North East pattern there are two fairly distinct sub-divisions. If we were to enter the District by way of the coast from the Buchan districts of Aberdeenshire and Banff we should not notice much, if any difference till we came to the mouth of the Spey, but if we came in through Keith we should soon observe that certain groups of words were being pronounced differently, especially bearing in mind the vowel systems mentioned above. Along the coastal area and inland over the Enzie, roughly, the parishes of Deskford, Rathven and Bellie, they say *steen* and *been* as in Aberdeenshire but in the middle and southern parts of Moray these sound as in central Scotland, with *-eh-,* i.e. as *stane, bane.* Similarly, in other words usually spelt with *-ea-,* and pronounced in Aberdeenshire as in English a *-ee-,* the main part of Moray says also *-eh-,* as in *clean, beast, meal, peat,* sounded like *clane, baste, male, pate,* though there is a tendency for this to be retreating now to the coastal strip.

The original long *o* sound which we saw became *ee* in the North-East generally as in *meen, speen, bleed,* etc. goes the same way in Moray too, except before *r* where for the Buchan *feerd, meer, peer,* i.e. ford, moor, poor, we hear *fyoord, myoor, pyoor,* not unlike standard English; no doubt this has something to do with the quality of the *r* itself which may not have been trilled in the same way as the Lowland Scots do, i.e. as in Italian. In Nairn for instance the *r* is very characteristic of Scotland north of Inverness, being pronounced with the tip of the tongue turned up and slightly backwards, a sure sign of Gaelic influence with its "palatal" *r,* and to this we can add the fact that in this part of our area the *r* often disappears altogether before a consonant as in *fist* for first, *hoss* for horse, *giss* for *girse,* grass, and probably most common of all, *haist* for *hairst,* harvest. Again before r the coast area pronounces the original long *i* like *i* in English *bite* but in the upland region it sounds more like *by,* as in *fire, tire, byre*; brother is *breether* inland, but *brither* by the sea, but normally in words ending in *-ther* in English, the coast pronounces *-der* as *fadder, midder.* Another feature of the dialect is to pronounce *v* at the beginning of a word as *w,* as wery, waluable, wast and weesable, though this is now only heard among older speakers among the fisher folk; and *speak* is pronounced as *spike.*

The western outpost of the coastal fringe is Lossiemouth. Beyond that at Howdman (Hopeman) and the Broch (Burghead) and Findhorn, the speech is not essentially different from the rest of the area. This seems to be because the fishing populations always tend to move coastwise and settled on the Moray coast from two different directions, people from the Banffshire seaboard moving westwards to set up house in Branderburgh, and another group from the Black Isle, Ardersier, Delnies, Nairn area sailing eastwards to meet them. This is a local tradition and appears to be borne out by the common surnames in the various villages.

The vocabulary of Moray dialect does not differ materially from the rest of the North-East area and an outsider would find it difficult to distinguish a speaker of one from a speaker of the other. But there are a number of words more commonly, if not exclusively, used in the western part of the new Grampian region, and the following will serve as an illustrative selection:

*bike,* the hook on a *swey* or fire crane, a local form of *beak*; *boldrites,* a glum or uncertain state, a lull; *caufie's mou,* a cowrie shell; a very distinctive word is *curneed* or sometimes *dorneed,* the youngest or weakest of a brood or family; *cheather,* a tier of peats set up for drying; *chye,* a chaffinch; *cowrack,* sowens or flummery (from Gaelic); *cyarlin,* a blank trip to sea, from *carline,* a witch, used in the fishing villages; *dabberlocks,* seaweed, rags and tatters; *doolie,* a marble; *dramlach,* a fishing-line (Gaelic); *drowlack,* a swing or hammock (Gaelic); *eeshan,* a tiny knot (Gaelic); *erick,* a starfish; *faik,* also *fyaak,* a shawl; *greesh,* the back of a fireplace (Gaelic); *hank o fish,* a string of fish; *heelie,* to be offended, to be scared off its nest, of a bird; *jallisie,* an illness, from *jealousy,* originally a fisher taboo usage;

*jo*, the wash from which whisky is made, a distillers' word; *jock hack*, a farm worker; *kellach*, a pannier; *kertin mary*, sea phosphorescence with an east wind (Gael. *caoir na mara*, 'sea flame'); *key*, a turret shell; *leep*, to hug the fire; *lonach*, a long cord or string; *loorach*, a rag, tatter (both Gaelic); *machreach*, a fuss, outcry (Gaelic); *mowrie*, gravel (Gaelic); *mouten*, to melt, clarify fat, etc.; *mummie*, grandmother, and *pawpie*, grandfather; *oof*, the angler-fish; *pegral*, an uncouth fellow, an oaf; *pullach*, a cod; *punnie*, crochet-hook; *reekiemyre*, a smoke-blower; *scantack*, a fishing-line; *seedack*, a hedge sparrow; *setterel*, short-tempered; *shaw*, hawthorn; *shiacks*, small fish; *slock-slaver*, a jellyfish; *smather*, to dawdle, footle; *sowd*, to curry favour; *speelack*, the tree creeper; *staff*, a bar of cloud across the sun; *syne*, a lull in the waves; *teetle*, a nickname; *tonie*, a jellyfish; *toors*, cumulus clouds; *treeock*, chaffinch; *trochie*, alley between houses; *windbell*, a ringing in the ears; *wisker*, a knitting-sheath; *yallock*, yellowhammer.

How many of these are still in everyday use or at least familiar will best be known to Moray readers themselves. The impact of two World Wars, the influx of many outsiders through posting to the many service installations in the area, the coming of new technological industries and the likelihood of their extension through the demands of oil, the assimilating influences of radio and television, have all combined to wear away the individual features of Moray speech, to cause confusion in its phonology and to obliterate its vocabulary. In the face of all the pressures for uniformity and against dialect, it is surprising that the speech of Moray has stood up so well. But the best way to preserve a language is to go on speaking it.

# FOLKLORE

## CRAWFORD HUIE

It seems no easy task to record the folklore of a District so varied and with such a mixed cultural heritage as Moray. The varying traditions of Celt and Norman Viking and Lowland Scot are mingled here, and the difficulty is not what to record, for alas, so much memorable tradition is gone and lost to us forever, but what to include and how to compress it into so brief a space as this chapter vouchsafes.

One can look at the names on an Ordnance Survey Map and speculate on their meaning with a world of regret for the traditions of a vanished past; in 1821 Colonel Stewart of Garth could write ". . . we still meet with Highlanders who can give a connected and minutely accurate detail of the history, genealogy, feuds and battles of all the tribes and families in every district or glen for many miles around, and for a period of several hundred years; illustrating their detail by a reference to every remarkable stone, cairn, tree or stream within the district; connecting with each some kindred story of fairy or ghost . . . ."

An explanation of the place names on the map of Moray reveals at once the mixed heritage of the area. Rural depopulation, evictions, the disastrous effects of the Jacobite Risings, the absorption of crofts into larger and more viable farming units and the break up of estates after two World Wars have all been destructive influences to folklore and tradition as have been the calculated destruction of the Gaelic language and the no less insidious destruction of local dialects in the Doric by the anglicising influence of the popular media.

In all Highland folklore the traditions of the Fingalian heroes immortalised by Ossian are among the most ancient. At the evening ceilidh the person who could recite the best poem, or sing the best song, or tell the longest and most entertaining tale, was the most acceptable guest. When a stranger appeared, after the usual introductions, he was asked "Can you speak of

the days of Fingal?" and it is only fitting that mention should
be made of the beautiful legend of Strathavon — "Strath-ath-
Fin" — The dale of the Ford of Fingal. The old stanza has it: -

"Chaidh mo bheans bhatha'
Ain uisg ath-fhin, nan clachan sleamhuin;
'S bho chaidh mo bheans' bhatha',
Bheirmeid ath-fhin, ain am amhuin."

"On the limpid water of the slippery stones
Has my wife been drowned,
And since my wife has there been drowned
Henceforth its name shall be The Water of Fingal."

Fingal, while hunting the red deer, crossed the river
successfully himself, but his wife who followed after was carried
away in the violence of the swollen stream.

While yet in the Highland region and indeed on the very
extremity of our boundary the mass of Ben Macdui rears with
its awe-inspiring tales of "The Grey Man", the grim giant who
haunts the mountain top and lures the unfortunate climber amid
swirling mists to the verge of a precipice. There have been many
accounts of the Grey Man through the years, and Macpherson
Grant of Ballindalloch writing of a sighting of this apparition
which he witnessed on the mountain on 10th October 1830
points out its similarity to the "Brocken Spectre" of Germany.
Seton Gordon states that the late Professor J. N. Collie, a former
president of the Alpine Club, asserted that he encountered this
spectre and heard the crunching of the giant feet of "Fear Liath
Mor" which followed him with dreadful persistency across the
plateau.

In writing of folklore there is the merging of an oral
tradition with the recorded facts of history and time and time
again such traditions have been proved true and supplied gaps
in documented historical knowledge.

Among the superstitions of the people there are a few more
interesting phenomena than "The Second Sight". This has been
the subject of study and curiosity for centuries and occupied
attention in the writings of such diverse characters as Samuel
Pepys, Martin, Dr. Johnson and Sir Walter Scott. Dr. Johnson
defined it as "an impression either by the mind upon the eye, or
by the eye upon the mind, by which distant and future things
are perceived and seen as if they were present." There has been
much argument about the good or evil origins of second sight and
while it has been alleged that persons possessing the gift came

by it by compact with the Devil "or converse with these Demons we call Fairies", it was undoubtedly possessed by such saintly men as St. Columba and the Rev. John Morrison, the Minister who is remembered as the Seer of Petty. The most famous Highland prophet was of course the Brahan Seer, Kenneth Odhar Mackenzie, burned in a barrel of tar at Chanonry Point at the instigation of Lady Seaforth in 1679. His remarkable predictions include the detailed fulfilment of his awesome curse on the Seaforth family nearly two centuries later, the Battle of Culloden, the Highland Clearances, the Highland Railway, the Caledonian Canal and the automobile.

Aubrey's "Miscellanies" of late 17th century date contain an account of one, "James Mack-Coil-vic-alastar, alias Grant in Glenbeum, near Kirkmichael in Strathawwin who had the second sight and was an honest man of blameless conversation. He used to look into the peat fire and fortell what strangers would come to his house the next day or shortly afterwards, describing their dress and weapons, and sometimes naming them. If goods or cattle were missing he could direct people where to find them and could tell if the beast were dead or would die before it was found. In the winter nights when people thronged to his fireside he would tell them to make room for others that stood unseen, or else they would be quickly thrown into the midst of the fire. It was suggested that he was referring to a Brownie or Mag Molach. Both of these were familiar spirits associated with Highland families and such creatures were sometimes helpful and sometimes mischievous. There is mention of Mag Molach, or "Hairy Hand" who was the familiar spirit of the Grants of Tullochgorum in the account of the raid on the Town of Keith by Petrie Roy MacGregor, the Freebooter, and his band in 1667. This sprite, often in the form of a small boy, uttered a dire and true prophecy concerning the fate of Petrie Roy who was captured and later barbarously executed on the Sands of Leith.

Closely allied to such traditions is the Fairy Lore and the fascinating subject of Witchcraft. Great was the respect for the Daon-Si, The Fairy Folk, or The Good People, of whom there are many accounts and there are Fairy Knolls and Fairy Hills, often ancient barrows, containing cist graves, scattered through-out the countryside. It might be relevant to refer to the farm of Sheandow, near Aberlour, (Sithean Dhu - The Black Hill of the Fairies), and sure enough within a short distance you will find marked, the Fairy Hill. The experience of Thomas the Rhymer, as recorded in Scott's "Minstrelsy of the Scottish Border" has other parallels in local lore:

> "Her shirt was o' the grass-green silk,
> Her mantle of the velvet fine
> At ilka tett of her horse's mane,
> Hung fifty siller bells and nine."

The similarity of the English nursery rhyme is striking and its relevance to witchcraft has been pointed out before: -

> "Ride a cock horse to Banbury Cross
> To see a fine lady on a white horse,
> Rings on her fingers and bells on her toes
> She shall have music wherever she goes."

In 1596, following severe penal enactments against witchcraft, as a result of the discovery of a plot to murder King James VI by occult means on his return voyage from Denmark, the Aberdeen Witch Trials took place. Among the accused was a self-confessed wizard, Andro Man of Rathven, near Buckie, who admitted that he had led his witch coven in their revels on the Bin Hill of Cullen and by the Loch and that he had consorted for years with the Queen of Elfland and the Devil whom he called "The Hynd Knight." Furthermore he could conjure up Satan by picking up a little black dog with his right hand, placing it under his left oxter and exclaiming — "Christsonday Benedicete Makpeblis! "

Prior to the Battle of the Hill of Fare in 1562 when the Gordons under the Earl of Huntly fought with the Royal troops under Queen Mary and the Earl of Moray, Huntly rode out to the Bin Hill of Huntly, which was then the principal resort of the local witch coven, to enquire how the forthcoming fight would go. Janet, the principal witch, prophesied that on the following night he would lie in Aberdeen without a mark on his body and taking this as a good omen the Earl set forth. The Gordons were of course overwhelmed by the Royal troops and, as a result of his exertions, the Earl who was a corpulent man fell off his horse with an apoplectic stroke and died instantly. That night his body lay in the Aberdeen Tolbooth.

Country people looked for signs and portents from natural and elemental causes. Spalding refers in his "Memorialls of the Trubles" to a great blazing star like a comet in the shape of a crab or cancer which appeared over Elgin and the country of

Moray in the year 1635, "Having lang broyndis or sprayngis spredding fra the samen". This was seen as a noteworthy warning of the great troubles in Scotland which were shortly to come to pass.

In some parts a field was set aside sacred to the Devil, known benevolently as "The Guidman" or "The Halyman". This piece of land, termed "The Guidman's Acre" or "The Halyman's Rig", was left uncultivated and it was believed that death or disaster would follow if it were ploughed. Offerings of salt and meal were placed there to ensure the securing of the harvest and to avoid famine and pestilence. The Farm of Killiesmont near Keith had one such "Guidman's Acre", while the Minister of Banff testified in 1641 that there was no plot of ground there dedicated to the Devil and left unlaboured. The imprint of the Devil's posterior is said to be seen on the rock at the Burn of Kinminity near Newmill.

> "At the Pot of Pittentoul
> Far the De'il gya youl."

Witchcraft is of course the survival of old pagan religion with its cults of the sun and moon, the Earth Mother and the spirits of wood and stream. Christianity was slow to penetrate to remote country parts, not least by the very difficulty of communications, and finally compromised with the old religion by naming ancient holy wells after the Saints and planting a church on the site of many a sacred grove or circle of standing stones. The Druid priests had evolved a highly organised religious society in their own right and were skilled in herb medicine. In time the Reformed Kirk declared remorseless war on witchcraft and old Kirk Session and Town Records are full of strange instances. Many of the accused were simply indulging in white witchcraft and trying to effect cures although there is no lack of examples of the other sort.

The witch Isobel Goudie, from Auldearn, is credited with telling her accusers, "There are thirteen persons in each coven". In fact the organisation consisted of The Devil (or his counterpart as a man in a beast's skin and horns); secondly, the Queen of Elfland (the fine lady on the white horse), then the Coven including the Maiden, a young and attractive girl who was the special attendant of the Devil or Halyman. There was also an officer who kept the roll and a number of male assistants and musicians. The witches had their 'familiars', i.e. such animals as dogs, cats, and toads and it was a common belief that a witch could turn into a hare. A curious instance occurs in 17th century Botriphnie of a woman accused of "yirding a cat with its legs in the air" for the better working of some spell. A coven in Forres in ancient times regularly roasted a wax effigy of King Duffus over a fire causing him to be 'sore afflicted in his body.' Dawn or cock-crow was the time for the revellers to depart.

William Duff of Dipple, ancestor of the Dukes of Fife, was the second son of Alexander Duff of Keithmore and was born in 1653. The night after the child's birth Keithmore sat near the fire in the bedroom with a candle before him reading his Bible. About midnight a tall woman in a green gown appeared upon the floor and walked up to the cradle in which the child was laid and stretched out her hand over it, upon which Keithmore arose, ran to the bedside and made the sign of the Cross, first on his lady and then on the infant, saying, "In the Name of the Father and the Son and the Holy Ghost may my wife be preserved from all evil," upon which the apparition immediately vanished. Presumably the fairy would have left behind a "changeling" or the child or the mother or both would have died otherwise.

A charm recorded as having been used by a man accused of witchcraft in Elgin runs: -

"The quaking fever and the trembling fever
And the sea fever and the land fever,
Both the head fever and the heart fever,
And all the fevers that God creatit
In St. John's name, St. Peter's name,
And all the Saints of Heaven's names,
Our Lord Jesus Christ's Name . . . . . . . ."

The above is of course an example of a spoken charm, but charm stones played a very important role in healing and a number of such stones survive, usually in the form of a clear rock crystal (Plate 32), mounted in silver or unmounted, perhaps the most famous of these being the Clach na Brataich of the Robertsons. The crystal was dipped three times (signifying the Trinity) in water from a Fairy Well or in clear running water taken from a burn near a bridge over which the living and the dead had passed. The water was then believed to have curative powers and was drunk by people with various ailments or used to cure animal diseases. St. Columba is recorded as having used a healing stone in this way and in the late 18th century a man called Willox in Tomintoul had a great local reputation for effecting cures which he accomplished by using a crystal ball and a brass hook said to have been cut from an elfin bridle worn by a water kelpie. Similarly in Dallas an "adder bead" was used to cure adder bites by immersing it in water three times. To ensure that a cow would give milk a silver coin (Plate 32) was regularly dipped in the milk pail and eel skin was used along the coast as a charm against drowning. Witches had a great fear of iron and cures were also effected with water in which iron ore or smithy cinders had been dipped. Flint arrowheads from primitive times were known as "elf-bolts" and were believed to be capable of causing harm. Cattle meeting with a mysterious end were believed to have been elf-shot and sometimes witches made actual use of them. Sometimes too the arrowheads were mounted in silver and hung around the neck as talismen.

Well worship is of very ancient origin and many holy wells exist which had famous healing powers. Some of these were of course chalybeate springs (springs where the water had a high iron content). Worthy of mention are St. Lawrence's Well at Rothes, St. Maolrubha's Well at Keith, Tobar na Chailleach on the Caird's Hill and the famous well of Our Lady at Orton. There was an ancient chapel here and regular pilgrimages were made from far and near, the worshippers approaching bareheaded and barefooted. Another remarkable well is to be found on the fortified headland at Burghead to which Roman, Danish and Pictish origins have been ascribed and near which the famous Bulls of Burghead were found (see Chapter 7). The stamping out of such pilgrimages was a source of great concern for post-Reformation Kirk Sessions who took a stern view of such superstitious practices; but tradition dies hard.

No account of the folklore of Moray would be complete without a reference to the Wizard Laird of Gordonstoun, Sir Robert Gordon, who was born in 1647. Like Michael Scot he is credited with having studied the Black Art as well as alchemy at the University of Padua, and like Faust he entered into a pact with the Devil there. Back at Gordonstoun he laid out the Round Square (Plate 23) as a mystic circle where he indulged in occult rites and it was said that he had a Fiend imprisoned who worked for him in a forge in the House of Gordonstoun. Tradition tells of a nightmare journey by coach across the Loch of Spynie on thin ice. The terrified coachman was warned

on no account to look round, but just as he reached the shallows
on the far bank he turned to see a huge bird like a raven perched
on Sir Robert's shoulder and the coach immediately sank to the
axles. In 1704 as he was on his way to Birnie Kirk one wild
night Satan claimed the soul of the Wizard Laird. A terrified
local minister, who later met a mysterious end, testified how he
had seen a fearsome black rider on a great horse with Sir
Robert's mangled body limp over the crupper, and stalked by a
dreadful hell hound which had torn out his throat with its
blood stained fangs. No doubt the country folk considered that
the Wizard Laird was but receiving his due in everlasting torment.

The Evil Eye was greatly feared (buidseach" in Highland
districts) and as a counter charm over byre doors and along the
eaves of farm touns were placed rowan sticks and red thread
which were a certain preventative. Little crosses of rowan twigs
bound with red thread were put in a person's clothing as a
safeguard and few houses did not have a rowan tree planted
near by.

> "Raan tree and red thread mak' the witches for to spread."
> "when she saw the new moon ran three times widderstones
> about and sat down upon her bare ars on the ground. Andrew
> Aikenhead saw her and suspects her of his skaith and health
> and also that his dog and cat ran wud (mad), and desired the
> Minister and Elders to make her take an oath that she
> neither did nor shall do him any wrong by witchcraft
> or sorcery."

Isobel Thomason, a witch known as "Premak" effected cures
with a plaster made of "swine's sawine, rossat, walx, black pepper,
honey and cannell." In 1601 a witch from Alves was burned
at Darnaway and in 1668 John Innes, at the request of the
bridegroom used a counter charm by putting a dirk between
the lock and the bar of the church door while the minister was
celebrating his brother's marriage, "to prevent any prejudice
that might occur."

The murder of the Bonie Earl of Moray at Donibristle in
1592 was very much a matter of local hatreds for it was John
Gordon of Buckie accompanied by the Earl of Huntly who
struck him down, allegedly at the order of King James VI for
reasons that the ballad makes obvious.

> "He was a braw gallant,
> And he played at the gluve;
> And the Bonnie Earl o' Murray,
> Oh! he was the queenes luve."

The old Kirk of Birnie occupies the site of the first cathedral in the diocese of Moray and there was a special reverence given to this ancient place which is said to be the oldest Kirk in Scotland in continued use. Prayers offered up there on three successive Sundays were sure to be heard. Also, when a person was ill or an evil-doer, there was a saying to the effect that 'You need to be prayed for thrice at the Kirk of Birnie that you may either end or mend." Noteworthy among churches too is the ancient Kirk of Mortlach which was extended by three spears' length by King Malcolm II in celebration of his victory over the Danes to which the famous Battle Stone bears witness. Pluscarden Priory too has a charming tradition of a monk who had attended Joan of Arc prior to her being burned as a witch at Rouen. As a last remembrance she gave him an inscribed ring; long after this monk found his way to Pluscarden where he worked and prayed until his life's end. Centuries after his death the silver gilt ring with the inscription "MARI IHS" was found at the Priory and identified.

The close-knit fishing communities of the coast have their own superstitions which have died hard, but since seafaring has become less hazardous by the use of powered boats with modern machinery and equipment many of the old beliefs have been forgotten. However it is still considered ill luck to have a minister aboard ship and Friday is a bad day to go to sea. No mention must be made of a rabbit or a cat and one would never take out a boat turning it widdershins to the sun. The picturesque ceremony of burning the Clavie at Burghead on 11th January, "Aul Eel", symbolises the ancient fire festivals of primitive man. The Clavie itself is a barrel filled with tar set up on a pole and carried ceremonially by a chosen Clavie Crew. Bonfires were lit at Beltane, the beginning of May, and this too was a time of pilgrimage to ancient wells where one could drop in a bent pin and wish a wish or tie a rag on a tree for luck. Carrying home the Clyack Sheaf and the Meal and Ale celebrations of harvest time are doubtless memories of traditional sacrifices to the Earth Mother.

Cullen is an ancient Royal Burgh with a peculiar association. Three prominent rocks jutting out into the sea are known as 'The Three Kings of Cullen" and elsewhere the Three Wise Men, The Magi from the East who followed the Star of Bethlehem, Caspar, Melchior and Balthasar, are venerated as

U

The Three Kings of Cologne. There is a magnificent shrine in the Cathedral in their honour there, for the bodies of the Three Kings were taken from Constantinople to Germany in the Crusades. In the medieval miracle plays performed in Aberdeen, however, "The Three Kings of Cullen" were represented.

Robert Burns made James Macpherson, the Highland Freebooter from Speyside, who was captured in the Kirkyard of Keith and hanged in Banff in 1700, a folk hero. The story goes that the Magistrates, spurred on by Duff of Braco, were so anxious to ensure his execution that they advanced the time on the Town Clock so that the pardon on the way would arrive too late. Thus perished a Highland Robin Hood who was also a noted violinist and composer.

> "Sae rantingly,
> Sae wantonly,
> Sae dauntingly gaed he,
> He played a spring
> And danced it round,
> Below the gallows tree."

Another remarkable Freebooter from Speyside who has become a legendary name is James of the Hill — Seumas an Tuim — whose long and chequered career included a remarkable escape from the dungeons of Edinburgh Castle. Unlike Macpherson he died peacefully at an advanced age. This man, James Grant of Carron, is celebrated in the Pipe Tune "The Breadalbane Gathering" the Gaelic words of which translated go: -

> "Ye women of the Glen
> Is it not time for you to arise?
> And Seumas an Tuim driving off your cattle."

The legend tells that this very tune was played by Campbell of Breadalbane's piper just before the Massacre of Glencoe, in the hope of warning the MacIans of their danger.

Near Forres is the famous "Blasted Heath" — the Hardmuir — traditionally the meeting place of the three Weird Sisters in "Macbeth". Forres as well as Elgin suffered at the hands of the infamous Wolf of Badenoch who sallied from his lair at Lochindorb to burn the Town in 1390 as he had burned the great Cathedral of Elgin a short time before.

Long forgotten historical and folk-lore legends are further commemorated by the great variety of standing stones and stone circles in our region telling of the resting places of Kings and Chieftains and ancient battles between Celt and Pict, Scot and Viking. Many other stone circles and standing stones have cup and ring markings associated with ancient rites in the dim mists of time and one of the most remarkable is to be found at Rothiemay where a great recumbent stone carries a pattern of cup marks which seems to indicate an astronomical chart of the heavens. Of the carved stones Sueno's Stone (Plate 15) near Forres is the best by far, displaying ancient craftsmanship in its processions of warriors and animals which may be associated with the Norse King Sweyn. There are symbol stones, too, carved with the mysterious patterns of double disc and Z-rod, serpent, mirror and comb, elephant, salmon and the rest, the significance of which is long forgotten.

Such then is an outline of the folklore of this land of Moray, a land steeped in legend, a land as haunted by its past as its haunted castles. People have dwelt in Moray from the earliest times leaving a wealth of history and tradition which could fill a separate volume. With this in mind there is great scope for the collector of old tales in every part of Moray and rich rewards of discovery.

# A SELECTED BIBLIOGRAPHY

## I  NATURAL ENVIRONMENT

Baxter, E. V. et alia, *The Birds of Scotland,* Oliver & Boyd, 1953.

Bremner, A., *The Glaciation of Moray and Ice Movements in the North of Scotland,* Trans. Edin. Geol. Soc., 13, 17 - 56, 1934.

Birse, E. L. & Dry, F. T., *Assessment of Climatic conditions in Scotland.* Soil Survey of Scotland, 1970.

Burgess, J. J., *Flora of Moray,* Elgin Courant & Courier, 1935.

Campbell, B. et alia, *A Field Guide to Birds' Nests,* Constable, 1972.

Caseldine, C. J. & Mitchell, W. A. (eds.), *Problems of the Deglaciation of Scotland,* Journal of St. Andrews Geographers, Special Publication No. 1, 1974.

Clapperton, C. M. & Sugden, D. E. in Gemmell, A. D., *Quaternary Studies in North East Scotland,* Dept. of Geography, University of Aberdeen, 1975.

Craib, W. G., *The Flora of Banffshire.* Reprinted from Transactions of the Banffshire Field Club, 1912.

Dunsire, A., *Frequency of Snow Depths and Days with Snow Lying at Stations in Scotland,* Meteorological Office, Clim. Memo. No. 70, 1971.

Fitzpatrick, E. A., *The Principal Tertiary and Pleistocene Events in North East Scotland,* in Clapperton C. M. (ed.) North East Scotland Geographical Essays, Dept. of Geography, University of Aberdeen, 1972.

Geological Survey — One Inch Sheet Memoirs.

*"The Geology of Mid-Strath Spey and Strathdearn."* (Explanation of sheet 74), 1915.

*"The Geology of West Aberdeenshire, Banffshire."* (Explanation of sheet 75), 1896.

*"The Geology of Lower Findhorn and Lower Strath Nairn."* (Explanation of sheet 84 and part of 94), 1923.

*"The Geology of Lower Strathspey."* (Explanation of sheet 85), 1902.

*"The Geology of Banff, Huntly, and Turriff."* (Explanation of sheet 86 and sheet 96), 1923.

*"The Geology of The Elgin District."* (Explanation of sheet 95), 1968.

Gordon, G. G., *Collectanae for a Flora of Moray,* 1839.

H.M.S.O., *Forests of North-East Scotland: Forestry Commission Guide,* 1963.

Holgate, N., *Palaeozoic and Tertiary Transcurrent movements in the Great Glen fault,* Scott. J. Geol., 5 (2) 97 - 139, 1969.

Johnstone, G. S., *The Grampian Highlands (Third edition) British Regional Geology,* H.M.S.O., 1973.

The Journal of the Scottish Ornithologists' Club, *Scottish Birds.*

Langmuir, E., *Snow Profiles in Scotland,* Weather 25(5) pp 205 - 209, 1970.

McCallum Webster, M., *A Check List of the Flora of the Culbin State Forest,* 1968.

MacInnes, H., *International Mountain Rescue Handbook,* Constable, 1972.

Mackintosh, H. B., *The Lossie and the Loch of Spynie,* Elgin, 1928.

Manley, G., *Mountain Snows of Britain,* Weather 26 (5) pp 192 - 200, 1971.

Manley, G., *Scotland's Semi-permanent Snows,* Weather 26 (11) 458 - 471, 1971.

Nethersole-Thompson, D. et alia, *The Cairngorms, their natural history and Scenery*, Collins, 1974.
Ogilvie, A. G., *The Phsiography of the Moray Firth Coast*, Trans. Roy. Soc. Edin., 53, 377 - 404, 1923.
Peterson, R. et alia, *A Field Guide to the Birds of Britain and Europe*, Collins, 1967.
Plant, J. A., *The Climate of the Coastal Region of the Moray Firth*, Meteorological Office. Clim. Memo. No. 62, 1968.
Sissons, J. B., *The Evolution of Scotland's Scenery*, Oliver & Boyd, 1967.
Steers, J. A., *The Culbin Sands and Burghead Bay*, Geog. J., 90, 498 - 528, 1937.
Steers, J. A., *The Coastline of Scotland*, Cambridge Univ. Press, 1973.
Synge, F. M., *The Glaciation of North East Scotland*, Scot. Geog. Mag., 72, 129, 1956.
Witherby, H. F. et alia, *The Handbook of British Birds*, Witherby, 1945.

## II  HISTORICAL

Benton, S., *The Excavation of the Sculptor's Cave, Covesea*, Proc. Soc. Antiquaries Scot., 65, 177 - 216, 1931.
Cant, R., *Moray in Scottish History*, The Elgin Society, 1952.
Cant, R., *Historic Elgin and its Cathedral*, The Elgin Society, 1974.
Cottam, M. B. & Small, A., *The Distribution of Settlement in Southern Pictland*, Med. Arch. 15, 1975.
Douglas, R., *Annals of the Royal Burgh of Forres*, Elgin, 1934.
Forbes, A. H., *Forres, A Royal Burgh 1150 - 1975*, Elgin, 1975.
Gordon, Rev. J. F. S., *The Book of the chronicles of Keith, Grange, Ruthven, Cairney & Botriphnie*, Glasgow, 1880.
Greig, J. C., *Cullykhan*, Current Archaeol. No. 32, 227 - 231, 1972.
McKie, E. W., *Radio-carbon Dates and the Scottish Iron Age*, Antiquity, 43, 15 - 26, 1969.
O'Dell, A. C. & Walton, K., *The Highlands and Islands of Scotland*, Nelson, 1962.
Ogilvie, A. G., *Loc. Sit.*
Rampini, C., *A History of Moray and Nairn*, Blackwood, 1897.
Ritchie, J. B., *The Pageant of Morayland*, Moravian Press Ltd., Elgin, 1938.
Roy, W., *The military antiquities of the Romans in Britain*, London, 1793.
Scott, J. G., *A Torc of twisted gold from Morayshire*. Proc. Soc. Antiquaries Scot. 87, 191 - 192, 1953.
Shaw, L., *History of the Province of Moray (3 vols)*, Hamilton, Adams & Co. Ltd. and Thorn. D. Morison, 1882.
Small, A. *Burghead*, Scot. Archaeol. Forum, 1, 61-68, 1969.
Small, A. & Cottam, M. B., *Craig Phadrig*, University of Dundee, Dept of Geography, Occasional Paper, No. 1, 57 pp, 1972.
Small, A., *The Hill Forts of the Inverness Area in Maclean, L. (Ed.), The Inverness Area*, Lerwick, 1975.
Smout, T. C., *A History of the Scottish People*, Collins, 1970.
St. Joseph, J. K., *Air Reconnaissance in Britain 1965 - 68*, J. Roman Stud., 59, 104 - 28, 1969.
St. Joseph, J. K., *Air Reconnaissance in Britain 1969 - 72*, J. Roman Stud., 63, 214 - 46, 1973.

Tranter, N., *The Queen's Scotland; The North East*, Hodder & Stoughton, 1974.

Walker, I.C., *The Counties of Nairnshire, Moray and Banffshire in the Bronze Age — Part 1*, Proc. Soc. Antiquaries Scot., 98, 76 - 125, 1967.

Young, H. W., *Notes of the ramparts of Burghead as revealed by recent excavations*, Proc Soc. Antiquaries Scot., 25, 435 - 47, 1891.

Young, H. W., *Notes on further excavations at Burghead*, Proc. Soc. Antiquaries Scot., 27, 86 - 91, 1893.

Young, H. W., *Discovery of an Ancient Burial Place and a Symbol-Bearing Slab at Easterton of Roseisle*, The Relinquary and Illustrated Archaeologist, 1, 142 - 50, 1895.

Young, R., *Notes on Burghead*, Elgin, 1868.

### III GENERAL

Alcock, J., *Two years improvements on the Estate of Aberlour*, (Privately printed), 1889.

Anderson, G., *Kingston on Spey*, Oliver & Boyd, 1957.

Anderson, M. L., *A History of Scottish Forestry*, Nelson, 1967.

Anson, P. F., *Fishing boats and fisher folk on the east coast of Scotland*, Dent, 1974.

Barrow, G. W. S., *The Acts of Malcolm IV, King of Scots, 1153 - 1165*, E.U.P., 1960.

Bell, H. G., *Life of Mary, Queen of Scots*, Constable, 1828.

Birse, E. L. & Dry, F. T., *Assessment of Climatic Conditions in Scotland*, The Macaulay Institute of Soil Research, 1970.

Brander, M., *The Original Scotch*, Hutchinson, 1974.

Brereton, H. L., *Gordonstoun*, Chambers, Edinburgh, 1968.

Cramond, W., *The Annals of Cullen*, W. F. Johnston, 1888.

Cormack, A. A., *William Cramond*, Aberdeen, 1964.

Coull, J. R., *Fisheries in the North-East of Scotland before 1800*, Scottish Studies 13, Pt. 1, 1969.

Cumming, G. C. F., *Memories*, Blackwood, 1904.

Daiches, D., *Scotch whisky, its past and present*, Deutsch, 1969.

Dickinson, W. C., *A New History of Scotland Vol. 1*, Nelson, 1961.

Donaldson, J., *General view of the agriculture of the County of Elgin or Moray*, Board of Agriculture, 1794.

Donaldson, J., *County of Banff*, Board of Agriculture, 1794.

Douglas, R., *Sons of Moray*, Elgin, 1930.

Douglas, R., *The Annals of Forres*, Elgin Courant and Courier, 1934.

Elton, Lord, *The Life of James Ramsay Macdonald*, Collins, 1939.

Fraser-Darling, F., *Natural History in the Highlands and Islands*, Collins 1947.

Gaskin, M., *North East Scotland*, H.M.S.O., 1969.

Gordon-Cumming, C. F., *The Lowlands of Moray*, National Rev. 4, 1884

Gordon, J. F. S., *The Book of the Chronicles of Keith*, R. Forrester, Glasgow, 1880.

Gordon, J. R., *Population changes in the Counties of Banff, Moray and Nairn 1755 - 1951*, . . unpublished M.A. (Hons) thesis, Aberdeen University, 1954.

Gordon, S., *Highways and Byways in Central Scotland*, Macmillan, 1948.

Gray, J., *Sutherland and Caithness in Saga-Time,* Oliver & Boyd, 1922.

Greenwood, D. & Short, J., *Military installations and local economics — a case study: the Moray air stations,* Aberdeen studies in defence economies No. 4, 1973.

Gregor, W., *Notes on the Folklore of the North-East of Scotland, especially Banffshire,* Folklore Society, 1881.

Grigor, J., *Arboriculture,* Edinburgh, 1868.

Henderson, E., *Life of James Ferguson,* Edinburgh, 1870.

Heyerdahl, T., *Fatu-Hiva: back to nature,* Allen & Unwin, 1974.

Huie, C. (Ed.), *Commemorating the County of Banff,* Keith, 1975.

Hutcheson, G., *Days of yore: or Buckie and District in the past,* Banffshire Advertiser Office, 1887.

Jeffrey, A., *Sketches from the traditional history of Burghead,* Aberdeen Newspapers Ltd., 1928.

Leslie, Rev. W., *General View of the Agriculture of the Counties of Moray & Nairn,* Sherwood, Keely & Sons, 1813.

Mackintosh, H. B., *Elgin Past and Present,* Elgin, 1914.

McLaren, M., *The Shell Guide to Scotland,* 1965.

MacRae, N. (Ed.), *Highland Second Sight,* G. Souter, Dingwall, 1908.

McVean, D. N., *in the Vegetation of Scotland. (Ed. J. H. Burnett),* Oliver & Boyd, 1964.

Mellor, R. E. H., *An excursion guide to the Moray coastlands,* North-East Scotland Geographical Essays, Dept. of Geography, University of Aberdeen (Ed. C. M. Clapperton), 1972.

Ministry of Transport, *Rural transport surveys,* Report of preliminary results, 1963.

Moray & Nairn Foresters' Society, *Journal No. 1, December,* 1927.

Morris, K., *The Story of Lord Mount Stephen,* London, 1922.

Murray, Rev. J., *The Kinnairds of Culbin,* Robert Carruthers, Inverness, 1938.

Murchison, C., *Dr. Hugh Falconer,* London, 1868.

New Spalding Publications, *The Records of Elgin (2 vols),* New Spalding Club, 1903.

New Spalding Publications, *The Annals of Banff (2 vols),* New Spalding Club, 1891.

Newte, T., *Prospects and observations on a tour in England and Scotland in 1785,* London, 1791.

O'Dell, A. C. & Walton, K., *Loc. Sit.*

Pococke, R. (Ed. D. W. Kemp), *Tours in Scotland 1747, 1750, 1760,* Scot. Hist. Soc. Vol. I, 1887.

Plant, J. A., *Loc. Sit., Registrum Episcopatus Moraviensis,* Bannatyne Club, 1837.

Ritchie, A., *The Scottish seine net fishery,* H.M.S.O., 1960.

Ritchie, J. B., *Loc. Sit.*

Ross, J., *Letter to C. Gordon,* Edinburgh, Gordon Castle letter books, 1776.

Sacks, B., *J. Ramsay Macdonald,* New Mexico, 1952.

School log books, *Scottish Charms and Amulets,* Proc. Soc. Antiq. Scotland, Vol. 3, 1892 - 93.

Shaw, A., *Letter to James Grant,* Castle Grant Papers G.D. 248, Vol. 677, General letter book of James Grant of Grant — 1769 - 1772.

Shaw, L., *Loc. Sit.*

Smith, A., *The Wealth of Nations (1776)*, Dent, 1910.

Smith, G., *Glenlivet . . . the annals of Glenlivet Distillery*, Smith-Grant, 1924.

Smout, T. C., *Loc Sit.*

Spalding Club Publications, *(a) Miscellany of the Spalding Club. Trials for Witchcraft. Vol. L. (b) Extracts from the Presbytery Book of Strathbogie, 1631 - 54. (c) Memorials of the Troubles in Scotland and in England 1624 - 45 (2 vols)*, J. Spalding, 1841.

Statistical Accounts, *1st (old) Statistical Account of Nairn, Moray and Banff*, 1791 - 99. *2nd (New) Statistical Account of Nairn, Moray and Banff*, 1845. *3rd Statistical Account of Scotland: The County of Banff*, 1961. *The Counties of Moray and Nairn, 1965.*

Stewart, D., *Sketches of the Character, Manners and Present State of the Highlanders of Scotland*, Constable, 1822.

Steven, H. M. et alia, *The Native Pinewoods of Scotland*, Oliver & Boyd, 1959.

Strachey, Lady, *Memoirs of a Highland Lady*, John Murray, 1898.

Symon, J. A., *Scottish farming, past and present*, Oliver & Boyd, 1959.

Taylor, A. & H., *The Book of the Duffs (2 vols)*, Wm. Brown, 1914.

Taylor, J., *A Memoir of Florence Wilson*, Elgin, 1861.

Tranter, N., *Loc. Sit.*

The Topographical, Statistical & Historical Gazeteer of Scotland, Fullarton & Co., Glasgow, 1842.

Vallance, H. A., *The History of the Highland Railway*, Stockwell, 1938.

Walton, K., *Population changes in North-East Scotland. Scottish Studies, Vol. 5 Part, 2., pp 149 - 180*, Oliver & Boyd, 1961.

Watson, J. & W., *Morayshire Described*, Elgin, 1868.

Watson, W. J., *The History of the Celtic Place Names of Scotland*, W. Blackwood & Sons, Ltd., 1926.

# INDEX OF PLACES